CAMBRIDGE

Brighter Thinking

Revolution and Dictatorship: Russia, 1917–1953

A/AS Level History for AQA
Student Book

Robert Francis and Hannah Dalton

Series Editors: Michael Fordham and David Smith

CAMBRIDGE
UNIVERSITY PRESS

University Printing House, Cambridge CB2 8BS, United Kingdom

Cambridge University Press is part of the University of Cambridge.

It furthers the University's mission by disseminating knowledge in the pursuit of
education, learning and research at the highest international levels of excellence.

www.cambridge.org
Information on this title: www.cambridge.org/ukschools/9781107587380 (Paperback)
                                        www.cambridge.org/ukschools/9781107587397 (Cambridge Elevate-enhanced Edition)

First published 2015

A catalogue record for this publication is available from the British Library

ISBN 978-1-107-58738-0 Paperback
ISBN 978-1-107-58739-7 Cambridge Elevate-enhanced Edition

Additional resources for this publication at www.cambridge.org/ukschools

Cambridge University Press has no responsibility for the persistence or accuracy
of URLs for external or third-party internet websites referred to in this publication,
and does not guarantee that any content on such websites is, or will remain,
accurate or appropriate. Information regarding prices, travel timetables, and other
factual information given in this work is correct at the time of first printing but
Cambridge University Press does not guarantee the accuracy of such information
thereafter.

Message from AQA

This textbook has been approved by AQA for use with our qualification. This means that we have checked that it broadly covers the specification and we are satisfied with the overall quality. Full details of our approval process can be found on our website.

We approve textbooks because we know how important it is for teachers and students to have the right resources to support their teaching and learning. However, the publisher is ultimately responsible for the editorial control and quality of this book.

Please note that when teaching the A/AS Level History (7041, 7042) course, you must refer to AQA's specification as your definitive source of information. While this book has been written to match the specification, it cannot provide complete coverage of every aspect of the course.

A wide range of other useful resources can be found on the relevant subject pages of our website: www.aqa.org.uk

Contents

About this Series

Cambridge A/AS Level History for AQA is an exciting new series designed to support students in their journey from GCSE to A Level and then on to possible further historical study. The books provide the knowledge, concepts and skills needed for the two-year AQA History A Level course, but it's our intention as series editors that students recognise that their A Level exams are just one step to a potential lifelong relationship with the discipline of history. This book has further readings, extracts from historians' works and links to wider questions and ideas that go beyond the scope of an A Level course. With this series, we have sought to ensure not only that the students are well prepared for their examinations, but also that they gain access to a wider debate that characterises historical study.

The series is designed to provide clear and effective support for students as they make the adjustment from GCSE to A Level, and also for teachers, especially those who are not familiar with teaching a two-year linear course. The student books cover the AQA specifications for both A/AS Level. They are intended to appeal to the broadest range of students, and they offer challenges to stretch the top end and additional support for those who need it. Every author in this series is an experienced historian or history teacher, and all have great skill in conveying narratives to readers and asking the kinds of questions that pull those narratives apart.

In addition to high-quality prose, this series also makes extensive use of textual primary sources, maps, diagrams and images, and offers a wide range of activities to encourage students to address historical questions of cause, consequence, change and continuity. Throughout the books there are opportunities to criticise the interpretations of other historians, and to use those interpretations in the construction of students' own accounts of the past. The series aims to ease the transition for those students who move on from A Level to undergraduate study, and the books are written in an engaging style that will encourage those who want to explore the subject further.

Icons used within this book include:

 Key terms

 Speak like a historian

 Voices from the past/Hidden voices

 Practice essay questions

 Chapter summary

 Taking it further

 Thematic links

About Cambridge Elevate

Cambridge Elevate is the platform which hosts a digital version of this Student Book. If you have access to this digital version you can annotate different parts of the book, send and receive messages to and from your teacher and insert weblinks, among other things.

We hope that you enjoy your AS or A Level History course, as well as this book, and wish you well for the journey ahead.

Michael Fordham and David L. Smith
Series editors

1 Dissent and revolution, 1917

In this section we will trace developments across 1917:

- the condition of Russia before the revolution of February/March 1917: political authority and the Tsar; the war effort; the economic and social state of Russia; discontent

- the February/March revolution of 1917: causes and the course of revolution; issues of leadership and the Tsar's abdication; the establishment of the Provisional Government and the Petrograd Soviet; the workings of the dual authority

- developments between the revolutions including: the return of Lenin; Lenin's ideology and the April Theses; the July Days; the Kornilov affair and the roles of the Provincial Government and Trotsky; Lenin and the Central Committee of the Bolshevik Party

- the October/November 1917 revolution: causes, course and extent of revolution; leadership and the establishment of Bolshevik authority; Sovnarkom and decrees and actions to December.

Introduction

For historians and for many of those who witnessed it, 1917 was an iconic year; the year that saw long-standing fault lines in Russian society finally rip it apart. It began with a tsarist regime established over centuries and ended with power in the hands of a few revolutionaries who, up to that point, had studiously avoided the responsibility of public office. The failure of the **Romanov** regime might have been avoided, particularly if Russia had not gone to war in 1914. The unexpectedly long-drawn-out war against Germany and Austria-Hungary had placed severe demands on an inadequate and poorly organised industrial infrastructure. As well as increasing the strains on the civilian population, it also spurred middle-class patriotic liberals, disliked by the regime itself, to begin attempts to better organise the war effort for fear of national defeat. Workers also looked to protect their interests through strikes and 'workers' control' of factories as inflation and scarcity took effect. The extent to which the urban working classes can be said to have shared the aims of revolutionaries seeking, in the main, a socialist transformation of society, has been debated by historians, but the atmosphere of protest and demand is well established.

The collapse of the tsarist regime in February 1917 and the troubles of the **Provisional Government** which succeeded it may simply be put down to the chaos created by war. Central authority continued to weaken after the 'February Revolution', not least because liberals and socialists within the government continued to prioritise the war effort above the demand for land reform and the provision of bread to the cities. Workers, peasants and soldiers increasingly took matters into their own hands. This opened the way for the Bolshevik Party, under Lenin, to seize power when the time was right. What many see as an opportunistic power-grab would become enshrined in Soviet history as the 'October Revolution': the founding act of what would become the Soviet Union. Under Lenin's successor, Stalin, this vulnerable regime established in October 1917 would become a world superpower which much of the world looked to as an example. This book will help you pick apart and understand that process. This first chapter will help you establish how the Bolsheviks were able to claim power in the first place.

The condition of Russia before the revolution of February/March 1917

Political authority and the Tsar

The tsarist regime under Nicholas II was highly resistant to political reform. Nicholas followed in the steps of his father Alexander III (Emperor from 1881 to 1894), who had essentially looked to reverse the limited reforms of his own father Alexander II (1855–1881). Nicholas was a somewhat reluctant ruler and much preferred the company of his family to that of his imperial ministers. This reluctance to rule sat very awkwardly with the supreme power that he held over his millions of subjects. It also meant that he was more likely to fall back on the repressive tactics of his predecessors in a crisis. Additionally, his wife Alexandra urged him, against the advice of reformist ministers, to maintain his **autocratic** powers.

Key terms

Romanov: The name of the royal family and household in Russia since 1613. In 1913, Nicholas II (the last of the Romanovs and last Tsar of Russia) celebrated the tercentenary or 300-year anniversary of the dynasty.

Provisional Government: Formed immediately after Nicholas II abdicated – intended to be a temporary body until the elections for the Constituent Assembly could take place later in 1917. Initially led by Prince Lvov and latterly by Alexander Kerensky.

Autocracy: The system of government that existed in Russia until 1917 under the tsars. All power was concentrated in the hands of the tsar who had no legal restraints on his power.

The October Manifesto, 1905

The political consequences of failing to bring about effective reform, as was made clear in 1905, involved separate reactions by a reformist liberal constituency on the one hand and a revolutionary socialist constituency on the other. The October Manifesto, written by Sergei Witte and issued by the Tsar on 17 October, convinced the newly formed liberal **Octobrists** and moderate **Constitutional Democrats (Kadets)** to, in effect, distance themselves from the working-class movements with whom they had some form of common cause during the year. Isolated, the Petrograd Soviet and striking workers were repressed over the next few months. In the Manifesto, the Tsar had promised greater political freedoms and the formation of a national parliament with limited powers, the **Duma**. This had passed some reformist legislation, including that of Pyotr Stolypin, but through a reform of the electoral law in 1907 it had become dominated by **Rightist** deputies.

Socialist politics within the constitutional set-up was therefore limited. Unlike in Germany, there was no broadly accepted social democratic party which brought together reformists and Marxists. Trades unions had only been officially accepted in 1905. By excluding socialists, the tsarist regime had perhaps limited their influence, but this had led to the dominance of more radical socialist elements within the workers' movement. Apart from more moderate labour parties such as the Trudoviks, the revolutionary left was dominated by three groups: the SRs, the Bolsheviks and the Mensheviks.

- The **Socialist Revolutionaries'** (SRs) outlook stemmed from 19th-century Russian populism, which favoured radical land redistribution for the peasants, but by 1917 they had a substantial urban base of support.
- Rival to the SRs were the **Social Democrats** (SDs), split from 1903 between Lenin's **Bolsheviks** and Martov's **Mensheviks**. The former emphasised the need for a small, disciplined party to educate and lead the industrial working class or proletariat in revolutionary action. The latter favoured a larger, mass-membership party to achieve the same end.

The impact of Marxism

The SDs were born of Russian **Marxism**, which had begun to gain traction in the 1890s. Inspired by the writings of the German **radical** Karl Marx, Plekhanov, the founder of Russian Marxism, had sought to apply West European Marxist thinking to the Russian context. Russia was not the first on the list when it came to likely contexts for Marxist proletarian revolution, because it had a relatively small working class (around 2.6 million in 1910 in a population of approximately 125 million) and a vast peasantry. Marxists nevertheless made headway in the illegal organisation of party cells in the major West Russian capitals of Petrograd and Moscow and in Finnish Riga. The significant point for Marxists is that they believed that the European war could simply collapse into a widespread international socialist revolution.

The European working classes, in and out of uniform, could theoretically stop fighting one another and turn their guns on their bourgeois and imperial masters (see Figure 2.2 in Chapter 2 and *Speak like a historian: Marxist terminology*, below).

Key terms

Octobrists: A group of conservative liberals formed during the 1905 revolution who called for Nicholas II to fulfil the reforms of the October Manifesto. However, they were fully committed to constitutional monarchy.

Constitutional Democrats (Kadets): Party formed of liberals in 1905 just after the announcement of the October Manifesto. Led by Pavel Miliukov, they favoured an eight-hour day but were committed to constitutional monarchy, so worked within the Duma.

Duma: Deriving its name from the Russian for 'consider', the State Duma was formed as a result of the 1905 Revolution under Nicholas II. It had legislative and advisory powers, but its power was to be severely curtailed under the Fundamental Laws issued by Nicholas II just before the opening of the Duma in May 1906.

Rightists: Supporters of the tsarist monarchy who were elected to the Duma during its existence between 1906 and 1914.

Key terms

Socialist Revolutionaries: Marxists who drew inspiration from the Narodnik/populist movements of the 1870s. The SRs were led by Victor Chernov from 1902 and thought that both peasants and workers could lead a revolution against tsarism. Although they sought to agitate peasants, they relied on political assassinations as a tactic to bring about a revolution.

Social Democrats: The Russian Social Democratic Labour Party was formed in 1898 to unite various Marxist groups within Imperial Russia. Members were Marxists and they opposed revolutionary populism – believing instead that the agents of the revolution would be the working class.

Bolsheviks: Meaning 'majority': these were a group of Social Democrats who split from the rest of the party because they disagreed on the leadership of the party. The Bolsheviks were led by Lenin.

Mensheviks: Originally part of the Russian Social-Democratic Labour Party, the Mensheviks (which means 'minority') were formed after a split between Julius Martov and Lenin, which occurred at the Second Congress of 1903. The Mensheviks opposed Lenin's idea of a vanguard party and wanted broad-based support within the party.

The war effort

The prosecution of the war (how it was organised and fought) was to play arguably the most important role in destabilising the government. At its outbreak in August 1914, there was overwhelming popular support for the Tsar. The expectation was for a rapid war of only a few months. The Russian army, the great 'Russian Steamroller', made up of nearly 6 million conscripted peasants, was mobilised faster than Germany and Austria-Hungary, their main enemies, had expected. Consequently, the armies made swift progress towards East Prussia in that first month. The German High Command, however, reacted with equal speed and inflicted defeats on Russian forces at Tannenberg in late August, and at the Masurian Lakes in September. The Russian advance on Silesia (an eastern German province) was halted at Lodz, at the end of November.

In 1915 Russia experienced its most dramatic reverses. Despite a successful campaign in May against Austria-Hungary in Galicia (to the south), between May and September, German forces advanced into the Russian Empire's western provinces, reaching Brest-Litovsk by 28 August and Grodno by 2 September. Unprepared for a drawn-out war, the Russian army found itself under-equipped. The regime insisted on continuing to buy expensive foreign armaments, rather than concentrating on building up the Russian industry. In addition, the higher ranks of the army were filled with aristocratic allies of the Tsar, rather than those promoted on merit.

An exception was General Alexei Brusilov. A capable career officer, Brusilov launched an offensive in June 1916 along the entire front. Such a comprehensive approach prevented the Germans from exploiting weak spots in the line. Between June and October, the line advanced up to 80 miles in some places. The Brusilov Offensive was a great success, but did not gain any strategic advantage. The Tsar's intervention (he had placed himself in charge of the war effort from September 1915 onwards) undermined Brusilov's strategy by ordering troops south. A further serious blow came from the defeat of Romania by Serbian forces in December 1916. Romania had been persuaded to join the war on the side of Russia and its allies in August and this has raised hopes of driving towards the ancient capital of the Ottoman Empire, Constantinople, now known as Istanbul.

By the beginning of 1917, though not hopeless, the prospect of victory over Germany was distant. Morale and discipline on the front line began to fracture. There were few links of loyalty between the mainly peasant infantry and an aristocratic officer corps. Military discipline was harsh and engendered resentment. Much discontent within the army, as we shall see, was in fact most evident in the garrisons of the major cities rather than at the front. Nevertheless, desertion (soldiers leaving the front without permission) and fraternisation (making friends with the enemy) became more common.

The economic and social state of Russia

Russia was not ready for war in 1914. There was a widespread sense of national unity following the declaration of war and the German military's high command were wrong-footed by the speed of mobilisation. Nevertheless, the Empire's

Speak like a historian

The political spectrum

Figure 1.1 shows the range of parties on the political spectrum from left to right. This is a way of understanding how different political ideologies (systems of political thinking) relate to each other. In simple terms:

- The Rightists were in favour of maintaining the power of the Tsar as an autocrat (a single ruler in complete control).

- Liberals, who only gained a political voice in 1905, favoured democratic reform through gradual constitutional (law-based) change, similar to the slow gains of British parliamentary democracy over many decades. This meant they wished for elected representatives (in the Duma) to have power over law-making and to limit the powers of the Tsar.

- The Kadets spanned a fairly broad range of opinion; many demanded radical reform. 'Radical' literally means 'from the root'. Another similar term is 'fundamental' – this means 'from the bottom up'.

- Further left, socialists rejected liberal reform as insufficient. In their eyes, liberals were still looking after the interests of the rich. Their solution was mass popular protest and overthrow of the ruling class: revolution.

Key terms

Marxism: The political and economic theory expounded by Karl Marx and Friedrich Engels. Their theory placed class struggle at the centre of historical development.

Radical: Someone who believes in drastic change from traditions or government policy.

industrial infrastructure was inadequate for a conflict lasting longer than a few months.

The state of Russia's industry

Under Sergei Witte, a loyal and reformist minister, Russia had undergone state-led industrialisation at a rapid pace. Between 1890 and 1914 56 400 miles of railway had been laid, coal production had more than quadrupled and steel production had risen almost tenfold during the same period. Russia's so-called 'backward' economy had expanded with the help of foreign loans, especially from its closest ally, France. The demand for armaments, however, benefited a favoured few industrialists and as the war developed, more common manufactured goods such as agricultural implements were neglected as they provided no guaranteed profit in wartime. Added to this was the fact that raw materials were not as effectively concentrated as in, for example, Germany. The railways could not deliver for both military and civilians. This was made substantially worse through poor management by the tsarist bureaucracy and ministers approved by the Tsarina. In August 1914 the wave of patriotism had brought a temporary lull to industrial unrest. But the revolution of 1905 and a subsequent upturn in strikes following the shooting dead of some 270 striking miners at the Lena Goldfields in April 1912 had created the basis for a radicalised and organised urban working class.

Russia's peasantry

The year 1905 had also seen the creation of peasant organisations, and the All-Russian Peasants Union was able to articulate their concerns nationally. Yet peasants were not easily controlled. Acts of defiance by peasant communities,

Key term

Mir: A traditional peasant commune, the basic unit of organisation in the countryside. It decided how land was distributed to each household. Pyotr Stolypin attempted to break the power of the commune by allowing kulaks (richer peasants) to buy their own land before the First World War. It remained popular until destroyed by collectivisation.

such as the temporary seizure of noble and church lands, and attacking and burning down property, were not uncommon, particularly following the repeated famines of the late 19th century. Although Alexander II had issued an Edict of Emancipation in 1861, freeing the serfs from their obligation to work for noble landowners, they were made to pay compensation through 49-year mortgages known as redemption payments. The institution that dominated peasant life was the commune or *mir*. It continued to provide a basic unit of self-governance and was responsible for the repartition or redistribution of strips of land to households every 10 to 15 years. This process ensured a periodic rebalancing of who got what to farm.

Pyotr Stolypin, Governor of Saratov province from 1903 and Prime Minister from 1906, had a dual approach to the peasantry. First, he brought harsh repression to Saratov and to peasants following the 1905 nationwide disturbances. Second, among his reforms he attempted to break at least some of the peasantry away from the commune by allowing them to withdraw and own their own consolidated plots. He had some success: 11% of households had separated from the commune by 1915, but the process had slowed after initial enthusiasm. Assassinated in 1911, Stolypin was unable to establish an efficient agriculture which brought the peasantry into the political nation. In 1917, peasant radicalism – the demand for the expropriation of private land – was arguably based on the conservative and xenophobic mind-set of the *mir*. During the war, the government could not afford to pay high prices for grain and there is little evidence to suggest that peasants felt a patriotic duty to produce for the war.

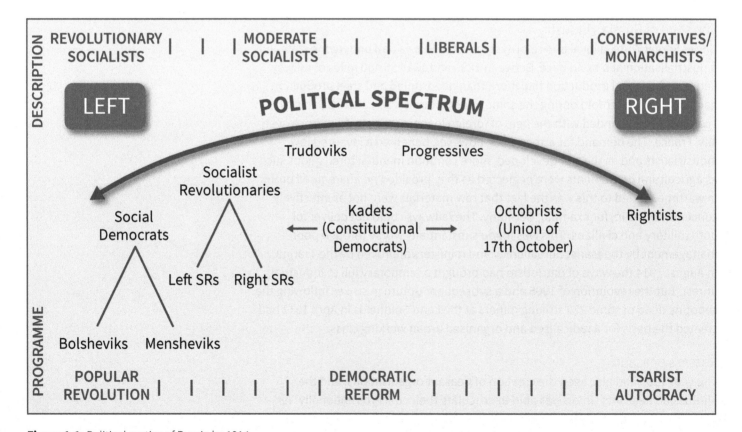

Figure 1.1: Political parties of Russia by 1914.

Discontent

The 'Progressive Bloc'

A major factor in the failure of the tsarist regime was the contempt in which tsardom's most likely liberal allies held the regime. They too had been alienated. In the words of Robert Service, the Tsar's 'court and government appeared incompetent and distasteful to an ever larger segment of the middle classes'.[1] The Duma had loyally dissolved itself in reaction to the outbreak of war. Not only the brutally repressive actions of the regime, but also the inability of the government to fight the war, effectively led to a middle-class intervention to attempt to rescue the situation. In 1915, a '**Progressive Bloc**' was formed, made up of Octobrists, Kadets and Progressives who had been sidelined in the Duma. Action to improve provision was taken at the local level where liberals had been able to gain influence, in the *zemstva* (local councils) and other voluntary bodies. These included Zemgor, the central organisation of the *zemstvo* headed by Prince Lvov and the Defence Council. The War Industries Committee was likewise used to improve the coordination of industry. This reaction was not without self-interest. Manufacturers who had not landed government contracts felt they had lost out and, as Service says, 'thin cats wanted to be fat cats'.[2] Although constructive in their reaction, liberals were essentially displaying their loss of faith in the tsarist regime.

The effects of the First World War

While the war was itself the main catalyst for the failure of the Romanov regime, it is generally argued that the popularity of a continued defence of the motherland was not at issue. Rather, the effects of the war demoralised all sections of society, including the landowners and the nobility, who saw their sons sacrificed for no gain. This lack of morale began to be focused on the regime, particularly as the Tsar left the capital to oversee fighting at **Stavka**, the military headquarters close to the front. The Tsarina, Alexandra, was left with responsibility for domestic government. Ministers were of course still appointed by, and responsible to, the Crown and Alexandra acted to replace the liberally minded with her own flattering, conservative favourites.

Her reputation suffered for other reasons. First, she was German and her loyalty to Russia in wartime was questioned. Second, her marital fidelity to the Tsar was also popularly questioned because of her close relationship with Grigori Rasputin. A so-called *starets* or holy man, he had become a trusted friend of the royal family after gaining the trust within noble circles in St Petersburg and claimed to be able to heal the Tsarevitch, the only son and heir to the throne, who had haemophilia. He was particularly distrusted by those in the nobility who sought, but failed to gain, influence with the court, and was murdered in December 1916. Anti-German sentiment was strongly in evidence. German-named businesses were attacked and the capital itself was renamed from St Petersburg to Petrograd ('town' in German is *Burg*; in Russian it is *gorod*). The regime itself pandered to this intolerance. **Anti-Semitism** and the prioritisation of Russian identity over the various nationalities within the Empire had long informed the regime's approach. Indeed the regime can be said not only to have provoked opposition, but also to have hindered the

Key terms

Progressive Bloc: Formed when the State Duma was recalled during the First World War – several members including the Progressists and the Kadets formed a political front to push Nicholas II to form a 'Government of Confidence' where they could take control of the domestic war effort.

Zemstvo: A form of local government created in Russia during the reforms following emancipation of the peasant serfs. Established in 1864, the *zemstva* were small elected councils in rural areas to provide social and economic services.

Stavka: General Military Headquarters. This name was used both for the tsarist army during the First World War and for the body created by Stalin in June 1941 following the German invasion of the Soviet Union.

Anti-Semitism: Racial hatred against Jewish people. This had been prominent in Russia and the Russian state had at times created laws to discriminate against Jews in the Russian Empire and supported attacks (pogroms) against Jewish communities.

Speak like a historian

Marxist terminology

Historians of political situations often use political terminology to describe processes, concepts and events (such as radicalisation, revolution, reaction, reform, democracy, conservatism, autocracy). In addition, they use the terminology of the historical actors themselves and in the case of the Russian Revolution, it is important to understand the Marxist terminology used by the Social Democrats and others to describe their own actions and the actions of others. For a fuller discussion of Karl Marx's theories, see Figure 2.2. Two key terms to understand at this point are the **bourgeoisie** (and bourgeois) and the **proletariat** (and proletarian). In simple terms, the bourgeoisie and the proletariat are the two opposing classes in society. To be 'bourgeois' is often understood as being 'middle class', but Marx really meant it to mean those in the ruling class under capitalism, who controlled industry and finance. Conversely, 'proletarians' are seen as the 'working class', but Marx meant them as those who worked for, and were ruled over, by the capitalist bourgeoisie. Marxists at this time therefore saw industrial society as divided into two classes with opposing interests. They believed that the proletariat were inevitably to be exploited (treated unfairly and paid too little) by the bourgeoisie until a crisis point where capitalism would fall apart and the bourgeoisie would be overthrown. Many at the time saw the war of 1914, between the major capitalist imperial powers, as the culmination of the crisis.

Key terms

Bourgeoisie: The ruling class under capitalism. Often translated as the 'middle class', for Marxists its most important members were the bankers and industrialists who, as they saw it, had power over the proletariat.

Proletariat: The industrial working class who, according to Marxists, would overthrow the rule of the bourgeoisie through revolution.

war effort by organising deployment of its forces on ethnic grounds. The Tsar's credibility as a war leader, not just as domestic ruler, was in doubt.

The February/March revolution of 1917

Causes and course of revolution

If the war acted as a catalyst in creating discontent, then losing control of his own troops was decisive in the fall of the Tsar in February 1917. Other factors clearly played a role in bringing matters to a head. Following two mild winters, that of 1916–1917 was bitter and this made providing for civilians more difficult. Two factors – the shortage of bread in Petrograd and a sudden lift in temperature at the end of February – combined to bring workers out on to the streets. International Women's Day on 23 February and the mild weather of minus 5 degrees created an atmosphere of holiday-like levity mixed with popular resentment. It was a dangerous combination that created an atmosphere of freedom and a willingness to ignore the threat of repression. This method – sending troops to end popular protest – though used effectively at the end of 1916, had resulted in a severe challenge to the Tsar's authority some years earlier, when unarmed protestors were shot on 'Bloody Sunday' on 9 January 1905.

It is fair to ask why the Tsar had not learned the lesson of 1905 when he ordered on 25 February that the protests be ended through force. The answer would seem to lie in his own sense of patriotism: how could civilians be allowed to undermine

Speak like a historian

The Progressive Bloc

The Progressive Bloc was formed of members of the Duma, which had been dissolved on the outbreak of war. They had been arguably the most cooperative members of the political class in trying to make the constitutional monarchy established in 1905 function effectively. Many had worked with Stolypin in his attempts to bring reform. They had a broadly patriotic purpose in wanting to help Russia win the war in the hope of future reform.

their own countrymen fighting at the front by engaging in self-indulgent protest at home? He was also some miles from the capital and even less able to understand the degree of crisis that was stirring. From this point events moved rapidly. Within a week the Tsar had given up his throne and the monarchy was abolished.

Timeline February–March 1917

14 Feb 1917	The Duma reconvened (for the first time since 1914).
23 Feb	International Women's Day – mass demonstrations in Petrograd.
24 Feb	200 000 idle workers joined demonstrations in Petrograd.
25 Feb	Demonstrations continued with an increasingly political character. Menshevik Duma deputies discussed the formation of a **Soviet**. Nicholas II sent a telegram for troops to restore order in Petrograd.
26 Feb	40 civilians killed or injured at rally in Znamenskii Square. Troops in Petrograd garrison voted to refuse to shoot civilians.
27 Feb	Three city regiments mutinied and occupied the streets with demonstrators. Nicholas II ordered General Ivanov to return to Petrograd with a battalion of elite troops to restore order.
28 Feb	Nicholas II began his return to Petrograd. His train was diverted to Pskov because of warnings of hostile troops en route. The Progressive Bloc Duma leaders formed the 'Provisional Committee for the restoration of order' including Rodzianko, Miliukov and Kerensky. Mensheviks and the Central Workers Group formed the Petrograd Soviet. An executive committee of the Soviet (**Ispolkom**) formed, including Kerenksy, deputy chairman of the Soviet.
1 Mar	Order No. 1 gave the Soviet control of the armed forces. General Alexeev recalled General Ivanov's expedition.

Key terms

Soviet: In late imperial Russia 'soviets' were workers' councils – the earliest being the St Petersburg Soviet formed in 1905. They were formed as a movement of workers independent of the government-sponsored Zubatov unions.

Ispolkom: The Executive Committee of the Petrograd Soviet. From February 1917, this body essentially represented the Petrograd Soviet in negotiations with the Provisional Government.

2 Mar	A Provisional Government formed, headed by Prince Lvov. Miliukov made Minister of Foreign Affairs. Kerensky made Minister of Justice (the only member of the Soviet in the Provisional Government). Negotiations between Ispolkom and the Provisional Government resulted in a document establishing so-called 'dual power'. Duma leaders and the commanders advised the Tsar to abdicate. Nicholas II decided first to abdicate in favour of his son, Alexis, with his brother Grand Duke Mikhael as Regent. Deciding his son was too ill, he agreed to abdicate in favour of Mikhael.
3 Mar	Mikhael refused the crown until a Constituent Assembly could offer it.
4 Mar	The republic proclaimed alongside the agreement between the Provisional Government and Ispolkpom. Nicholas joined his family at Tsarskoe Selo near Petrograd.

Issues of leadership and the Tsar's abdication

Historians differ on who bears the responsibility for the fall of the Romanovs:

- the Tsar himself in ordering a crackdown without fully knowing the situation in Petrograd and being persuaded to abdicate
- the General Staff and Duma leaders in pushing for abdication
- the workers of Petrograd in demonstrating and challenging authority

Voices from the past

The Programme of the Progressive Bloc, 25 August, 1915

The undersigned representatives of factions and groups in the State Council and State Duma, convinced that only a strong, firm and active government can lead our country to victory, and that such a government can only be one that is based upon the confidence of the people and is capable of organising the active cooperation of all citizens, have come to the unanimous conclusion that the most important and urgent task of creating such a government cannot be fulfilled unless the following conditions are met:

1 The formation of a united government which enjoys the confidence of the country …
2 Radical change in the methods of administration employed to date, which have been based on a mistrust of public initiative, in particular:
(a) strict observance of the principles of legality in government;

(b) abolition of the dual authority of the military and civil authorities in questions which have no immediate bearing on the conduct of military operations;

(c) the renewal of the personnel of local administration;

(d) a rational and consistent policy to maintain civil peace and the elimination of discord between nationalities and classes.[3]

Discussion points
1. What criticisms of how the government works are implied in this programme?
2. Why do you think members of the Progressive Bloc believed they could contribute to a government 'based on the confidence of the people'?
3. Does this extract suggest that the Progressive Bloc was more concerned with military victory or internal reform?

- the troops of the Petrograd garrison for mutinying and joining the demonstrations
- socialist leaders in politicising the protestors.

It is possible to paint the Tsar as weak and indecisive, but his reason for stepping down (he did not foresee his brother's refusal of the crown) was to pacify the crowd in Petrograd and enable Russia to fight on to victory. While this was a miscalculation for him personally, those persuading him to go sought the same outcome of Russian victory. Some argue that this was a soldiers' rather than a workers' revolution. Certainly, mutinous troops played an essential role. However, the munity took place because the troops wished to show their solidarity with workers' demonstrations. Revolutionary socialists played a somewhat minor role in leading revolt. Many, such as Lenin, were not present.

The establishment of the Provisional Government and the Petrograd Soviet

Nevertheless, those who were present took full advantage of the situation. Ispolkom, the newly founded Petrograd Soviet's executive committee, issued Order Number 1 claiming for itself control of the armed forces – the Soviet must approve orders from the Provisional Government. The two rival bodies – the Soviet and the Provisional Government – met in opposite wings of the Tauride Palace, where the Duma had previously met. Despite their rivalry, the two bodies agreed on a document that gave official responsibility to the Provisional Government and the power to essentially veto its legislation to Ispolkom, in the name of the Soviet. This mainly involved questions over the control of the military and its democratic structure. The majority opinion in Ispolkom was that Russia was not ready for a socialist revolution, but rather must undergo a lengthy stage of bourgeois development. This demonstrates both the timidity of the Duma leaders in the face of popular discontent and the hesitancy of socialists to participate in government. Only Alexander Kerensky, the Socialist Revolutionary demagogue, had a foot in each camp.

The workings of the dual authority

As you will see from the sources at the end of the chapter, the relationship between the Provisional Government and the Petrograd Soviet meant that governmental authority in Russia did not seem to be located fully in either of these bodies. This gave rise to the expression 'dual authority'. This is to say that neither body had full authority, and each relied on the other in order to influence national policy. Nevertheless, at a national level, the Soviet seemed to have greater influence over the people and the liberals who made up the Provisional Government seemed to need the assistance of the Soviet in order to bolster their legitimacy to rule; hence Minister Guchkov's claim that the Provisional Government's directives were 'carried out only to the extent that it is permitted by the Soviet … which enjoys all the essential elements of real power'.

Two men played central roles in defining the reality of 'dual power'. The first was Prince Georgy Lvov. He had been heavily involved in the coordination of *zemstvo* attempts to aid the war effort and domestic administration in the preceding years. This made him a natural choice to replace Rodzianko as the Prime Minister of

Speak like a historian

Political bodies

There are a number of political institutions or 'bodies' that it is important to be able to identify:

- The Duma was the Russian elected assembly or parliament set up in 1905. It did not have quite as many powers as other countries' parliaments.

- The zemstva were provincial councils established in 1864 with limited powers to run local affairs – this is where some of the liberals gained political experience before 1905.

- The Provisional Government was a 'provisional' or temporary government that expected to be replaced once a Constitutional Assembly had been elected to write a new constitution for the new republic (which the Russian Empire became following the fall of the monarchy in February 1917).

- The Petrograd Soviet acted almost as a rival national power from February to October 1917, but there were thousands of Soviets set up across the country, which were literally 'councils' of workers, soldiers, sailors and peasants' representatives.

Newly set-up institutions often had their names shortened for convenience. Three such during this period were:

- Ispolkom, the Petrograd Soviet's executive committee (a smaller body set up to undertake the business of the Soviet)

- Milrevkom, the Petrograd Soviet's **Military Revolutionary Committee** or armed force, also referred to as the MRC

- **Sovnarkom**, the Council of People's Commissars, which replaced the Provisional Government in October 1917.

the Provisional Government following the Tsar's abdication. Lvov was in some senses well placed to help steer a pragmatic government, but these same reasons undermined his ability to provide a decisive lead. He was used to working with different parties who all wished to work in the national interest and so was unsuited to dealing with competing political agendas and parties. He retained what might be termed an 'optimistic liberalism', trusting in the good sense of the Russian people despite the revolutionary turmoil. It was for this reason that he insisted on a methodical drawing-up of arrangements for a Constituent Assembly, which brought delay and undermined what confidence existed in the 'dual authority' to deliver.

Ispolkom's attitude towards the Provisional Government seems relatively clear: this was not the moment for revolutionary government, and a Soviet with influence but without responsibility was the most advantageous role for socialists. Lvov felt that the Soviet support lent much-needed legitimacy to what was after all a temporary government. Events in February indicated that the socialists were the Duma liberals' only effective intermediary to the more volatile elements of the mass of people. There was some belief and hope that once the democratic reforms of March were enacted, the Provisional Government would become less reliant on revolutionary democratic committees in order for its writ to run. Events would prove otherwise.

In July Lvov resigned and was replaced by Alexander Kerensky. Kerensky was a Socialist Revolutionary in the Petrograd Soviet and, to begin with, was Minister for Justice in the Provisional Government. His position was therefore unique. He regarded himself as an essential lynchpin, although Orlando Figes[4] suggests that he was much more at home with liberal politicians than socialists and that his role in the Soviet was mainly to make grand speeches. It could be argued that Kerensky enjoyed listening to the sound of his own voice and encouraged a cult of personality around himself. When eventually it came to his elevation to the head of government, he took on the role of 'saviour of the nation'. Other socialists, such as Chernov and Tsereteli, were eventually willing to take part in government, but Kerensky can be said to have acted as a lynchpin between the liberals and socialists who were broadly united in wanting to save the social gains of the revolution without allowing the Russian nation to fall apart in political chaos and military defeat.

Developments between the revolutions

The return of Lenin

Events in April 1917 underlined the problems of the liberal-dominated Provisional Government. On 3 April Lenin, who had been in exile, arrived in Petrograd, courtesy of the German government, who had agreed to send him to Russia on a sealed train. From their point of view, they hoped that Lenin would act to cause further disturbance in Petrograd and contribute to taking Russia out of the war. Lenin did indeed advocate peace, but he also persuaded the Bolshevik faction of the Social Democrats to absolutely rule out further cooperation with the Provisional Government. He made the programme clear in what has come to be referred to as the April Theses. It was a very effective message: peace (for the soldiers), bread (for the workers) and land (for the peasants). Its genius, other than its simplicity, was that it demanded (and promised) an immediate resolution to the people's problems, irrespective of the difficulties of ending the war.

Lenin's ideology and the April Theses

The solution was also simply put: 'All power to the Soviets'. This was similarly vague, and it suggested that the answer lay in boycotting the bourgeois Provisional Government and seizing power for the Soviets. Lenin was re-writing the Marxist model, by claiming that Russia could move immediately from bourgeois revolution to proletarian revolution. Orthodox Marxists, especially the Mensheviks, insisted that Russia had not developed sufficiently to be ready for the next historical stage of revolution (see Figure 2.2). Lenin was thus proposing, in some people's eyes, to shortcut Marx's model. As a popular message 'All power to the Soviets' was very successful and Bolshevik support began to increase. Lenin was convinced of the need for a seizure of power by the Bolsheviks and this may

Key terms

Military Revolutionary Committee (MRC or Milrevkom): The armed force of the Petrograd Soviet. It was used by Trotsky to organise the Bolshevik seizure of power in October 1917.

Sovnarkom: Council of People's Commissars formed shortly after the October Revolution in 1917. It was the legislative body, chaired by Lenin, charged with restructuring government systems to build the Soviet Union. There were eleven members called 'commissars' instead of 'ministers'. It became the Council of Ministers under Stalin in 1946.

have been his prime motivation. The first step towards this aim was to distance the Bolsheviks from other socialists, particularly the Mensheviks and the Provisional Government.

Lenin arrived at the Finland Station, in the heart of the working-class Vyborg District of Petrograd, on 3 April (Figure 1.2). His journey to Russia had been facilitated by the German government in the hope of further destabilising the situation in Russia and removing them from the war.

Figure 1.2: The arrival of Communist leader Vladimir Ilich Lenin (facing crowd with hat raised) at the Finland Station in Petrograd, Russia, April 1917. Joseph Stalin, who was not actually present at the event, is fictitiously depicted standing behind Lenin. Soviet painting, 1930s.

The July days

The June Offensive

In a sense, the German government played into Lenin's hands. On 18 April Miliukov, as Foreign Minister, assured the Allies in a memorandum that Russia would not only not seek a separate peace, but also look to gain land from the Ottoman Empire in a future Allied victory. The publication of this note resulted in demonstrations which were only quelled through the influence of the Petrograd Soviet. 'Miliukov's note' ended in his resignation from the government and triggered negotiations with moderate socialists. As a result a new liberal-socialist coalition government was formed, which included Kerensky as the dominant Minister for War. Six socialists entered the Cabinet of 16, possibly out of patriotic duty and in the belief that they might speed some reform. Their policy on the war, however, remained unchanged. It was decided that there would be a determined effort to make progress in the war through a renewed offensive in June.

Kerensky (shown in Figure 1.3) was active, as was his manner, in giving speeches to rally the troops. He sold the conflict as a war in defence of the February revolution.

Given the weaknesses of an army that was poorly equipped and subject to the demands of soldiers' committees, it is fair to question why it was attempted. The answer would seem to be that the coalition, under pressure from their Allies to attack, agreed on the same solution for different ends. The Right hoped to use war to destroy the revolution; the Left intended to win enough ground to sue for a passable peace and save the revolution. Launched on 16 June, there were two days of advances on three fronts, but they could not be sustained and the Germans counter-attacked. Kerensky's motivational speeches were not enough. The failure of the offensive led to the collapse of the coalition and a period of political crisis known as the July Days.

ACTIVITY 1.2

Consider how Lenin's return is portrayed in Figure 1.2 and its likely accuracy.

You may wish to research the event further.

Figure 1.3: Alexander Kerensky (standing in car) inspecting the troops in 1917.

This poorly directed challenge to the government was sparked, as in February, by the mutinous action of the Petrograd garrison. Order Number 1 had guaranteed that the garrison would not be ordered to the Front, but would stay in the city to protect against any attempts as 'counter-revolution'. When ordered on 20 June to send a detachment of machine-gunners to the Front, it refused. Encouraged by Bolsheviks in the garrison and most militant working-class district of Vyborg,

 Voices from the past

Alexander Kerensky

Alexander Kerensky was born into a middle-class family in 1881. He grew up under the repressive Alexander III and his parents were friends with the Ulyanovs (Lenin's family). He became a lawyer and worked as counsel to those accused of crimes during the 1905 revolution. Kerensky was elected as a Trudovik (Labour Party) candidate to the Fourth Duma in 1912, but by 1917 had joined the Socialist Revolutionaries and called for Nicholas's removal. He became first Minister of Justice, then Minister for War and eventually Prime Minister of the Provisional Government, but was also a member of the Petrograd Soviet. His aim to bridge the gap between moderates and radicals during 1917 proved impossible.

Key terms

Kronstadt: The fortified naval base of Petrograd (later Leningrad), which was situated at the edge of the city's Baltic Sea port. The sailors of Kronstadt were strong supporters of the Bolsheviks in 1917, but turned against them in March 1921, accusing them of betraying the revolution and instead creating a dictatorship.

Central Committee: The sovereign body of the Communist Party, elected by the Party Congress. While many of its responsibilities were given to other important bodies such as the Politburo, it was in theory where, ultimately, the policy of the Communist Party was decided.

workers, soldiers and sailors from the Kronstadt naval base acted much as they had in February: they marched on the city centre on 3 July, this time with the sufficiently vague slogan, 'All Power to the Soviets'. When confronted with the opportunity to head up this movement, Lenin and the Bolshevik Central Committee gave it their general support but were hesitant to do anything more.

In this situation, the Provisional Government took the initiative and called in loyal troops to end the demonstrations and to arrest Bolshevik leaders and clear their headquarters. Kerensky, in particular, propagated the idea that Bolsheviks were part of a German plot to undermine the achievements of February. By 7 June, Lenin had gone into hiding and Trotsky, who had joined the Bolshevik ranks, was under arrest with several other Bolsheviks – and the crisis was over. Kerensky formed a new coalition government on 9 July, replacing Lvov as Prime Minister.

The exact role of the Bolsheviks during the July Days is disputed. Lenin seems to have been ambivalent about whether the time was right. It is possible to say that faced with the opportunity for power, he lost his nerve. Alternatively, it could be that, as the supreme opportunist, Lenin knew that this was not the right time to strike. While the July crisis was used by the Bolsheviks' rivals to damage their name and hinder their activities, it could be argued that it benefited them by again demonstrating their difference from all the other parties and their uncompromising stance against the Provisional Government.

Subsequent events and decisions by others played an essential part in giving the Bolsheviks the upper hand. Kerensky still portrayed himself as the saviour of the revolution and the nation. Nevertheless, the 'bourgeois' industrialists and their allies in the press and the military were buoyed by the defeat of the Bolsheviks, seeing the opportunity to curb the enemies of the Provisional Government and to restore order among the troops. It was this that precipitated the Kornilov affair.

The Kornilov affair

The affair seems to have been the result of mistrust and miscommunication between Kornilov and Kerensky. Kornilov began to doubt that the Provisional Government could be trusted with military secrets, following remarks in a meeting on 3 August. Kerensky, on the other hand, bristled at the enthusiastic reception Kornilov received at a state conference on 14 August. What brought matters to a head were fears of another Bolshevik-inspired uprising. Through the fateful actions of one Vladimir Lvov, who acted as an unsolicited emissary between the two men, Kornilov was led to believe that Kerensky was prepared to allow him to declare a military dictatorship and send troops to secure the Provisional Government, dispersing the Soviet if necessary. Kerensky had no such intention, but through a conversation by teleprinter at cross-purposes, Kornilov dispatched a force to Petrograd on 27 August to secure the Provisional Government. On learning of this, Kerensky, fearful for his own position, dismissed Kornilov and ordered his arrest. He then decided that it was necessary to mobilise the popular forces of Petrograd to defend the revolution against what he claimed was a military coup, accusing Kornilov of treason. He released Bolsheviks from prison and distributed 40 000 guns. There was, however, no confrontation. Kornilov's troops were met on the way by a Soviet delegation that persuaded them to halt their advance.

The effect of the Kornilov affair was to undermine the authority of both the Commander-in-Chief and the Prime Minister. In undertaking what looked like a coup, Kornilov was painted as a danger to the revolution (in all fairness, he had no problem with the idea of military dictatorship). In siding with 'Red Petrograd', Kerensky lost the trust of his generals and demonstrated his weakness by calling on the support of the Bolsheviks. With both men discredited, there was a power vacuum into which the Bolsheviks could now step.

The Provisional Government and Trotsky

Kerensky's resort to the very forces he had opposed in July in order to defend his own power base became a major factor in the final collapse of his coalition. Leon Trotsky (shown in Figure 2.3) became a significant actor in events at this point. Having possibly played an ambiguous role in the July Days, he welcomed his arrest and imprisonment, hoping to use his trial as a public platform. When Kerensky appealed for the help of the Kronstadt sailors against Kornilov, Trotsky was consulted in his cell at Kresty prison. He encouraged the sailors to side with Kerensky for now, because he sensed the Prime Minister would not last long.

On his release, Trotsky was to play a key role in turning radical popular opinion against the Provisional Government and realising Lenin's now impatient call for an immediate armed seizure of power by the Bolsheviks. It was becoming increasingly clear that the uncompromising position of the Bolsheviks, particulary regarding the war, was winning them popularity. In February, Bolshevik membership stood at around 10 000. By October, it is estimated to have been as great as 300 000. This was most apparent in early September, when they began to win majorities in the urban Soviets in and around the two capitals and other industrial centres.

Other socialists began to look for an alternative power base and proposed a Democratic Conference, which was eventually held on 14 September. Kerensky looked to use this event to bring socialist opinion behind his government by means of a pre-parliament. Bolshevik opinion was split as to whether to take part in the conference. It was Trotsky who defined the Bolshevik response. Before this point he had not explicitly associated himself with the Bolshevik faction, but he now moved quickly towards Lenin's position and limited the Bolsheviks' role at the conference to denouncing the Provisional Government (and those socialists prepared to take part in it) and calling for all power to be transferred to the Soviets (as stated in the April Theses). Trotsky then managed to persuade the Bolshevik Central Committee to withdraw from the conference by 5 October. Kerensky went on to form another coalition with the liberal Kadets and essentially lost all purchase with the far left from this point.

Assess the position of the Provisional Government by October 1917. The decisions of the Provisional Government are very often blamed for their consequent loss of power. Reread the sections on the Provisional Government and add to Table 1.1.

Decision	Advantage	Disadvantage
Example: accepting 'dual power' with the Petrograd Soviet	The Provisional Government was able to maintain the support of the workers' movement.	The Provisional Government was unable to act without the approval of the Soviet – It had responsibility without full power.

Table 1.1: Decisions made by the Provisional Government

Lenin and the Central Committee of the Bolshevik Party

The Bolsheviks had replaced the SRs and Mensheviks as the majority socialist party in the Petrograd and Moscow city Dumas (city councils) and the Soviets in September. Some Bolsheviks, Kamenev for example, believed that they could gain power within the Soviet movement, rather than through a separate coup. Lenin became convinced that cooperation with fellow socialists was pointless. In the public mind, they were associated with a failed government. Throughout September he sent messages from exile in Finland urging the Central Committee to take action. He eventually lost patience and returned to Petrograd where, in meetings on 10 and 16 October, he won votes in favour of a small force taking power, without recourse to a mass uprising. Only Kamenev and Zinoviev voted against. They hoped to gain power through the Second All-Russian Congress of Soviets scheduled for 20 October. Lenin did not want to risk this.

Trotsky had played a key role in driving Bolshevik opinion towards a seizure of power and had been appointed Chairman of the Petrograd on 8 October. On 16 October, the Soviet established a Military Revolutionary Committee on the basis of defending the Soviet from counter-revolutionary assaults. From this point, it was obvious to Kerensky that he needed to organise his own forces. Kamenev and Zinoviev, alarmed at their isolation in the Central Committee, revealed the plans for an uprising in a newspaper article. Trotsky quickly denied the rumours at the Petrograd Soviet on 18 October. Zinoviev and Kamenev added their voices to confirm the denial in the hope of changing policy. Trotsky, however, was in reality undeterred and assured Lenin that arrangements were in place. He rushed from barracks to factory shoring up support from the most radical elements in the army and workforce.

The October/November 1917 revolution

Causes, course and extent of revolution

March to October: The collapse of authority and the struggle for power

The Provisional Government had limited influence against the Soviet. Orlando Figes, however, suggests that this was less about 'dual power' and more about the fragmentation and breakdown of authority.[5] As the message that the monarchy had fallen filtered out to the provinces and countryside, various bodies stepped in to claim control. In towns this mainly involved members of the *zemstvo* and Soviets or factory committees. In the countryside, those who had broken away from the *mir* quickly found themselves under pressure by commune elders who were keen to claim all private land for common use. The greatest instance of power being seized seems to have been in the armed forces, where there was a sudden rise in the number of councils and Soviets claiming democratic control over their units. This was an important way of ensuring that those troops who had mutinied would not be disciplined under military law. In such a situation there were many asserting power, but who had it was not obvious.

The need for peace

The Provisional Government may have produced legislation to create new citizens of a 'free Russia', but its overriding priority was the war. The United States, the newest ally against Germany, was the first to recognise the Provisional Government as the legitimate successor to the monarchy. Its authority stemmed from elections to a now defunct body, the Duma. The fourth point of the agreed document promised the 'immediate preparation for the convening of the Constituent Assembly'[6] by means of fair elections. These would eventually take place in November, after the Provisional Government had lost power.

It is possible that liberals within the government were aware that they would most likely lose influence following such elections, or that they simply believed they could not be properly held in the midst of war. They hoped to create an orderly form of constitutional government, but the conditions for doing so were becoming less and less favourable. The fact was that workers, soldiers and peasants were already, to some extent, taking what they wanted. The matter of land reform (liberals hoped for a peaceful and legal process rather than straightforward expropriation or seizure by peasants) was the most problematic. Were private land to be granted to the peasants before the end of hostilities, the Provisional Government feared that troops, composed mainly of peasants, would simply desert the front line in order to ensure they gained their piece of land. Land reform was therefore put off until a Constituent Assembly could carry out the process legally and gradually. There was no clear clamour for a peace at all costs. Surrender to Germany and the consequent loss of land in the west was unpalatable to those who had fought for a free Russia in February. Socialists did, however, advocate a speedy peace without annexations (the claiming of captured Russian land by the victorious Germans) – a solution that was very unlikely to be acceptable to Russia's Western allies.

ACTIVITY 1.4

Research the role of each of these individuals in the evolution of the Provisional Government. Place them on a timeline from February to October 1917.

- Mikhail V. Rodzianko (Octobrist Prime Minister, February)
- Prince Georgy Y. Lvov (Kadet Prime Minister, February to July)
- Pavel N. Miliukov (Kadet Foreign Minister, February to April)
- Irakli Tsereteli (Menshevik Minister of Interior under Kerensky and member of Ispolkom).

Timeline August–December 1917

Late August/ early Sept 1917	Bolsheviks gained majority in Soviets in Petrograd, Moscow, Riga and Saratov.
14 Sept	Democratic Conference held between Kadets and Socialists to negotiate a new coalition.
24 Sept	A new liberal-socialist coalition was formed under Kerensky.
10 Oct	Lenin returned to Petrograd from Finland to hold a secret meeting with the Bolshevik Central Committee and gained agreement to prepare for an uprising.
16 Oct	Lenin gained agreement for an armed seizure of power by a small, disciplined force. Kamenev and Zinoviev resigned in protest.
18 Oct	Newspapers carried stories of the Bolsheviks' plans.
20 Oct	The Military Revolutionary Committee of the Soviet was formed to prevent the removal of the Petrograd garrison to the front.
24 Oct	Lenin left hiding in the evening to convince Central Committee at the Smolny Institute to undertake the seizure of power immediately.
25 Oct	MRC deployed to strategic bridges and telephone exchange; entered Winter Palace to arrest the remainder of the Provisional Government. A total of 670 delegates of the Second All-Russian Congress of Soviets met in the Tauride Palace (rescheduled from 20 Oct). Bolsheviks declared that power had been seized by Sovnarkom. Mensheviks and some Socialist Revolutionaries walked out in protest. Winter Palace was taken with very little resistance.
26 Oct	Decree on Land and Decree on Peace.
27 Oct	Decree on the Press: banned opposition newspapers.
29 Oct	Bolsheviks opened talks with socialist parties; eventually abandoned. Decrees on the Eight-Hour Day and Popular Education.
2 Nov	Declaration of the Rights of the Peoples of Russia.
12–14 Nov	Elections to the Constituent Assembly were held.
14 Nov	Decree on Worker's Control: handed power to factory committees.
2 Dec	Creation of Supreme Council of the National Economy.
5 Dec	Creation of the **Cheka** under leadership of Felix Dzerzhinski.
14 Dec	Nationalisation of all banks.

Leadership and the establishment of Bolshevik authority

Most historians are quite clear that when the moment came, the Bolsheviks seized power through a coup: the stationing of Bolshevik **Red Guards** at strategic points around Petrograd and the deposing of the government by force. While there was some resistance on the day chosen, 25 October, the opposition melted away and Kerensky escaped in a car and eventually made his way into exile. This then contradicts the idea spread by the subsequent Bolshevik regime that a popular revolution took place in October as it had in February. The choice in many workers' minds was between the forces for or against the revolution and what it had won them.

The Soviet leaders, aware of Lenin's intentions, delayed the meeting of the Congress by five days, but this worked instead to Lenin's advantage. If he were able to seize power just before the Congress met, then he could claim to be doing so in the name of the Soviets. The circumstances, it seems, had changed since July, particularly as Trotsky now had control of the Soviet's Military Revolutionary Committee, which itself gained the control of the Petrograd garrison. The so-called 'Storming the Winter Palace', represented by the Bolshevik regime later as a mass invasion, in reality involved a relatively small number of armed persons on either side. Those charged by the Provisional Government to defend Petrograd at key points against the Bolsheviks, mostly military cadets, were ordered to retire – many simply left their posts. Before he fled, Kerensky tried unsuccessfully to raise a force from the front.

In the early hours of 25 October, Lenin declared himself Chairman of the Council of People's Commissars (Sovnarkom), which was to be the new government of Russia. To begin with it comprised only Bolsheviks, with Trotsky in charge of Foreign Affairs and Stalin in charge of Nationalities. The seizure of power was based on sheer assertion and the great majority of the country had no idea it had occurred. Indeed, when the decision was presented to the Soviet Congress that met that day, it was couched in the terms of the Soviet (rather than the Bolsheviks) taking power from the Provisional Government. Mensheviks and the so-called **Right SRs** again made the Bolsheviks' new hold on power stronger by walking out of the Congress in protest, consigning themselves in Trotsky's words 'to the dustbin of history'. **Left SRs**, although subsequently critical, supported Sovnarkom and were given a minority of places in the new government later in the year. The Bolsheviks succeeded by allowing the broad impression that Soviet power had been established, but those in the Congress on 25 October who acclaimed the new government and condemned those who had left, had handed power to Lenin.

Reasons for Bolshevik success

- Bolsheviks identified as the sole party opposed to the Provisional Government
- Kerensky's loss of support from left and right
- the Provisional Government failure to bring land reform, win the war or create a Constituent Assembly
- 'Dual power' undermined the authority of the Provisional Government
- Lenin's leadership and insistence on seizing power
- the popularity of the slogans from the April Theses

Key terms

Cheka: (All-Russian Extraordinary Commission against Counter Revolution and Sabotage), formed on 20 December 1917, was the Bolsheviks' secret police force. It was responsible for carrying out the 'Red Terror' mass oppression during the Russian Civil War of 1918–1922. Its founder and leader was Felix Dzerzhinsky.

Red Guards: A paramilitary organisation within the Bolshevik Party, made up of factory workers, peasants and ex-soldiers. Reorganised into the Red Army during the Civil War beginning 1918.

Right SRs: The Socialist Revolutionaries split in 1917, between those who supported the Provisional Government (established during the February Revolution) and those who supported the Bolsheviks (the Left SRs). When the majority of SRs left the Congress of Soviets in October 1917 when the Bolsheviks took over, they were labelled by the Bolsheviks as 'Right SRs'.

Left SRs: The Socialist Revolutionaries split in 1917, between those who supported the Provisional Government (established during the February Revolution) and those who supported the Bolsheviks (the Left SRs). In 1918 they revolted against the Bolsheviks, who had signed the Treaty of Brest-Litovsk.

- the association of the Mensheviks and Socialist Revolutionaries with the Provisional Government through coalition
- the refusal of the Soviet to take power in its own name.

Sovnarkom and decrees and actions to December

Despite the apparent ease with which it was established, Sovnarkom's rule was not immediately secure. Leading Bolsheviks thought that at any point a rival force might simply arrest them. When Trotsky arrived at the Ministry of Foreign Affairs announcing himself in charge, the staff laughed and went home. Other such civil service strikes occurred, but were, bit by bit, suppressed by armed men arriving and persuading them to cooperate or be arrested.

From the start, opposition to the new regime was dealt with through arrest and censorship. Opposition newspapers were banned and the Military Revolutionary committee (MRC) of the Soviet was used to arrest Menshevik and SR leaders. This would be replaced on 7 December by the Extraordinary Commission for Struggle against Counterrevolution and Sabotage, the 'Cheka' – a new secret police. Sovnarkom ruled not by vote but by decree (in a sense comparable to the Tsar's rule by edict) and asserted its ability to do so without the approval of the Soviet and the waning Ispolkom.

Repression was not, however, universally obvious, nor was the transfer of power immediate. Sovnarkom allowed elections to the **Constituent Assembly** to take place in November. Lenin had been desperate to seize power before these could

Hidden voices

Lenin

The following call to action is an extract is taken from Lenin's letter to the Central, Petrograd and Moscow committees and Bolshevik members of the Petrograd and Moscow Soviets, in October 1917.[7]

Dear Comrades,

Events are prescribing our task so clearly for us that procrastination is becoming positively criminal.

The peasant movement is developing. The government is intensifying its severe repressive measures. Sympathy for us is growing in the army …

In Germany the beginning of a revolution is obvious, especially since the sailors were shot. The elections in Moscow – 47 per cent Bolsheviks – are a tremendous victory. Together with the Left Socialist Revolutionaries we have an obvious majority in the country.

The railway and postal employees are in conflict with the government. Instead of calling the Congress for 20 October, the Liberdans [Lenin's derisory phrase for Menshevik leaders and their followers] are already calling it at the end of October etc. etc.

Under such circumstances to 'wait' would be a crime.

The Bolsheviks have no right to wait for the Congress of Soviets; they must take power at once. By doing so they will save the world revolution …

If power cannot be achieved without insurrection, then we must resort to insurrection at once.

Discussion points:

1. What is Lenin's reasoning for seizing power at once?
2. How useful is this source in assessing Lenin's role in the lead-up to the Bolshevik revolution?

take place and the results demonstrated why: the Socialist Revolutionaries gained a clear majority of 38% to the Bolsheviks' 24%. This stated, the ballot papers did not distinguish between left and right SRs, so that this referendum on the Bolshevik seizure of power may not be seen as such a defeat for the new government. It also held out the possibility that Sovnarkom would be replaced once the Constituent Assembly met. It may have been part of Lenin's plan to allow this perception to remain widespread in order to allay fears of wholesale dictatorship.

Public opinion, where it mattered, was also convinced of Bolshevik sincerity by the immediate decrees on Land and on Peace. The Bolsheviks had no means to enforce these decrees, but this was not necessary. They simply reflected the reality on the ground:

- The Decree on Land legitimised the seizure of private land by peasants that had been taking place throughout the summer. It borrowed directly from the SRs' programme and declared the land 'socialised'. At the same time, the All-Russian Peasants Congress, which had been independent of the Soviets, was merged with the Soviet of Workers and Soldiers Deputies on 12 December.
- The Decree on Peace was simply a statement that Sovnarkom would seek a peace without annexations. It was highly unlikely that Germany would be so generous, but it drew a clear line under the war and bought the Bolsheviks time to negotiate. Germany was more concerned with transferring its troops to the Western Front. Importantly, at the same time, Russia declared war on the Ukraine, which sought independence. This demonstrates not only that Bolshevik policy on those nationalities eager to break free of the Russian grip was unlikely to find favour, but that the **Civil War** was underway. This was more than apparent to the wealthy, who were subject to government-sponsored harassment as bourgeois enemies of the working class.

Conclusion

Given what came next, the final months of 1917 look like an incredible failure of the Bolsheviks' opponents. Central authority itself had collapsed in February. The Provisional Government allowed what power it had to leech away by failing to win, or end, the war and by failing to bring about a Constituent Assembly earlier. The Bolsheviks took power under the guise of the Soviets and made use of vague populist rhetoric in an increasingly polarised and war-weary society that demanded simple solutions. Moderate voices were endangered and unlikely to get a hearing. The threat of counter-revolution by the Right, as illustrated by the Kornilov affair, acted as a factor in undermining the Provisional Government. Kerensky was aware of the importance of defending the gains of February, but lost all credibility. By the end of October, the Bolsheviks could claim to hold power, but it would take a very serious struggle to establish it and to keep it.

Key terms

Constituent Assembly: The first democratically elected legislative body in Russian history, formed just after the October Revolution of 1917. It met for 13 hours before the Central Executive Committee (under Lenin's orders) dissolved it.

Civil War: A conflict in which two or more groups within one country fight each other. The Russian Civil War began in 1918 and lasted until 1922. It was fought mainly between the 'Reds' and 'Whites'. Red victory ensured the consolidation of power by the new communist regime. Another relevant example is the Spanish Civil War (1936–1939), fought between socialists and nationalists.

This timeline of 1917 lists the key events of each month summarised in just one or two words. Look back over your notes and complete the timeline.

Timeline 1917

Month	Event
January	Strikes
February	
March	Laws
April	
May	Coalition
June	
July	Days
August	
September	Bolshevik majority
October	
November	Elections
December	

Further reading

For an excellent introduction to the revolutions and why they occurred when they did, Orlando Figes' *Revolutionary Russia 1891–1991* (Pelican, 2014) is a good choice because he succinctly delivers an interesting narrative, with fantastic vignettes and descriptions that reveal more about particular characters at the time. Richard Pipes' *A Concise History of the Russian Revolution* (Vintage, 1997) begins with the revolution of 1905 but describes, in great detail, the events which took place in 1917. However, you should be aware that he is extremely critical of the Bolsheviks in the October Revolution. Robert Service's *Lenin: A Biography* (Pan, 2010) details a wonderful account of Lenin the public figure as well as the private man in this biography and is useful for gaining an insight into his commitment to Marxism.

Practice essay questions

1. 'The February Revolution occurred because the Russian military lost faith in the Tsarist regime.' Assess the validity of this view.
2. 'The seizure of power by the Bolsheviks in October 1917 was achieved without widespread support.' Explain why you agree or disagree with this view.
3. 'By 1914 the tsarist regime was on the verge of collapse.' Assess the validity of this view.
4. With reference to the sources below and your understanding of the historical context, assess the value of the three sources to a historian studying authority in Russia in 1917.

Source A

War Minister Guchkov, Army Commander-in-Chief, March 1917 (in Fitzpatrick, S., *The Russian Revolution*, p. 17).

The Provisional Government does not possess any real power; and its directives are carried out only to the extent that it is permitted by the Soviet of Workers' and Soldiers' Deputies, which enjoys all the essential elements of real power, since the troops, the railroads, the post and telegraph are all in its hands. One can say flatly that the Provisional Government exists only so long as it is permitted by the Soviet.

Source B

Resolution of the Conference of the Petrograd Socialist Revolutionaries, 2 March 1917 (in Evans, D. and Jenkins, J., *Years of Russia, the USSR and the Collapse of Soviet Communism*, p. 218).

The conference considers that support for the Provisional Government is absolutely necessary, whilst it carries out its declared programme: an amnesty, the granting of individual freedoms, the repeal of estate, religious and national restrictions and preparation for the Constituent Assembly. The conference reserves the right to change its attitudes should the Provisional Government not adhere to the implementation of this programme.

Source C

Extracts from Order Number 1 of the Petrograd Soviet (adapted from Vernadsky, G., *A Source Book for Russian History, Volume 3*).

The Soviet of Workers' and Soldiers' Deputies has decided:

- *In all companies, battalions, squadrons and separate branches of military service of all kinds and on warships, committees should be chosen immediately.*

- *The orders of … the State Duma [Provisional Government] shall be carried out only when they do not contradict the orders and decisions of the Soviet of Workers' and Soldiers' Deputies*

- *All kinds of arms, such as rifles and machine guns, must be under the control of the company and battalion committees and must in no case be handed over to officers even at their demand.*

- *The addressing of officers with titles such as 'Your Excellency', 'Your Honour' etc., is abolished and these are replaced by 'Mr General', 'Mr Colonel' and so on.*

Chapter summary

By the end of this chapter you should be able to:

- establish and prioritise the causes of the February Revolution
- assess the influence and popularity of the Provisional Government in relation to revolutionaries, opponents of revolution, popular movements, and the armed forces
- establish the reasons for the success of the Bolshevik seizure of power in October
- define the nature of early Bolshevik rule.

End notes

1   Service, R., *The Penguin History of Modern Russia: From Tsarism to the Twenty-First Century*, p. 40.
2   Service, *The Penguin History of Modern Russia*, p. 49.
3   Cited in Kowalski, R., *The Russian Revolution, 1917–1921*, pp. 21–22.
4   Figes, O., *Revolutionary Russia, 1891–1991*.
5   Figes, *Revolutionary Russia*.
6   In Kowalski, *The Russian Revolution*, p. 49.
7   Cited in Acton, E. and Stableford, T., *The Soviet Union: A Documentary History, Volume 1, 1917–1940*, p. 56.

2 Bolshevik consolidation, 1918–1924

In this section we will investigate the consolidation of the newly established Communist regime and the creation of the Soviet Union:

- the consolidation of the Communist dictatorship: the establishment of one-party control; the removal of the Constituent Assembly; the end of involvement in the First World War

- the Civil War: causes and course; the Red Army and the role of Trotsky; the murder of the Tsar; the Red Terror; reasons for the Red victory

- economic and social developments: state capitalism; social change; conditions in cities and countryside during the Civil War; war communism; revolts and the Red Terror; the NEP and its political and economic impact

- foreign relations and attitudes of foreign powers: the break-up of the Empire; foreign intervention in the Civil War; Comintern; the Russo-Polish War; the Rapallo Treaty; Britain and the Zinoviev letter; Lenin's rule by 1924.

Introduction

The seizure of power in the name of the Soviets and the early decrees, which seemed to deliver the promises of the April Theses, ensured that the Bolsheviks were for some time regarded as the defenders and guarantors of what had been achieved for the people in 1917. For many, 1917 had seen the successful defeat of tsarist autocracy and liberal compromise. The political and economic rights (workers' control, the seizure of land and democratic freedoms) were the result of a popular revolution which had been defended against its enemies, as celebrated in, for example, Figure 2.1. It was, however, already clear that the Bolsheviks did not enjoy the support of the whole of the population. Having taken power in the name of the Soviets, it very soon became apparent that those on the revolutionary left who did not submit to Bolshevik leadership would be met with exclusion and repression.

Although the regime had extricated itself from the First World War by March 1918, it already faced armed and organised opposition outside its 'heartland' of the industrial north-west of the former Empire. Its geographic position gave it a crucial advantage over the so-called white armies which were established to the south-east and north. Once the threat of military defeat had declined, Lenin still faced economic disaster and opposition from workers, soldiers, sailors and peasants whose interests the state purported to manifest.

The consolidation of the Communist dictatorship

The establishment of one-party control

'The dictatorship of the proletariat'

In light of the evidence of Lenin's practical political ability, it is possible to forget the role political theory played in the decision-making of the Bolshevik regime. In his book *Imperialism, the Highest Stage of Capitalism* (written in 1916) Lenin had set out his belief that revolution would take place first in less industrially developed countries such as Russia and then spread to the centre of the industrialised world. In *The State and Revolution* (1917) he argued in favour of what Marx had called 'the dictatorship of the proletariat'. What this meant was that it was time for the industrial proletariat (working class) to seize power in Russia and that a period of severe repression of those who opposed the revolution was a historical necessity.

Lenin was turning theory into reality. Within this ideological context, the Bolshevik regime took some very practical steps. The leaders of the Bolshevik regime began to encounter the same problems as the Provisional Government: concluding the war with Germany; dealing with the threat of political opposition; feeding the cities; and establishing its authority. The early decrees had gained the Bolsheviks a great deal of credit and were an important factor in their retaining power over the following years.

Figure 2.1: A Soviet propaganda poster celebrates the 15th anniversary of the 1917 Revolution.

Marx – development and revolution

Any summary of Marx's theory involves simplification, and it is worth reading a translation of the original German text of *The Manifesto of the Communist Party* by Karl Marx and Friedrich Engels, first published in 1848. It is fairly brief and gives you a good taste of Marxist language and rhetoric. In the *Manifesto*, Marx and Engels set out their theory that the organisation of society was based on who controlled 'the means of production' – that is, the way goods and wealth were created, such as agriculture and industry. They set out a model of historical and social change that involved 'class struggles'. They suggested that as trade and industry developed, the 'ruling class' would be challenged by the 'revolutionary class' below it, because this revolutionary class was becoming stronger and more powerful and in a position to challenge the ruling class through revolution. You can see from Figure 2.2 that this had already happened once, according to Marx – with the rise of the 'bourgeoisie' and the creation of 'capitalism'. He suggested, however that, just as the bourgeoisie had displaced the monarchs and aristocrats, so they in turn would be displaced as the ruling class, by the 'proletariat'. This would be achieved by the expropriation of (literally 'taking ownership of') the means of production or, in simpler terms, occupying the factories and seizing the land.

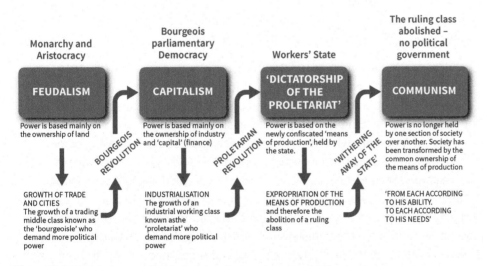

Figure 2.2: Marx's theory of historical development and revolution.

The tightening of control

The Bolsheviks acted to exclude other parties from the apparatus of government very early after their seizure of power. Alongside the new provisional government of Sovnarkom, the second Congress of Soviets had created the **Central Executive Committee** (CEC) which included members of the non-Bolshevik parties. It was supposed to act as a restraining force on Sovnarkom (made up entirely of Bolsheviks) and drew its legitimacy from the Congress. Lenin claimed that Sovnarkom must be able to pass decrees independent of the Central Executive

Central Executive Committee: Formed in 1922, this was the highest governing body of the Soviet Union until 1938, when it was replaced by the Supreme Soviet. It was part of the Soviet state apparatus rather than the party apparatus.

Politburo: An abbreviation of 'Political Bureau of the Central Committee of the Communist Party of the Soviet Union'. Founded in October 1917 by Lenin with seven members who would decide on questions too urgent to await the Central Committee.

The Russian Soviet Federated Socialist Republic (RSFSR): The name for Russia after the Bolshevik Revolution until 1922, when it became a republic of the Soviet Union.

Committee. Lenin justified this on the grounds of urgent necessity and doing away with 'bourgeois formalism'. Based on two very close votes on 4 November 1917, the Bolsheviks got their way. This essentially gave Lenin the power once enjoyed by the Tsar. After this point, the CEC automatically approved Sovnarkom's decisions.

From the seizure of power in October 1917 onwards, Lenin acted on the assumption that Bolshevik Party policy should be regarded as the law. Over the following years policy would become the reserve of a small number of those on the party's Central Committee. This control was formalised in early 1919 into the **Politburo**, initially comprising only five members. While Lenin was meticulously organised, an observer of Sovnarkom meetings suggested that much of the pre-revolutionary underground organisation's method was retained: true to Lenin's distaste for formalism, it was run as an exclusive conspiratorial cabal (a small, exclusive and tight-knit group), rather than as a constitutionally bound body.

The removal of the Constituent Assembly

Those who wished to see the Constituent Assembly succeed and become the sovereign body of what had been referred to as 'free Russia' were well aware that the Bolsheviks and Left SRs would attempt to frustrate them. The Bolsheviks had maintained a strong support base among troops in the capital and had prepared detachments in order to deal with demonstrations in favour of the Constituent Assembly. The day before the assembly was due to meet, 4 January 1918, Petrograd was declared to be under martial law and gatherings near to the Tauride Palace were forbidden. A regiment of Latvian riflemen, loyal to the Bolsheviks, was deployed to disperse 50 000 demonstrators who gathered in defiance. Troops shot at the crowd, killing at least 10 and injuring many more.

Lenin did not, however, prevent delegates from meeting on 5 January 1918. He allowed Viktor Chernov, a Right SR and former member of the Provisional Government, to attempt to chair the session. Chernov found this difficult for two reasons. First, he was proposing legislation in the name of the Constituent Assembly, which had already been enacted by Bolshevik decree. This demonstrated the powerlessness and, in Bolshevik eyes, irrelevance of the Assembly. Second, he faced jeering from Bolshevik delegates and troops throughout the day. As at the Second Congress of Soviets on 25 October 1917, intimidation played its part in weakening the position of the non-Bolshevik socialists. Lenin sat in the ministers' gallery allowing the situation to play out. Eventually at 6 a.m. the next day, the sitting was adjourned, on the grounds that the guards were tired. Later that day, when deputies attempted to re-enter the palace, they found it locked and discovered that the Central Executive Committee had dissolved the Assembly. Sovnarkom now proclaimed itself the permanent and legitimate government of Russia.

Remaining socialist opposition

The Left SRs had been an important component in supporting the Bolshevik-dominated government. They did, however, remain independent and had a major role in drafting a new constitution for the **Russian Soviet Federated Socialist Republic (RSFSR)**. As has been suggested, real influence lay with the Bolshevik

Party, but the new constitution reflected what, in theory, was the new settlement: that power resided in the Soviets.

In the first few months of 1918, the Bolsheviks began to assert their influence more fully in as many Soviets as they could and looked for obedient executives rather than pluralistic discussion-based councils allowing a variety of political parties and opinion. Elections to the central Russian city Soviets during the spring of 1918 demonstrated that the Bolsheviks were facing greater opposition from workers and soldiers who had supported their victory in October. The Bolsheviks' response was to declare the election results invalid and to re-run them until a better result was achieved. The Bolsheviks also disqualified Mensheviks and SRs from running in the elections. In Petrograd, the so-called Assembly of Plenipotentiaries was formed by workers as an alternative to the Soviet, but was disbanded by troops loyal to the Bolsheviks.

The end of involvement in the First World War

March 1918 was a turning point for the Bolshevik regime. In that month it made peace with the German government, which resulted in the Left SRs leaving Sovnarkom and great division within the Bolshevik Party itself. In the same month the regime moved to Moscow from Petrograd and in a symbolic consolidation of the one-party nature of the regime the Bolshevik Party was renamed the Communist Party. This placed them firmly within Marx's historical model. At this point, it was expected that the revolution would, at the very least, spread throughout Europe, and there were promising signs of Soviet-style revolution in parts of Germany.

The war against Germany had of course been both the burden and destabilising factor for the Provisional Government. One of the reasons that Russia had remained in the war, other than to avoid the shame of defeat, was the funding offered by the Allies. Following the Armistice of November 1917, Trotsky had attempted to draw out negotiations with the Germans for as long as possible. First, he wished to maintain the prospect that Russia might recommence hostilities against Germany and thereby continue to receive funding from the Allies. Second, he knew that however popular the slogan 'a just and democratic peace', the reality was likely to be politically and economically very costly. They remained confident that by stalling for time, they would provide an opportunity for industrial workers in Germany and elsewhere to replicate the revolution. They had some reason to be hopeful as there was growing industrial unrest in Germany in January 1918. By February, the Kaiser was convinced by his general staff that if there was to be no peace treaty, then the advance east must be renewed and the Bolshevik regime (which the Kaiser of course detested) should be overthrown and Russia occupied.

The Treaty of Brest-Litovsk, March 1918
Trotsky publicly advocated a policy of 'neither peace nor war' in which Russia would, unilaterally (without the agreement of its Allies), pull out of the war and allow the Germans to expose themselves as imperialists by advancing east. He hoped this would then stir up the Russian population to counter such an advance. In Lenin's eyes, this was entirely unrealistic. He argued, in the face of opposition on the Central Committee, that Russia must come to terms with Germany. He

Hidden voices

Patriarch Tikhon

It was not just attacks on political opposition that occurred in the first few months of Bolshevik rule, as this document illustrates. The extract is taken from an epistle from Patriarch Tikhon, 19 January 1918.[1]

Come to your senses you fools, and cease your bloody reprisals, for what you are doing is not only cruel but truly satanic, for which you will suffer the fires of hell and hereafter and in this earthly life be cursed by posterity. By the authority given to us by God we forbid you the Sacraments and excommunicate you, even if you still have Christian names and even though from birth you belong to the Orthodox Church … A most terrible hue-and-cry has been raised against Christ's Holy Church: the blessed sacraments that illumine human birth and Christian marriage are being openly declared unnecessary and superfluous; holy churches are being subjected to destruction by artillery or to plunder and blasphemous contumely; holy and revered abodes are being seized by the godless lords of darkness of this age and declared some kind of national property …

Discussion points:
1. Who are the 'godless lords of darkness'?
2. Why is Tikhon so upset?
3. How valuable is this source to the historian studying life in Bolshevik Russia?

continued to be outvoted until it became clear that German forces were advancing on Petrograd. Trotsky then gave in. In a panic, Lenin made an unsuccessful attempt to seek assistance from the Allies. Even now, with the German ultimatum, the Central Committee agonised. Nevertheless, Lenin eventually got his way and on 3 March 1918 the **Treaty of Brest-Litovsk** was signed with highly punitive terms. Russia had to give up a great swathe of territory in the west of the old Russian Empire, including Finland, the Baltic states, Poland and the Ukraine, whose independence must also be recognised. This included a quarter of the population, nearly a third of industry, over a third of harvestable land and three-quarters of available coal and iron. Less than a week later, Lenin relocated Sovnarkom to the Kremlin fortress in Moscow, still wary of the potential German advance.

The treaty was extremely unpopular, and had the Allies not defeated the Germans in November, this negotiated surrender may well have destroyed the regime. As it happened, as soon as the Germans had been defeated, Lenin cancelled the Treaty and rejected its conditions. This meant Lenin could claim that it had only ever been a temporary sacrifice. From another point of view, it was a gamble that paid off. The treaty also served to redefine Lenin's regime. Alongside the repression of rival socialists in the following months and the further empowering of the Cheka, Lenin began to define the interests of international communism on the basis of the security of his regime. This was manifested in the holding of the Third Communist International Conference in Moscow the following year, in which Lenin called for socialist parties to break away from their reformist social democratic comrades and work for worldwide proletarian revolution. This, though, in effect meant that the Communist regime of Russia should be viewed as the 'socialist fatherland'. This would remain a divisive issue for the party.

The Civil War

Causes and course of the war

Russia could be considered to have been in a state of civil war from the middle of 1917. There is much evidence to suggest that Lenin, Trotsky and others viewed war against the opponents of the revolutionary regime as part and parcel of the revolutionary process, and that conflict was inevitable and desirable. This process had begun with press censorship, government-sanctioned expropriation (seizure of land) and harassment of the 'bourgeoisie', the banning of the Liberals and the establishment of the Cheka. Nevertheless, alongside what might be termed 'internal repression' there was also a military conflict developing, involving organised armed forces.

The campaigns of the White armies and alternative regimes

The so-called 'White' opposition to the Bolsheviks began very modestly. The terminology of anti-Bolshevik '**Whites**' (versus pro-Bolshevik 'Reds') stemmed from the French Revolution, where forces in favour of the restoration of the Bourbon monarchy, whose symbolic colour was white, struggled against the revolutionary regime. Red was the colour of socialism, and as we have seen had already been used in reference to the February Revolution (hence the defence of 'Red Petrograd' during the Kornilov affair).

Aleksеev's Volunteer Army
General Alekseev, who had in fact encouraged the Tsar to abdicate in February, had escaped to Rostov in the Ukraine after the Bolshevik seizure of power. There

Voices from the past

Leon Trotsky (1879–1940)

Leon Trotsky was born Lev Bronstein in 1879 in to a Jewish family in the Ukraine. The Bronsteins escaped poverty by going into commercial farming.

Figure 2.3: Portrait of Trotsky (The Grainger Collection, New York).

Lev was also provided with schooling that encouraged him to develop his formidable intellectual abilities. In his youth, he developed radical populist sympathies and became involved with a revolutionary group in Nikolayev, Ukraine. He became attracted to the ideas of Marx and Lenin and organised a workers' union. These activities resulted in his arrest in 1898 and imprisonment, in Ukraine then Moscow. This was

followed by exile to Siberia, though he escaped in 1902 to London, where he changed his name to Trotsky.

He became a prominent writer for the Social Democrat newspaper *Iskra* (*The Spark*), where he met Lenin, Martov and Plekhanov and other members of the Russian Social Democratic Labour Party, or Social Democrats (founded in 1898). Following the 1902 split of the Social Democrats into Bolsheviks and Mensheviks, Trotsky sided with Mensheviks, which put him at odds with Lenin, but distanced himself from the Mensheviks in 1904, claiming to be non-factional. In 1905, as revolutionary turmoil developed, he travelled to St Petersburg and worked with Social Democrats to form the first Workers' Soviet, of which he became Deputy Chairman.

Following the defeat of the Soviet in December 1905, Trotsky went into exile in Vienna. There he began writing for *Pravda*, a new Social Democrat newspaper. Involved in the various arguments within the party, he wrote a letter in 1912 denouncing Lenin and the Bolsheviks, which would later be used against him. He remained in exile until 1917, by which time he was living in New York. He returned to Petrograd in May 1917 and found himself increasingly associated with the Bolshevik position and allied to Lenin. Trotsky played a major role in organising the October seizure of power by the Bolsheviks and then went on to command the Red Army during the Civil War as Commissar for War.

Trotsky had established a reputation as one of the foremost Bolshevik leaders and regarded himself as the natural successor to Lenin. He did not have the support of all of the party, however. Despite his intelligence, and his abilities to lead, organise and speak, many regarded him as arrogant. His Jewish background made him unpopular in the broadly anti-Semitic culture of the party. He found himself isolated and outmanoeuvred by his enemies. He was eventually exiled from the Soviet Union in 1929 and murdered by the Soviet regime in 1940 in his home in Mexico. Many on the left who became disillusioned with the Soviet Union became followers of Trotsky (and were referred to as Trotskyists).

Key terms

Treaty of Brest-Litovsk: Signed on 3 March 1918 between Germany and the Bolshevik government of Russia effectively signified a Russian surrender and withdrawal from the First World War.

Whites: The Whites formed as a loose confederation of anti-Bolshevik forces who fought for control of Russia from 1917 to 1922. Some wore the white uniforms of imperialist Russia but some chose white to be distinct from the Bolshevik Reds.

he established a Volunteer Army of around 3000 men, including General Kornilov and other anti-Bolshevik officers. Temporarily forced south by Bolshevik forces, the Volunteer Army recruited among the Cossacks from the Kuban and retook Rostov, establishing it as their base. General Denikin, who had replaced Kornilov – killed in the retreat – concentrated on securing this southern region, ignoring Alexseev's advice to push north-east towards Tsaritsyn and join up with those resisting Bolshevik rule in the east. Nevertheless, by September 1918 he had a force numbering up to 40 000 men and could consider an assault on Moscow.

The role of the 'Czech Legion'

During 1918, political and military opposition to the Bolshevik regime developed in the east. This began with a group of Czech and Slovak prisoners of war who had been fighting the Russian Empire. With the fall of the Tsar, they had negotiated a passage east to Vladivostok in order to eventually return to Europe and fight for the independence of a new Czechoslovak nation, in anticipation of Austro-Hungarian defeat. In March 1918, the Czech legion travelled east in an armed convoy, having agreed not to intervene in internal Russian conflict. It got as far as Chelyabinsk before being unwisely challenged by local Bolsheviks in May 1918. Trotsky, the new Commissar for War, looking to demonstrate Bolshevik authority in the region, ordered that the group be forced to join the new Red Army. Having been broadly supportive of the regime's cause and fearing they would be handed over to the Germans, they now turned against the communists and occupied the area of the mid-Volga. Under their protection, SRs ejected from the Constituent Assembly in January and who had a good deal of support in this region, proclaimed a new government based in the city of Samara, and known as Komuch. This rival regional government reinstated civic freedoms but confirmed the socialisation of land.

Right SRs and Kadets

Similarly, a coalition of Right SRs and Kadets formed a government in Tomsk, in Siberia, again cancelling Bolshevik laws including, in this case, the seizure of the land, which was returned to its previous owners. For a brief period the two regional governments merged in September 1918 to form a five-man Directory of SRs and their sympathisers. This, however, fell apart after two months owing to disagreement and was left weakened when the Czech legion withdrew from its defence in order for the main part to return to Europe. A group of conservative officers in the newly created Russian People's Army decided to stage a coup. The Directory was replaced by its Minister of War, Admiral Kolchak, who with the Cabinet of Ministers was proclaimed 'Supreme Leader'. The creation of what seemed like a reactionary regime in Omsk (to which the government had moved) persuaded many socialists to throw their weight behind the Bolshevik government.

The progress of war

The Bolsheviks now had opposition on two fronts: Kolchak to the east and Denikin to the south. A third, rather modest, army, led by General Yudenich, would also threaten the Bolshevik regime by attacking Petrograd from Estonia. Cooperation between these forces, though theoretically possible, was difficult and unlikely. Although the opposition forces should not be underestimated, being based on the periphery of the former Empire disadvantaged them. Another important failure of these anti-Bolshevik regimes is that they were led by military men and thus provided no clear political alternative (see *Reasons for the Red victory*, below).

In 1919 there were large-scale offensives by the White armies on all three fronts, posing a severe threat to the Communist regime, gaining large tracts of land as they attempted their respective advances on Moscow (see Figure 2.4). Given the size of the land mass both sides competed to control, advances were mainly made by rail, the fronts were thousands of miles wide and occupation of land taken was, at best, patchy. They encountered hostility from local peasant populations and independent armed groups.

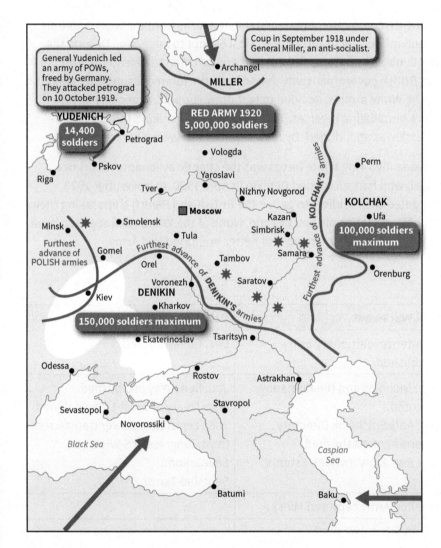

Figure 2.4: Key battles of the Russian Civil War.

One of the reasons for Kolchak's advance in the spring of 1919 was the priority of the Red Army to deal with the Volunteer Army in the south, and in particular the Don Cossack region. Denikin decided to split his forces, sending General Wrangel to advance on Tsaritsyn and possibly link up with Kolchak advancing from the east, and he himself countering the Reds in the Donbas. As before, however, his priority was to secure the south. The dramatic advance by Kolchak from the

Some key events have been already been added to the Civil War timeline below. Go back through your notes and add other events that will allow you to build a chronological picture of how the Civil War unfolded.

east in the early part of 1919 is partly explained by the speed of travel by rail. By April he had crossed the Ural Mountains and was within a hundred kilometres of the River Volga, which was a very approximate eastern boundary to Bolshevik-controlled Central Russia. The Red Army responded by sending a large number of reinforcements and began to drive Kolchak back by June. Chelyabinsk, east of the Urals, was taken in late July.

In July, Denikin decided on an all-out offensive on Moscow – his 'Moscow Directive'. The offensive had three prongs, the strongest being the central and most direct, via Kharkov, Kursk, Orel and on to Moscow. This was a risk as his armies were outnumbered by three to one, including reinforcements. By September the central prong had advanced to Kursk. At this point a newly created Polish army, which could have threatened the Red Army from the west, and thus facilitated Denikin's advance, agreed with Moscow not to intervene. Despite the advance, Denikin's army lacked reserves and enough men to defend the front. In addition, the British government, which had been the foremost supporters and suppliers of the White armies, decided to withdraw support, especially having seen Kolchak's humiliating reverses. This demoralised Denikin's forces. In mid-November Kursk was abandoned. By mid-December so were Kharkov and Kiev.

The final episode involving White forces was the chaotic evacuation of Crimea under Wrangel, who had succeeded Denikin in April 1920. In November 1920 civilians competed with soldiers to get on the British and French ships taking them to the safety of Constantinople and beyond. None of the White advances had been sustainable against a better-manned and better-equipped Red Army.

Timeline

Year	Civil War event	Other event in Soviet Union
1917	Counter-revolutionary army established.	Dec: Cheka formed.
1918	July: Nicholas and the Romanovs executed. Sep: Anti-Bolshevik Directory government established. Nov: Red Army invaded Estonia.	Jan: Red Army established. Mar: Treaty of Brest-Litovsk signed. July: Legislative power transferred from Congress of Soviets to Sovnarkom. Sep: Red Terror.
1919	Jan: Red Army captured Minsk.	
1920	Jan: Kolchak executed. Jul: Latvia and Lithuania declared independence.	
1921	Feb: Red Army invaded Georgia. Aug: Makhno and his commanders arrested and executed.	Feb: Gosplan created. Kronsdadt rebellion. Mar: Lenin introduced NEP.
1922		Feb: Famine. Stalin appointed General Secretary.

Key term

Gosplan: The State Planning Committee which was responsible for economic planning in the Soviet Union, particularly from 1928 onwards. It was set up under the authority of the Council of Labour and Defence in 1921.

The Red Army and the role of Trotsky

Resistance to Alekseev in late 1917 had been an improvised affair. By the following March, the Communist regime began organising a Workers' and Peasants' Army, but this too proved insufficient. In April, having achieved Brest-Litovsk, Trotsky was made Commissar for War and turned his energies to organising the defence of the Soviet 'heartland'. Many Bolsheviks still saw this as a revolutionary war to be taken beyond the borders of the former Empire. In October 1918, it was agreed that a professionally organised and conscripted army of at least 3 million men was necessary to counter the threat from the south and the east. This was controversial among the veteran revolutionaries of the regime because it involved the re-employment of 75 000 officers and 775 generals from the imperial army. This reversed the democratisation of the army that had been such an essential part of the revolutionary movement in 1917. Strict discipline was reintroduced, as was saluting and the death penalty. This was not, however, a full reversion. 'Tsarist' officers were, in the main, those who had come up through the ranks during the course of the First World War and as such were not overly bound to the former regime. The fact that the regime threatened to harm their families, essentially treating them as hostages, and was prepared to hand out severe punishment for even the suspicion of disloyalty, ensured their cooperation.

Trotsky's role as Commissar for War was arguably more that of propagandist and terroriser than of an organisational genius. He certainly facilitated the prosecution of the war in practical terms by – particularly through making use of his personal train – intervening and providing ammunition and authoritative decisions and orders on the ground where necessary. As head of the political body that oversaw the professional staff, he was responsible for confirming the generals' strategy, but the majority of practical military planning was undertaken by the military and went mainly unchallenged. Trotsky's most significant role was, in simple terms, to provide encouragement, giving speeches and threatening punishment. Desertion from the Red Army was substantial, but its remedy was effective. As well as a major propaganda effort through 'agit-trains' disseminating leaflets, the Red Army also relied on political commissars attached to each unit, and repeated rhetoric regarding a soldier's duty to shoot a deserting comrade. The logic was that it was better to risk possible death in the field than certain death if deserting.

The murder of the Tsar

Lenin also, as seems clear now, ordered that the Tsar be killed. The Tsar and his family, under house arrest, had been moved to the western Siberian city of Tobolsk and then to Ekaterinburg. In June the Tsar's brother, Mikhail, in exile in Perm, had been shot by the Cheka. In the early hours of 17 July 1918, the Tsar and his family, along with their small number of servants, were taken down to the basement of the 'House of Special Designation' and shot repeatedly. Their bodies were disposed of nearby. The process was overseen by the local Soviet, and it is possible that Lenin did not intend the whole family to be murdered. However, once the facts were reported to Moscow the matter was seen as closed.

The murder of the Tsar with his whole family was obviously a symbolic event. The family had been repeatedly moved, seemingly as a response to the growing threat from Kolchak in the east. The Bolsheviks obviously feared that the rescue of the Tsar by the Whites would be a major propaganda coup, if not the basis for the restoration of the monarchy. The exact nature of events surrounding the executions is not wholly clear, but the broader significance of the murder of the royal family was to prevent any return of Romanov rule.

The Red Terror

The trigger for the unleashing of mass terror seems to have been an attempt on Lenin's life by Left SRs. This took place on 30 August 1918. After Lenin had spoken to workers at a Moscow factory, he was about to leave when three shots were fired. Lenin was shot in the neck but survived and recovered in a few months. The woman arrested and held responsible was named Fannie Kaplan. She claimed to have acted on her own, and was executed, but this gave Lenin an excuse to arrest all Right SRs. In early September he issued two decrees that ordered the taking of hostages, the use of mass executions where necessary and the confinement of 'class enemies' to concentration camps. He had ordered these to be constructed on a permanent basis in August. By 1921, 84 had been constructed; by 1924 there were 315.

Indiscriminate terror carried on until April 1919. Its causes were paranoia and an instinctive desire to root out counter-revolution. The method was intended to scare the population into compliance. In the words of an official at the Commissariat of Justice: 'We must execute not only the guilty. Execution of the innocent will impress the masses even more.' The Cheka became, as Richard Pipes describes, 'a state within a state'[2] with agents in every sector of administration. By 1920 it had a separate military force of around 250 000 men. It is important to note that there were instances of what has been referred to as '*White* Terror'. The name stems again from the French Revolution. There is a question as to whether actions by White forces should be equated with the government-sanctioned murder and persecution of the Communist regime. Nevertheless, there is clear evidence of excessive cruelty on both sides.

Reasons for the Red victory

There were three sets of reasons for the defeat of 'White' forces by the Red Army by the end of 1920. The first could be classed as military advantages, the second as geographical advantages, and the third as political advantages.

Military advantages
Militarily, the Reds had a more effective leadership and control over the most advantageous territory. As shown, discipline extended over both the army and the civilian population. To be in the Red Army was, however, arguably a better bet. The regime's economic policy was based on ensuring that the army had first claim to resources, especially food. The general staff of the career officer S.S. Kamenev was in the main able to carry out operations unimpeded, and indeed supported, by the regime. In some cases, this actually involved their ignoring Trotsky's advice.

Geographical advantages
The geographical factor, however, was possibly the most important. This 'heartland', sometimes referred to as 'Sovdepia' (under the control of the deputies

of the Soviets) by their enemies, held many advantages. It contained the major industrial centres of the former Empire and its arsenals, which meant that it had access to ready-made materiel (resources) for war. The White armies depended far more on weapons and equipment provided by their Western allies, particularly Britain. Being at the heart of Russia's industrial production also meant that the Communist regime was able to control the major railway junctions and routes out to the less well-connected periphery. Other than through Tsaritsyn, where no timely victory was gained, Denikin and Kolchak could not have linked forces other than by penetrating Communist territory. Control of the two capitals, Petrograd and Moscow, was symbolically important given the relative ethnic homogeneity of this region.

Political advantages: government and control in wartime

Motivation to fight was obviously also among the political factors behind Red victory. Both sides deployed terror against the peasant communities through which they moved. There is less evidence of a centrally directed and deliberate policy of terror under the Whites in the south, but clearly Denikin did little to prevent Cossacks carrying out anti-Semitic pogroms (which drove a number of Jews into supporting the Communists) in the south. While this remains disputed by historians (and it is likely that later Soviet historians will have sought out anti-White testimonies), there is fair evidence that either through indiscipline or sheer brutality, forces under Kolchak acted indiscriminately against peasant populations. Major General William S. Graves, the commander of the American Siberian expedition, was highly critical of the indiscipline and cruelty of White forces there. Terror won short-term compliance from populations but, at the same time, created deep resentment.

 Hidden voices

Commissar Petrovsky

The People's Commissar for Internal Affairs gives the order on 4 September 1918 to enact reprisals for the attempted assassination of Lenin:

A decisive end must be put to such a situation. An end must be put immediately to slackness and softness. All Right SRs known to local soviets must be immediately arrested and a considerable number of hostages taken from among the bourgeoisie and officers. Unconditional mass shooting must be carried out at the slightest sign of movement in White Guard circles. In this respect local guberniya executive committees must show particular initiative. Through the offices of the militia and Cheka, administrative departments must take all necessary measures to root out and arrest all those hiding behind

false names, unconditionally shooting any involved in White Guard activities …

The rear of our armies must be finally cleansed of White Guard elements and all vile conspirators against the power of the working class and poor peasantry. There must not be the slightest hesitation or indecisiveness in the application of mass terror.

Discussion points:

1. Using your own knowledge and with reference to the source, why was there a need for such violence at this time?
2. How valuable is this source for a historian studying the nature of Bolshevik governance?

ACTIVITY 2.2

Go back through this section and note down reasons why the outcome of the Civil War was in favour of the Bolsheviks. Draw up a two-column table with the headings 'Reasons for Red success' and 'Reasons for White failure'.

There remain two key areas in which Reds had a political advantage. The first was having a clear political programme that they actively promoted in the territories they held. Quite apart from the policies the Communist regime offered was the fact that they imposed political control at all. The White generals were not interested in civil administration and gave it little thought. The second aspect was closely related. While some of the 'White' SRs initially wished to confirm the seizure of land by the peasantry, the popular perception in those areas of 'Sovdepia' threatened by White advances, particularly by Denikin in late 1919, was that the only way to retain what they had seized was to join the Reds – they did so in the form of 1 million new recruits. On the question of nationalities within the former Russian Empire, it was not that the Communist regime offered independence (although Lenin had made easy promises in his Decree on Nationalities), but that the overriding vision of the White generals was 'Holy Russia' undivided. As was clear from the temporary deal between Poland and the Communist regime, Lenin was prepared to make promises in order to concentrate on the more pressing problems in the south and east.

Economic and social developments

It is perhaps not surprising that economic policy should have been a central matter for debate within the Bolshevik (then Communist) Party. Despite the increasing intolerance of non-communist dissent by the regime, the question of how to organise the revolutionary or post-revolutionary economy was a difficult one. A great deal of what occurred was a result of improvisation within economically chaotic and politically hostile circumstances. This said, it is difficult to overestimate the extent to which policy was informed by communist doctrine. The outcome was a combination of both ideology and improvisation.

State capitalism

Conventionally, the period prior to the onset of civil war, roughly from October 1917 to June 1918, has been referred to as 'state capitalism'. It is again important to remember the context of these early months, in which many Bolsheviks hoped for, and expected, an international revolution and economic transformation as a result of the expropriation (seizing land and property) from capitalists and landowners. Lenin's initial plans, however, involved, to some degree, gaining the cooperation of employers. Certain measures were undertaken to assert the power and role of the state. This involved the seizure of the state bank and subsequent nationalisation and amalgamation of all private banks into the People's Bank of the Russian Republic in November 1917. The regime also refused to pay any foreign debts.

In December 1917 a body subordinate to Sovnarkom was created. It was called the **Supreme Council of the National Economy**. Its role was to attempt to organise production and consumption and essentially to be the owner of nationalised industry. Its departments and its personnel proliferated rapidly, but its actual ability to regulate the economy was very limited, as was the case for Sovnarkom's political control. While the state was able to seize control of the railways from an independent trade union in March 1918, control of industry and

Key term

Supreme Council of the National Economy: Set up in December 1917 under the authority of Sovnarkom, this was the first body responsible for attempting to create a planned economy. It set up many subordinate bodies to deal with a wide range of economic issues.

agriculture had become radically localised and therefore less and less productive. 'Nationalisation', in terms of workers taking control of factories, even at very small concerns, continued rapidly during the first half of 1918. This was part of the 'disruptive localism' which the regime found increasingly frustrating. It acted to ban further 'nationalisation from below' without permission in January 1918 and again in April, but such decrees were ignored.

In June, Lenin issued a new decree on nationalisation, which began to put an end to the chaos of workers' control (which he had arguably encouraged through his November decree of that name). The Supreme Council had included some managers and owners in its various departments (or *glavki*), particularly, for example, in the textiles department. In April 1918, Lenin encouraged Meshcherski, an iron and steel magnate, to put forward a joint ownership project. It was not that Lenin wished for a prolonged 'mixed economy' model, but he saw the value of using, as he put it, 'bourgeois methods' to build up socialist industry. This, it could be claimed, was 'state capitalism' and critics on the left who had seen Brest-Litovsk as too great a compromise (the Left SRs resigned from the government on this matter in March) continued to complain.

Social change

Having undergone war and revolution, early Soviet society was already in a turbulent state. The ravages of civil war would bring yet more disruption. 'Soviet Man' as dreamt of by communist idealists was in reality created through severe hardship. The First World War had meant economic dislocation, shortages and an influx into the main cities of refugees from captured Western territories. The February Revolution, with its new freedoms, brought a challenge to social hierarchy. The egalitarian form of address, 'citizen', was adopted. Under the communist regime, political freedom (for the regime's opponents) was attacked, but there were many elements within the new government who saw it as their role to liberate humanity from social oppression and, in particular, to emancipate women.

Alexandra Kollontai, People's Commissar for Social Welfare from October 1917 and head of the party's 'Womens' Department' *Zhenotdel* from 1919, was a prominent advocate of redefining relations between the sexes. Her influence was limited and her views on sexual promiscuity were unpopular with Lenin. Nevertheless, the Civil War years saw the introduction of the Family Code in October 1918, which legalised divorce, the legalisation of hospital abortion in 1920 and the promotion of women's education and employment through childcare provision. Patriarch Tikhon denounced the Bolsheviks' social policy which flew in the face of traditional Orthodox Christian teaching. The persecution of the Church, the confiscation of its lands and promotion of atheism did not in fact prevent a demand for traditional religion. The League of the Militant Godless was established in 1921 as an attempt to convert the nation to atheism. Despite some popular rural resistance attacks on the Church's property, priests were easily accused of being 'counter-revolutionary', and the Church's power was severely weakened and its position precarious.

Conditions in cities and countryside during the Civil War

While it is important to acknowledge changes in social attitudes, the overwhelming priority of the inhabitants of the former Russian Empire during the Civil War was survival. Following the mass migration of refugees into towns during the war, the deprivation caused by economic collapse during 'war communism' saw a mass migration out of urban centres. The major industrial cities under Bolshevik control saw the most dramatic drops in population. The combined populations of Petrograd and Moscow fell from 4.3 million in 1917 to 1.86 million in July 1920.[3] This exodus was caused by the newly imposed blockade of the northern ports by the Allies, the capture of food-producing regions in the south by the Whites and the severe reduction of industrial production (including armaments), and the consequent unemployment, collapse of wages and hunger. Hunger and lack of fuel gave rise to epidemics of typhus, typhoid, dysentery and cholera. The great majority of deaths during the Civil War were a result of disease rather than fighting.

The working class who had participated in revolution now left for the villages in order to survive. The rural population had already been swelled by demobilised soldiers looking to claim their share of the newly available land seized from landowners. Christopher Read describes the villages as 'the national safety net' and the 'redoubt in which Russia survived from 1918 to 1922/3'.[4] This is not to claim that conditions were easy in rural Russia. In the central black earth of the provinces in which the rail lines intersected, rural populations were heavily affected by fighting and terror. Grain requisitioning also drove peasants to grow crops for their own consumption, rather than grain for sale or other cash crops. Even after the end of hostilities, the Volga region and North Caucasus and Ukraine suffered a catastrophic famine as a result of the confiscation of seed grain in the preceding years. This saw the migration of refugees to the north and west during 1921 and 1922 and led to further starvation and disease in the towns. Deaths from famine and disease between 1918 and 1920 are estimated at 8 million. The estimated figure for 1921 to 1922 is a further 6 million.[5]

War communism

However useful 'state capitalism' is as a label, communist economic policy was to gain a new name from around June 1918, that of '**war communism**'. Again, as a label, it might be treated with care as it originated as a convenient name for the policies enforced during the main period of the Civil War; policies which were, by necessity, abandoned in early 1921. Nevertheless, it is not wholly inaccurate to say that war communism was introduced as a means of fighting the Civil War.

Lenin's policy of requisitioning grain

The true origins of war communism, it might be argued, lie in Lenin's attitude to the peasants. The overriding priority of the regime during economic decline was the provision of bread to the cities, and latterly to the army. Rationing had been in place since 1916 and as paper money became less and less valuable, the bread ration, though very meagre, was essential to survival. The ration also suited communist ideology as it imposed equality of provision. It was in fact used

Key term

War communism: The economic system introduced by Lenin that existed during the Civil War. It was a combination of Marxist ideas and emergency measures and involved nationalising the land and banks.

Speak like a historian

The peasantry

The peasantry did not fit easily into the Marxist model, but the Bolsheviks were bound to include them within a class analysis of the society they sought to rule. Lenin's response was to fit them into three categories:

- the 'poor peasant' (bednyak)

- the 'middle peasant'

- the 'rich peasant' (kulak.)

The natural allies of the urban workers were the poor and middle peasants. The kulaks, on the other hand, were to be associated with bourgeois capitalist interests and treated with suspicion. There was undoubtedly a diverse range of peasants and their property and incomes varied. The kulaks had been part of Stolypin's plans to reform agriculture from 1906 onwards. He wished to create an independent class of land-owning peasants who were free from the influence of the commune or *mir* and would support the tsarist authorities (see *Russia's peasantry* in Chapter 1). With communal land seizures during 1917, the influence of the traditional commune had been reasserted and there was some resentment of those who had taken up Stolypin's offer to break away. This said, Lenin's attempt to turn peasant against peasant was not particularly successful. Alec Nove cites Teodor Shanin in stating that 'intergenerational mobility and intermarriage caused real peasant attitudes to diverge from the oversimplified "class" categories used in party debates'.[6] In other words, these 'classes' of peasants were, above all, convenient labels for the purposes of party control and propaganda. The demonisation of the kulaks would become a major part of repression under Stalin.

to punish the propertied classes and anyone perceived to be 'bourgeois' (they received a smaller ration).

Lenin's hatred for the bourgeois was equalled by his hatred of the rich peasant or 'kulak'. As early as February 1918, Lenin voiced his detestation of this perceived class of peasants, who in his mind were responsible for hoarding and withholding grain in order to get the highest price. He denounced them as 'speculators'. This led to one of the main planks of war communism: grain requisitioning. This policy of sending out 'food detachments', squads from the cities under the control of the Cheka who would seize what they defined as 'surplus' grain, began in earnest in June 1918. Lenin intended to promote class war between the poorer peasants and their better-off neighbours. A decree in that month tasked 'committees of the poor' with achieving the expropriation of the **kulaks**. The consequences of this process were that peasants, knowing their surplus will be seized, sowed smaller acreages and more actively hoarded and hid their grain. The reaction of the food detachments was to confiscate any grain they could, including seed grain that was required to sow the following harvest. This created a vicious cycle of lower grain production and ever more punitive requisitioning.

As an economic policy and a way of feeding the cities, grain requisitioning was a failure. Under war communism, the black market was an essential means of survival. In June 1918 it became officially illegal to trade privately, particularly in grain. Nevertheless, most of the means of subsistence in cities was provided by 'sack men': black marketeers who found their way past patrols with sacks full of goods on illegal street markets. Life in the cities became desperate. The winter of 1917 to 1918 was particularly harsh. Wooden buildings and pavements

Key term

Kulaks: A group of relatively affluent farmers that grew during Stolypin's reforms. According to Marxist-Leninist philosophy they were class enemies of the poorer peasants. Under Lenin, kulaks meant anyone who refused to hand over grain during requisitioning. Under Stalin they were terrorised during collectivisation.

were dismantled to be used as fuel. The urban population reduced substantially through starvation, typhus and workers leaving for their former villages. It can be argued that, as it failed to feed the cities, the main value of grain requisitioning to the Communist regime was as an instrument of terror.

Abandoning money

The other main aspect of war communism was the 'moneyless' system of production and consumption that came about during 1919 and 1920. Again, those on the left began to believe they were at the forefront of creating a new stage of economic history by having a system that dispensed with money, which was the basis of capitalist trade. Paper money remained in use, but severe scarcity and the increased printing of money by the regime in order to pay debts meant that black-market prices kept going up and the value of the currency kept going down. As money became useless as a form of currency (grain was far more useful) those parts of the economy under state control traded with each other without money. Charges stopped being made for use of the postal service, the telephone and trams; rents were no longer collected; and the ration, such as it was, was free. In such a situation there was a proliferation of state bureaucracy, which worked ceaselessly to deal with the inevitable failures of supply. A **Council of Labour and Defence** was created, headed by Lenin, which became superior to the Supreme Council, whose main aim was to provide for the war.

Government and control

The development of war communism could be seen as an integral part of the Communist regime's attempt to impose its authority on the territory it held during the Civil War. It was in some senses simply a means of overcoming the 'disruptive localism' that had flourished from the middle of 1917 and had enabled the Bolsheviks to topple the Provisional Government. It has been suggested that this determination to impose state authority, in the context of economic crisis and armed resistance, was partly why the Reds prevailed over the Whites.

As with economic policy, political terror stemmed from principle as well as necessity. Lenin's older brother had been executed by the tsarist authorities in 1892; Felix Dzerzhinsky had spent years in a tsarist jail; Marx himself had praised the Terror of the French Revolution, but these revolutionaries of the early 20th century were determined not to suffer Robespierre's fate. (Having overseen the period of mass executions – known as the Terror – during the French Revolution, Robespierre himself was executed in 1794.) Terror was also part of the logic of the seizure of power in October 1917, as Trotsky admitted in his 1920 book *Terrorism and Communism*.

While the popularity of the party may have declined, the first half of 1918 saw the consolidation of control over the local Soviets and greater central party control. Sverdlov, Chairman of the Party Secretariat and of the Central Executive Committee, oversaw this process.

The growth of executive organs of local Soviets allowed for more effective administration. Provincial executives were a crucial means of control and are described by Evan Mawdsley as 'the government's islands in the peasant sea'.[7] This consolidation of Communist power was an important precursor to the outbreak of

Key term

Council of Labour and Defence: Set up under the authority of Sovnarkom in November 1918 to help administer the wartime economy. It brought together the most important individuals involved in the war effort including the chairman of the Supreme Council of the National Economy.

Red Terror. Having left Sovnarkom in March 1918, Left SR sentiment turned against the communists and in July there was an unsuccessful armed uprising in Moscow. Their leaders were arrested or went into exile. Following the growth of opposition in the south and east, Lenin believed his regime to be in peril. That month he issued the decree 'The Socialist Fatherland in Danger', which ordered the summary execution of 'enemy agents, speculators, burglars, hooligans, counter-revolutionary agitators and German spies'.

Revolts and the Red Terror

Workers' and peasants' revolts of 1920–1921

In attempting to discern the various fronts and campaigns of the Civil War, it is possible to oversimplify the shifting nature of the conflict and the degree of control over territory. It has rightly been called a 'railway war' because troops could be dispatched quickly to deal with reported threats. The Communist regime was likely to label any resistance to its rule as 'White'. There were, however, a number of localised forces, mainly peasant bands, who resisted both Red and White incursions into their territory. The Cossacks, it should be remembered, were a semi-independent force who were most concerned with defending their territory in the south.

The Ukrainian anarchist Nestor Makhno led another significant force. Such peasant movements, hostile to both sides, have been referred to as the 'Greens', but in other than a very few cases, they did not act under central leadership. Makhno's partisans mainly acted to frustrate Denikin's forces up to the end of 1919. However, as the White threat receded, Makhno's ranks swelled with peasants now keen to throw off Communist control.

Rural resistance and the Tambov revolt

This resistance became a more generalised problem in 1920. Once it became clear that the White threat to return land to its former owners was over, peasants set about attempting to overturn the rule of the Communists in favour of the self-rule they had experienced in 1917. Grain requisitioning and its associated brutality remained Lenin's policy. Tambov province, to the south-east of Moscow, had been one of the most productive regions for grain. It had suffered at the hands of the Communists' 'food detachments'. In mid-1920, a partisan armed resistance developed, under the leadership of Alexander Antonov. Using guerrilla tactics it attacked communist targets in raids, and then dissolved into the forests or into the villages. By the beginning of 1921, Antonov had tens of thousands of followers and much of the countryside was ungovernable. Lenin responded with Cheka units who resorted to collective punishment of villages and poison gas to drive the 'bandits' out of the forests.

 Thematic link: Terror and communism

The geography of the Soviet Union had a huge bearing on how leaders tried to rule over it. The sheer size of Russia (around 22 400 000 square miles) and its short growing season created many difficulties for both the tsarist regime and the Communist Party, but significantly for the citizens too. Some historians have suggested that the perpetual struggle most ordinary people experienced simply to feed themselves could be one explanation as to why Russia's rulers have found it so easy to exert such strict control over the people.

Opposition from workers and the Kronstadt rising

Alongside this crisis of rural control, a **Workers' Opposition** developed within the party, calling for an end to centralised control, the predominance of 'bourgeois specialists' and the use of trade unions to ensure labour discipline rather than represent workers' interests. Those within the party who shared these views put forward their ideas at the Ninth Party Congress in 1919. They also demanded that every communist should spend a quarter of the year undertaking manual work. This was a very obvious challenge to the Bolsheviks' claim to speak for the working class. It could be argued that workers' democracy had never played a significant role in the party, other than to approve what the leadership had already chosen to do. Lenin denounced the Workers' Opposition as 'syndicalist deviation'. They were 'deviating' from the correct revolutionary path by wanting 'syndicalism' – a less disciplined and less centralised form of organisation.

Worker unrest in Moscow and Petrograd was triggered by a reduction in the bread ration in February 1921. There were strikes and calls for the legalisation of private trade, the civil freedoms of February 1917 and the restoration of the Constituent Assembly. By the fourth anniversary of the February Revolution, the revolt reached the Kronstadt naval base. There the sailors, who had been the foremost supporters of the Bolsheviks in 1917, created a Provisional Revolutionary Committee in support of a general strike and prepared for the inevitable military reaction. This began on 7 March and was overseen by Trotsky. The Kronstadt sailors accused the Communist regime of betraying the revolution and creating a tyranny worse than Tsarism. Between 16 and 18 March 50 000 Red Army troops were sent over the ice against 17 000 sailors. Trotsky had placed loyal machine-gun units behind his advancing troops. The Kronstadt Mutiny was defeated.

New Economic Policy (NEP) and its political and economic impact

With the defeat of the White armies achieved by 1920, it has been suggested that Lenin might have ended grain requisitioning and war communism earlier. In the context of the workers' and peasants' revolts, its continuation might be seen as part of Lenin's attempt to retain control. However, it became obvious to him by March 1921 that these policies were dangerously unpopular outside the party elite and were leading to economic collapse. War communism had been introduced as a means of asserting Communist control and to prioritise the needs of the military. True to his tactical and pragmatic nature, Lenin abandoned it in favour of his overwhelming priority of holding on to power. At the Tenth Party Congress, the **New Economic Policy, or NEP** as it was called, was introduced. It replaced requisitioning with a tax in kind well below the amount of produce demanded in the previous year. It enabled peasants to sell their surplus grain legally. Initially intended to be restricted to 'the local market', the policy inevitably led to the full legalisation of private trade. As a result, small-scale traders known as 'Nepmen' took advantage of the situation and stepped in where the black market had been.

Key terms

Workers' Opposition: The political faction which formed during 1919 to 1920 to protest against the decrease of influence of working-class democratic institutions under the Communist regime.

New Economic Policy (NEP): Introduced by Lenin in 1921 after it had become obvious that war communism had failed. NEP was controversial because it allowed the peasants to sell some of their produce for profit and allowed small independent businesses to flourish once more.

While the 'commanding heights' of the economy, banks, foreign trade and large-scale industry were retained in state hands, a decree of May 1921 removed blanket nationalisation. Decrees in July allowed for the formation of small-scale industry in private hands and the leasing of previously nationalised enterprises to private owners by the Supreme Council. This led to the closure of many state enterprises and was bitter medicine, but it made state industry commercially viable. Large industries were broken up into trusts, which had to compete with each other and with the private sector. Wages were reintroduced and rationing was abolished in November. Inflation, however, continued and trusts were unable to pay their workers, resulting in rising unemployment. In July 1922, a new currency, the chervonets, was introduced backed by gold. The previous currency, the rouble (renamed the sovnak or soviet token under war communism) remained in circulation until February 1924. A new state bank was created at the end of 1921. There was some very limited foreign investment and in 1922 a trade deal was struck with Britain, and others followed.

Difficulties remained with fuel and transport and above all, in 1921, with a lack of food. Chiefly the legacy of an intensified requisitioning programme up to the beginning of the year, millions died as a consequence of famine. The grain harvest in 1920 was half that of 1913. In 1921 it was even lower. Efforts were made to provide food to the worst-hit regions, including a cancellation of the tax in kind and contributions from the American government, but this was insufficient. In 1923, however, the tide began to turn. A new problem that developed as a result of grain production recovering faster than industrial production was the so-called 'scissors crisis'. This saw industrial goods at three times the price of their relative agricultural goods compared with the pre-war situation. The Supreme Council retained a controlling role in the economy but was less assertive and began to redefine and devolve its role.

NEP was politically controversial, but Lenin explained it as based on one step back in preparation for two steps forward. He had, after all, been proved right before when arguing in favour of temporary setbacks; the most notable example had been signing the Treaty of Brest-Litovsk. The introduction of NEP, however, was to create another fault line in the party.

ACTIVITY 2.3

Go through your notes and see if you can identify why NEP was so controversial. To do this you will need to look at Marxist economic principles, features of war communism and NEP. You may want to create a mind-map to illustrate the links between these policies.

One has been started for you in Figure 2.5, but you will need to use your notes to complete it.

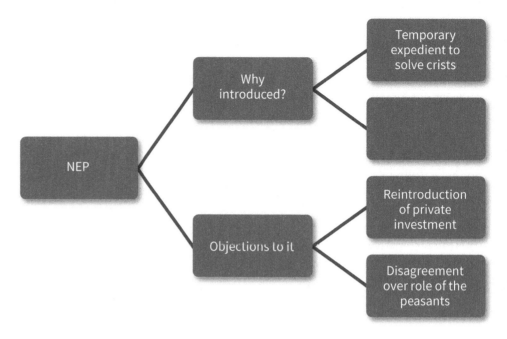

Figure 2.5: Assessing the NEP.

Foreign relations and attitudes of foreign powers

As has been emphasised, what became known as the Soviet regime (the 'Soviet Union' was not constituted until 1922) looked to export the revolution from as early as possible, primarily to central and western Europe, and possibly further. There are three aspects to consider regarding the new state's standing in the world. First is the Moscow-based regime's attitude to the various 'nationalities' (with diverse ethnicities, languages and religions). Second is its attempts to spread communist revolution. Third is its relationship with foreign countries, notably Britain and Germany. Between 1917 and 1924, the regime shifted reluctantly from a position of propagating revolution to consolidating the newly founded **Union of Soviet Socialist Republics (USSR)**.

Newly independent nations – the break-up of the Empire

The context for the assertion of independence by a number of nations, mainly down the western edge of the former Empire, is twofold. The first was Lenin's Declaration of the Rights of the Peoples of Russia of early November 1917. His intention, alongside that of Stalin, Commissar for Nationalities, was to allow independence (as the declaration stated) and then welcome them into a new multinational *'voluntary and honourable union'*. This was on the assumption that revolutionary regimes would quickly be established and wish to be part of a pan-European socialist state. The second part of the context was the final year of the First World War and allied negotiations at the Paris peace conference of 1919. In early 1918 Ukraine then Finland, Lithuania, Latvia, Estonia and Transcaucasia declared independence. The last of these became independent Georgia, Armenia and Azerbaijan in May. Moscow fought for and regained these three territories by the end of February 1921. Ukraine, supported by occupying Germany, had for a time a nationalist government in Kiev, but descended into chaos before Denikin's invasion and eventual Red victory and the repression of its various warlords.

Foreign intervention in the Civil War

Four countries – Britain, France, the United States and Japan – intervened in the Civil War, broadly on the side of White forces. It is been argued that they did so primarily to secure or advance their own interests rather than with the determination to defeat the Bolshevik regime. This was most clearly the case for Japan, who landed forces in the Pacific west with the intention of securing land and ports for themselves. They had, after all, coveted that region since the end of the Russo-Japanese war in 1905. The United States did so for slightly different reasons. It too sent a force of just under 8000 men under the command of William S. Graves to Siberia with the main task of protecting US military assets provided to the pre-Bolshevik regime and of assisting the evacuation of the Czech Legion. Britain and the United States had a brief involvement in the north-west, landing 8500 troops at Arkhangelsk in August 1918. The British also enforced a naval blockade of Petrograd. The French and the British also sent troops to the Black Sea to intervene in Ukraine with Odessa as the main base for French forces.

Although army surplus was supplied, there was very little actual fighting by foreign troops. At the beginning of 1919 the British recognised Kolchak's regime as the legitimate government of Russia, but as Kolchak's fortunes began to reverse in the second half of the year, Lloyd George (the British Prime Minister) decided that there was little sense in throwing good money after bad. The French pulled out in April 1919 and Britain normalised relations with the Soviet regime in November. US and Japanese forces withdrew in early 1920. The episode should be seen within the context of a war-weary set of Allied governments and a basic assumption that the Soviet regime was distasteful but not dangerous.

Winston Churchill (then an army minister) was a lone advocate of overthrowing the Communist regime, but his viewpoint was not popular. Allied attention at this point was still based on the future of central Europe and dealing with a defeated Germany. The Soviet regime was therefore left to establish itself among the economic ruins of war communism.

Comintern

In March 1919, 35 delegates, the majority of them from Russia, met at the First Congress of the **Third (Communist) International**. This was shortened to **Comintern**. The First and Second Internationals had been loose federations of European socialist parties. Comintern was to be distinct from these. Lenin intended for it to be an instrument of worldwide revolution. While the Commissariat of Foreign Affairs established itself as a legitimate part of international diplomacy, Comintern was intended as a means to subvert foreign governments by the creation of communist parties loyal to the Moscow regime.

During 1918 and 1919 there were signs of sympathetic revolution in western Europe, including short-lived communist regimes in Hungary, Finland and Bavaria, south Germany. Grigori Zinoviev, a senior and influential member of the Communist leadership, was made chairman of Comintern. The Second Congress

Key terms

Union of Soviet Socialist Republics (USSR): Formed officially in 1922 and disbanded in 1991, the USSR was a single-party, communist state consisting originally of the RSFSR, Transcaucasian, Ukrainian and Belorussian Soviet Socialist Republics (SSRs). Other SSRs were subsequently formed and joined the Union. It is often referred to as the Soviet Union.

Comintern (Third Communist International): An international organisation created in 1919 whose purpose was the promotion of worldwide revolution. The First and Second Internationals had been loose federations of European socialist parties, whereas this was under the direct influence of the Communist Party of the Soviet Union (CPSU). It was dissolved in 1943 and succeeded by Cominform in 1947.

was held, again in Moscow, in the summer of 1920. By this point there were 217 delegates from 36 countries. It met as the Red Army advanced on Warsaw. Józef Piłsudski had agreed a treaty with the Nationalists in Ukraine and invaded in April 1920. In May they had taken Kiev, but in June Red cavalry pushed the Polish back. The British Foreign Secretary, Lord Curzon, stated that Britain and France would intervene if the Communists crossed into Polish territory. Despite this they pushed on and headed for Warsaw. The progress of the Red Army reignited hopes of a military campaign to expand the revolution. As the Second Congress ended, there were clear hopes of establishing a pro-Moscow regime within days. British dockers refused to load ships bound for Poland in sympathy with Moscow. Nevertheless, Piłsudski struck back, dividing the two prongs of the Red advance.

A possible reason for this sudden reverse in Communist fortunes was an overambitious policy of splitting and weakening their forces in order both to take the newly established Polish corridor (agreed at the Treaty of Versailles) and to head south towards Hungary and Czechoslovakia. The Red Army's rear was threatened and Moscow was forced to sue for peace, which was concluded by March 1921. In so doing it lost territory it might have kept.

Defeat in the war against Poland was a decisive factor in turning Lenin away from westward expansion and towards the consolidation of Soviet territory. He still intended to make use of Comintern and, at the Second Congress, had passed 21 articles that required affiliating parties to adhere strictly to central Comintern policy, which meant taking orders from the Communist Party in Moscow. These were deliberately demanding terms, as he wished to split the revolutionary European left away from their social democratic and more moderate socialist comrades. He was successful in this in many cases. Separate communist parties were set up and in some cases struggled to remain loyal to the Soviet regime.

The Russo-Polish war

The western border remained in question, in particular the status of Poland. As described above, Piłsudski, leader of the Polish nationalist army, had held back his forces in order to allow the Red Army to defeat Denikin in 1919. Once this had been achieved, he went on the offensive in Ukraine, to gain a 'buffer zone' between Poland and Russia. Lodged between Russia and Germany, Poland had gradually been subsumed into the Russian Empire by 1900 and was treated as a province; as with Finland, its government and culture were 'russified'. The Russo-Polish or Soviet-Polish war that ensued became part of Lenin's short-lived initiative to spread the revolution.

 Thematic link: Communist revolution

The interconnectedness of political change is an important point to remember when studying the past: we may study one state in isolation, but events rarely happen that way. The revolution in Russia generated waves of fear throughout the rest of Europe. Across Britain, France and Germany, industrialisation had led to workers' movements which demanded greater political involvement and representation, and leaders worried that these could quite easily become radical socialist movements.

The Rapallo Treaty

There is a strong case that the Bolshevik regime's survival in 1918 was highly dependent on the German imperial government. The German Foreign Office advised the Kaiser that by supporting the Bolsheviks they would continue to keep Russia weak and divided, and ripe for eventual German domination. This had been the rationale for assisting Lenin to return in April 1917. This was very clearly a marriage of convenience, as the two regimes were ideologically diametrically opposed. In November 1918, circumstances changed when a new civilian government in Berlin signed an armistice with the Allies. In the ensuing years Germany and what became the Soviet Union found themselves in a similar predicament: as outcasts of international diplomacy. Germany was subjected to the punitive terms of the Treaty of Versailles in 1919 and was excluded from the newly established League of Nations. This led to a partial reconciliation. In April 1922 German and Russian delegations met at Rapallo, having attended an international conference in nearby Genoa where the French had demanded the Soviet regime repay its pre-war debt. The two parties signed the Treaty of Rapallo on 16 April which re-established diplomatic relations, cancelled all the territorial and financial claims of either side and promised greater economic cooperation. This was one of the building blocks for the Soviet regime's recovery.

Britain and the Zinoviev letter

Another of these building blocks was the improved relationship with Britain. Following the signing of the Treaty of Versailles, Lloyd George looked for the stabilisation of relations with Russia and to end the blockade of Petrograd. Negotiations began in London in May 1920 between Krasin, Commissar for Foreign Trade, and members of the British cabinet. These continued on through the summer with Kamenev, a member of the Politburo, joining the trade delegation. The Anglo-Soviet Trade Agreement was signed on 16 March 1921. It drew a line under British intervention, ending the blockade and facilitating trade between the two countries, promising to 'remove forthwith all obstacles … placed in the way of the real trade … in any commodities which may be legally exported … or imported … and not to exercise any discrimination against such trade … or to place any impediments in the way of banking, credit and financial operations'.[8] The Anglo-Soviet Trade Agreement clearly went beyond trade matters, dealing also with the return of British subjects and Russian citizens to their respective countries and the prohibition against encouraging propaganda against each other outside their own borders. In other words, this ran counter to the main reason for the existence of the Comintern.

Britain's position in relation to the Soviet Union remained a matter of controversy. The trade union movement in Britain was broadly supportive of what it regarded as a working-class government in Russia and was influenced by the Communist Party of Great Britain (CPGB), which had been founded in 1920–1921 as a result of the foundation of Comintern. This party attempted to influence the moderate socialist Labour Party, which briefly held office as a minority government in 1924 and recognised the Soviet Union in February of that year. Ramsay MacDonald, the Labour Prime Minister, however, was defeated in a motion of no confidence in October, and called a general election. Four days before the election the *Daily Mail* published a letter allegedly written by Zinoviev, head of the Comintern, to the CPGB urging the extension of 'Leninism' to Britain. Zinoviev immediately claimed the letter had been forged, but his denial was not published in Britain until December. Historians have since established that the letter was most likely the work of anti-communists. While it did not have a significant impact on the Labour Party's vote, the Conservative government returned to office was wary of diplomatic support for the Soviet Union and remained so throughout the 1920s.

Lenin's rule by 1924 and his legacy

In December 1922, the Union of Soviet Socialist Republics (USSR) was formed. It was composed of the Russian Soviet Federative Socialist Republic, Ukrainian Soviet Socialist Republic, the Belarusian Soviet Socialist Republic and the Trans-Caucasian Socialist Federative Soviet Republic. The Union Treaty provided for the possible inclusion of new republics in time.

In May of that year, Lenin suffered a stroke as a result of endless work. Another stroke followed in December and then again in March 1923. This removed him from having any part in politics. After his first stroke he dictated a number of papers, including what became known as his Testament. It was critical of several of his closest and highest-ranking comrades, including Joseph Stalin, who had by necessity begun to lead the government alongside his comrades Kamenev and Zinoviev. They formed a 'triumvirate' hostile to Trotsky, who was a clear contender to succeed Lenin.

One of the key issues at stake was the position of the Soviet Union in the world. As the Soviet Union again became internationally isolated, there was a move by Stalin and those of like mind towards building up the Soviet Union as a socialist state, rather than looking to prioritise the spread of the revolution. This shift away from the broad revolutionary, internationalist and even utopian vision of the early years towards creating a strong and prosperous socialist state was to define the following years of Russia's history.

Further reading

Evan Mawdsley offers a lucid account of the complex Russian Civil War in his book titled *The Russian Civil War* (Birlinn, 2008), which provides a balanced analysis of why the Communists were the victors. Christopher Read's *From Tsar to Soviets* (UCL, 1996) is highly readable and provides fascinating insight into the experiences of ordinary people during the early years of Bolshevik power. For an in-depth explanation of Marxism, *The Communist Manifesto* (Penguin, 2004) is an excellent starting point. The introduction by Gareth Stedman Jones in the Penguin edition is a detailed account of the genesis of Marx's thought and its historical context.

Practice essay questions

1. 'The introduction and continuation of the NEP saved Bolshevik Russia from collapse.' Explain why you agree or disagree with this view.

2. 'By 1921 the Bolsheviks had successfully established a one-party dictatorship over Russia.' Explain why you agree or disagree with this view.

3. 'The Communists maintained power in Russia 1917–1924 because they established a successful apparatus for repression.' Assess the validity of this view.

4. With reference to the sources below and your understanding of the historical context, assess the value of these three sources to a historian studying the extent of popular support for the Bolsheviks during the Civil War.

Source A

Petition of Stepan Efimovich Iakitin, a peasant from Staro-Slavkino village, May 1919 (in Atkin, N., *Daily Lives of Civilians in Wartime Twentieth-Century Europe*, pp. 63–64).

I, as a working peasant, working only with my family and my own callused hands, •
had one of my two horses confiscated, leaving me only one horse, and they also took
16 funt [sacks] of wool, all without payment. I ask you, comrade representatives, to
defend my rights as you should defend the interests of all working peasants, and I ask
you to consider why the comrade leaders took my horse and wool, when I have only
two horses, and whether I can really be a kulak with only two horses, and whether I can
exploit the labour of others when I do not have enough animals and tools for myself.
Surely my interests, the interests of a working peasant, will be defended by comrade
Lenin, surely I will be defended by you, representatives of the higher authorities.

Source B

Provisions Commissar of Kozlov Uezd (Tambov Province), summer 1919 (in Figes, O., *Peasant Russia Civil War*, p. 246).

More and more often one hears not only bourgeois and kulaks, but also members of
the rural poor and workers comparing Soviet power unfavourably with the old regime
… The enormous number of government orders, the proliferation of official institutions
and commissions, the thousands of party bosses with lists of warrants and orders three
years long who travel around the country terrorizing the peasants – all this has placed a
heavy burden on the population, and has caused the people to grumble and curse and
become bitter. It has even driven some of the peasants to destroy their grain, meat, and
other foodstuffs rather than give them to the Communists.

Source C

Proclamation by the political leadership of the Stavropol Soviet in its newspaper *Izvestiya*, April 1919.

Comrades, peasants, and citizens of Soviet Russia! You are right to resist the domination of a few Communists since this political party of Bolsheviks and Communists contains many tramps and hooligans, in the spiritual and physical sense, who are not even able to look after themselves and their own comrades honourably. Peasants, now you are eager to fight and if necessary die in the struggle against these rascals, but remember that you still have the soviets. The soviets are your flesh and blood, the means by which you threw off the chains of servitude … Citizens-intelligentsia! Help the peasants understand their movement; direct them towards the wisest path! Join the peasants and help them in their difficult task!

Taking it further

1. Carry out some research on the Church in Soviet Russia. Does Patriarch Tikhon (see *Hidden voices*, earlier) have good reason to be upset?
2. Carry out your own research into the Red and White terrors. What kinds of people became victims of both sides?

Chapter summary

Having studied this chapter you should be able to:

- identify in what ways the Bolshevik regime removed its remaining political opponents and developed its power base
- identify the different stages of the Civil War
- identify and prioritise the reasons for 'Red victory' in the Civil War
- trace the development of 'war communism' and methods of terror and assess their economic and social effects
- identify the reasons for, and impact of, the New Economic Policy from 1921
- assess the internal and external security and stability of the regime by 1924.

End notes

1 Cited in Acton, E. and Stableford, T., *The Soviet Union: A Documentary History, Volume 1,* pp. 85–86.
2 Pipes, R., *A Concise History of the Russian Revolution*, p. 226.
3 Davies, Harrison and Wheatcroft, *The Economic Transformation of The Soviet Union 1913–1945*, p. 62.
4 Read, C., *War and Revolution in Russia, 1914–22*, p. 161.
5 Davies, R.W., Harrison, M. and Wheatcroft, S.G. (eds), *The Economic Transformation of The Soviet Union*, p. 64.
6 Nove, A., *An Economic History of the USSR*, p. 97.
7 Mawdsley, E., *The Russian Civil War*, p. 106.
8 *The World War I Document Archive*, from Brigham Young University, wwi.lib.byu.edu.

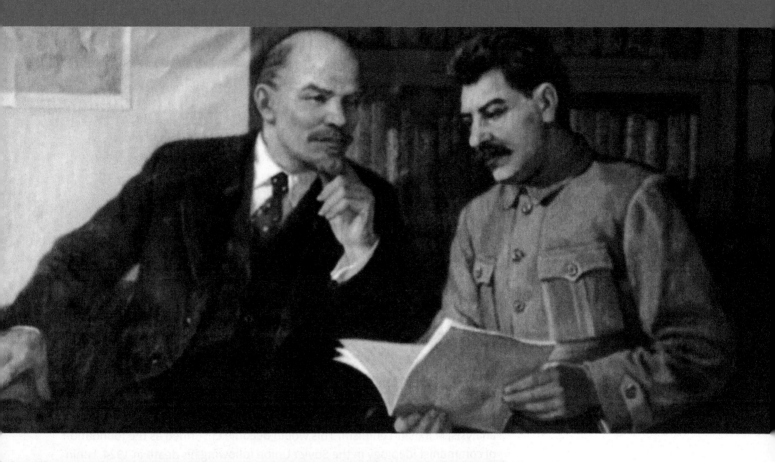

In this section we will investigate Stalin's rise to power during the 1920s:

- the power vacuum and power struggle: ideology and the nature of leadership; Lenin's Testament; divisions and contenders for power; character, strength and weaknesses of Trotsky, Stalin, Zinoviev, Kamenev, Bukharin, Pyatakov, Rykov and Tomsky

- ideological debates and issues in the leadership struggle: NEP and industrialisation; 'Permanent revolution' versus 'Socialism in One Country'; how and why Stalin became party leader and the outcomes for the other contenders

- economic developments: reasons for the impact of the Great Turn; the economic shift; the first five-year plan and the decision to collectivise

- government, propaganda and the beginning of the Stalinist cult: Stalin's attitude to foreign powers; changes in Comintern.

Speak like a historian

Changes in party culture

In some senses, the broad membership of the Communist Party of the Soviet Union, as it grew in size and influence during the 1920s, was increasingly driven by practical considerations rather than ideology. Mark Sandle notes that with the changing composition of the party, the membership became 'overwhelmingly short on education and long on pragmatism'.[1] The party became more and more dominant in public institutions and natural careerists discovered that joining the party was the means by which to gain promotion in their profession or community. This led to an increasing role for patronage and clientism: senior figures acted as 'patrons', building networks of loyal party members (their *'clients'*), who would support them in return for promotion and favours. This, in turn, led to corruption (bribes and favours for personal gain) and the growth of personality cults. These came about through constant praise and adulation (flattery) of the figure concerned in hope of gaining promotion and fear of being disadvantaged. In such a situation, open criticism could become dangerous. The supreme example of this was Stalin, but it is important to note that other major figures, such as Trotsky, had similar followings, as did some local and regional figures.

The power vacuum and power struggle

Ideology and the nature of leadership

By 1921 Lenin had come to be regarded as undisputed leader of the Communist Party, the Soviet Union and the 'revolution'. His official positions were Chairman of Sovnarkom and de facto Chairman of the Politburo. His authority, however, rested on his reputation both as the successful leader of the world's first 'communist' revolution and its foremost theorist. Through his adaption of the Marxist model to the circumstances of Russia in 1917, he was the author of the new version of analysis, Marxism-Leninism. This would become enshrined as the foundation of communist ideology in the Soviet Union following his death in 1924. Lenin expected there to be debate within the higher ranks of the party, but he expected to win that debate through force of argument and secret arrangements, if necessary. It is important to establish this model of leadership before considering what would follow. His involvement in running the party and the country began to wane, along with his health, from late 1921 onwards. To some extent a 'party machine' already existed and a transition to 'collective leadership' was underway during the three years before his death.

The state and the Communist Party by 1924

Leading Bolsheviks, not least Lenin and Trotsky, were wary of the revolution becoming 'bureaucratised'. This is to say that, in the process of assuming power, the new regime could lose the dynamism, passion and flexibility of the revolutionary group. With a retreat on the economic front, many on the left of the party feared slipping back into tsarist ways and its slow-moving bureaucracy in which official processes frustrated the ability of the government to act quickly. The state itself had expanded substantially as a result of war communism. This occurred not only in economic institutions but under others, such as the Commissariat of Enlightenment in charge of education, propaganda and the arts. In an economically unstable situation, government jobs provided a guaranteed income. This created what Richard Pipes terms a 'bureaucratic caste' separated from the working class.[2] Alongside state apparatus, and increasingly more important, was the Communist Party. By March 1920 it had 600 000 members compared with only 24 000 at the beginning of 1917. As intolerance of non-communists grew, the party became the most obvious place for career advancement. In addition, the Communist Party gradually began to dominate 'non-party' public and state institutions. Party members began to organise themselves to ensure that party policy was accepted, by ensuring the appointment of dependable individuals in key positions.

In March 1919, the Central Committee created the Politburo and the **Orgburo** to work alongside the Party Secretariat. It was also during this time that the Executive Committees of local and provincial Soviets gained decisive power and were less dependent on the votes of full meetings of the Soviets. This created a powerful body of powerful officials or 'party cadre', sourced substantially from the lower middle classes and numbering about 15 000 by 1922. It was this alienation from the working classes that drove the Workers' Opposition in 1920 and 1921. Lenin, however, was not concerned by the lack of democracy within the party.

Faced with the alternative of socialist disunity within a hostile capitalist world, he opted for party discipline (thus the ban on factions at the Tenth Congress in 1921). There was logic to the centralisation of power (see Figure 3.1), which led to the appointment of party officials and of delegates to the party congresses by Moscow.

Key term

Orgburo: Organisational Bureau of the Central Committee of the Communist Party of the Soviet Union. Created in 1919, this body was responsible for party administration and membership. It was also in charge of the Party Secretariat which became an important part of Stalin's power base when he became General Secretary of the Secretariat in 1922.

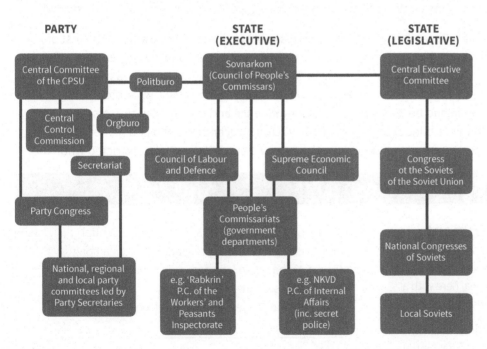

Figure 3.1: Key party and state bodies. (Adapted from Sandle, M., *A Short History of Soviet Socialism*, p. 75.)

Lenin's Testament

Lenin regarded the revolution as a collective achievement. He had not been widely known as its 'leader' before the attempt on his life in late 1918. At that point others began to use his image to serve as an icon of the revolutionary cause, but it is doubtful that he sought a cult of personality for himself. In some ways the

Speak like a historian

The party and the state

Under the Treaty of Union (1922) and the subsequent Constitution of the Soviet Union (1924), the party (**CPSU**) and the state (USSR) were officially separate. In reality, the party came to dominate the state, both executive (government bodies) and legislative (those bodies responsible for agreeing laws). This domination of state organs by party members and party policy and the banning of all other political parties gave rise to the phrase 'one-party state'. This process was aided by the centralisation of power to the party hierarchy. A major part of the process was the creation in 1922 of three bodies that stemmed from the Central Committee, which gained its authority from the Party Congress. The Politburo began as a five-member committee to deal with urgent issues for the Central Committee. It gradually became the focal point of power. The Orgburo was also an important body, under the Politburo and Central Committee, which was responsible for party administration and membership. It in turn controlled the Party Secretariat, which was made up of secretaries from other Central Committee bodies. Stalin became its General Secretary. Two other powerful bodies were the party's Central Control Commission and the People's Commissariat of the Workers' and Peasants' Inspectorate, known as Rabkrin. These had similar roles in investigating complaints against party officials (CCC) and government officials (Rabkrin).

leadership of the regime was already 'collective', but Lenin's absence did create a question of succession. As undisputed leader of the Communist Party, Lenin had been able to throw his personal authority behind, for example, the NEP, which remained controversial within the party (see *NEP and industrialisation*, below).

From December 1921, Lenin was less able to direct policy owing to the first of three strokes which took him away from work, into convalescence. An unofficial 'triumvirate' (group of three) of Stalin, Zinoviev and Kamenev was formed to guide the party and essentially to resist the influence of Trotsky. By September 1922 Lenin had become wary of Stalin's influence and reached out to Trotsky to assist him in a 'bloc against bureaucracy'. On 15 December Lenin had his second stroke and returned to Gorki under the supervision of Stalin. Stalin restricted whom he

Voices from the past

Extract from Lenin's Testament

I have in mind stability as a guarantee against a split in the immediate future, and I intend to deal here with a few ideas concerning personal qualities.

I think that from this standpoint the prime factors in the question of stability are such members of the Central Committee as Stalin and Trotsky. I think relations between them make up the greater part of the danger of a split, which could be avoided, and this purpose, in my opinion, would be served, among other things, by increasing the number of Central Committee members to 50 or 100. [...]

In my opinion, the workers admitted to the Central Committee should come preferably not from among those who have had long service in Soviet bodies ... because those workers have already acquired the very traditions and the very prejudices which it is desirable to combat.[3]

Discussion points

1. Why do you think Lenin believes enlarging the Central Committee will help to guard against a split in the party?
2. What do you think Lenin means by 'the very traditions and the very prejudices which it is desirable to combat'?

could see, so Lenin dictated a number of notes to his secretaries, one of whom was his wife, Krupskaya. These notes became known as his Testament, but his intention was to communicate his concerns to his comrades in preparation for the Twelfth Party Congress. The notes touched on three main issues: the new constitution of the USSR (the parameters of which were laid down in the Union Treaty of 30 December 1922); the need to 'democratise' the party (to counteract its bureaucracy); and the suitability of various leading members of the party (in the light of Lenin's likely demise).

All of these, to some extent, reflected poorly on Stalin. While Lenin had essentially gone against his original 'Declaration' on nationalities, his intention was to allow the newly recovered republics to become part of the existing Federation (RSFSR). This would give them equal status. Stalin, on the other hand, wished to subordinate them to the Russian government and allow them a degree of autonomy. To Lenin's frustration, Stalin essentially got his way with the Union Treaty, although the constitution was not formalised until 1924.

It is arguable that, as with the nationalities question, Lenin's proposals to bring greater scrutiny from below the party hierarchy was a little like shutting the stable door after the horse had bolted. In his notes he suggested adding 50 to 100 new members from lower down in the party to the Central Committee, and allowing it to question the actions of the Politburo. This clearly ran counter to the broader culture of excluding dissenters so apparent in the ban on factions. Lenin most probably had in mind a means by which a collective leadership might be maintained after his death. He was perhaps aware that he had performed a unique role.

The third and most explosive element of Lenin's notes was brief assessments of the strengths and weaknesses of the members of the Politburo. His comments, if shared, would undoubtedly have influenced who succeeded him. None of his characterisations were overwhelming endorsements. This was perhaps to ensure some degree of fair-handedness, but more to demonstrate the need for a balancing of power. The key contenders for power, and Lenin's view of them, are detailed below. The actual influence of Lenin's Testament on the struggle for power will then be discussed.

Divisions and contenders for power: character, strengths and weaknesses

Trotsky

Leon Trotsky (born Lev Bronstein) was possibly the most obvious candidate to succeed Lenin because of his personality, experience and high rank in the party. He had masterminded the seizure of power in October 1917, ended Russia's involvement in the First World War as Commissar for Foreign Affairs, and spearheaded Red victory in the Civil War. His energetic speechmaking made him popular with young party enthusiasts, and his association with the army brought him support there. Students also admired Trotsky's intellectual ability. Lenin referred to him as 'perhaps the most capable man in the present Central Committee' and, alongside Stalin, as one of 'the two outstanding leaders'.

Key term

Communist Party of the Soviet Union (CPSU): The ruling party of the Soviet Union. All other political parties had been banned by 1921. Its power structure was closely integrated with the organs of state in the Soviet Union. Originally, it was the Bolshevik faction of the Russian Social Democratic Labour Party and then the Russian Communist Party (Bolshevik) before the creation of the Soviet Union in 1922.

Trotsky would not have appreciated being placed on a par with Stalin. Trotsky's arrogance, both real and perceived, was to prove a major weakness. Lenin stated that he 'displayed excessive self-assurance' and it seems clear that Trotsky underestimated Stalin as a threat. For some time Trotsky regarded Zinoviev as the more serious rival and failed to challenge Stalin when he might have. Trotsky also failed to build alliances with his fellow leading Bolsheviks. He had come late to the Bolshevik fold (attempting to be a non-factional Social Democrat until October 1917). His loyalty could therefore be questioned, although it was he who sided with Lenin in favour of an immediate seizure of power, against the viewpoint of Zinoviev and Kamenev. His cool relationship with this strategic pair was to have important consequences.

Stalin

It was perhaps astute of Lenin to recognise Stalin as one of the outstanding leaders of the Politburo. In comparison to Trotsky, Stalin lacked charisma and personality. His reputation was built on administrative efficiency and party loyalty. Born into a poor Georgian family, Joseph Dzhugashvili took the name Stalin (which means 'man of steel') because of his tough reputation: he was exiled and imprisoned several times as a result of his revolutionary activity for the benefit of the Bolsheviks. He became a member of the Central Committee in 1912 and unlike other leading Bolsheviks, including Lenin, Trotsky and Zinoviev, was present for the February Revolution. He quickly became convinced of Lenin's programme, and although he played no great role in the October seizure of power, he became Commissar for Nationalities and was an original member of the seven-man predecessor of the Politburo. It was Stalin's appointment as General Secretary in April 1922 that gave him control over party membership and chairmanship of the Secretariat. His relative anonymity was to serve him very well in the long term.

That year, the Orgburo and Secretariat appointed 10 000 provincial officials. Over the following years, Stalin was able to promote his supporters and sideline or even expel his detractors. Additionally a 'Lenin Levy' party recruitment drive, undertaken in 1924 and 1925, added 440 000 'proletarian' workers to the party. The ideological intention was in a sense to respond to previous criticisms of the gulf between the party and the proletariat, but in fact it produced an influx of 'practical' men and women to whom Stalin's apparently moderate, less intellectual stance appealed.

Stalin's ability to ensure that he was perceived as a unifier and a moderate during the ideological debate of the mid-1920s was an essential part of his slow accumulation of power. Lenin had nevertheless noted that Stalin had 'unlimited authority concentrated in his hands' and was unsure whether he was able to exercise it with 'sufficient caution'. He went further, though, and in a postscript recommended that Stalin be removed from his post as General Secretary and replaced with someone with 'greater tolerance, greater loyalty, greater courtesy and consideration to comrades'.[4]

Zinoviev and Kamenev

Those primarily responsible for playing down Lenin's criticism of Stalin were Grigori Zinoviev and Lev Kamenev (and later Nikolai Bukharin). As part of the Zinoviev–Kamenev–Stalin 'triumvirate' that began to take the reins of power, the key internal concern was preventing the rise of Trotsky. This perhaps blinded Zinoviev and Kamenev to Stalin as a potential threat.

Both Zinoviev and Kamenev were long-standing Bolsheviks. They also both had strong and important local power bases. Zinoviev had held influential positions within the workers' movement in Petrograd since February 1917. He went on to become Party Secretary in the city, once it had been renamed Leningrad, in honour of the dead leader. Similarly, Kamenev (see Figure 3.2) had become Chairman of the Moscow Soviet in 1918 and subsequently Party Secretary. Kamenev was a full member of the Politburo from its creation in 1919; Zinoviev from 1921. Both had held positions related to the international standing of the new state: Kamenev as Commissar for Foreign Trade (he was part of the negotiations with Britain) and Zinoviev as Chairman of the Comintern from its inception in 1919. They also both served as deputies to Lenin in different roles: Kamenev as Deputy Chairman of Sovnarkom from 1918 and its acting chairman during Lenin's illness, while Zinoviev delivered reports to the Twelfth and Thirteenth Congresses, which was ordinarily the role of Lenin.

Despite these senior roles, neither man was a member of Sovnarkom from the outset, owing to their strong opposition to Lenin's demands for an immediate seizure of power in October 1917. This 'October episode' was not forgotten and was briefly referred to in the Testament as 'no accident' (as was Trotsky's non-Bolshevik past). This, and their collaboration with Stalin, has resulted in their often being paired. They did, however, seem to have different personalities and attributes. Zinoviev was seen as the more ambitious. He spoke well but was not popular, nor was he rated as capable. Kamenev, on the other hand, was intellectually capable but unwilling to lead. Both men were associated with the left wing of the party, but, possibly owing to personal rivalry, did not unite with Trotsky in this regard until late.

Figure 3.2: Trotsky, Lenin and Kamenev at the Second Party Congress of the Communist Party of Russia in 1919.

Bukharin and Pyatakov

Nikolai Bukharin and Yuri Pyatakov were not a strategic pair, but were the final two to be mentioned by Lenin in the Testament and were in some ways similar as younger members of the party still in their 30s. Despite his youth, Bukharin played a major intellectual role in the party. A Bolshevik from 1906, he wrote *Imperialism and World Economy* (1915), which is likely to have influenced Lenin's better-known work. In October 1917 he became editor of the party newspaper *Pravda* and continued to produce theoretical works, in particular *The ABC of Communism* (1919). Deeply concerned with economic theory, Bukharin quickly converted from a Left Communist stance during the Civil War, to one in favour of NEP. Lenin clearly rated Bukharin and acknowledged his popularity: 'a most valuable and major theorist of the party' and 'rightly considered the favourite of the whole party'. However, he then went on to suggest that his 'scholastic' nature made him politically, even ideologically, questionable. He could, Lenin wrote, 'be classified as fully Marxist only with great reserve'.[5]

Pyatakov was described by Lenin as 'a man of outstanding will and outstanding ability' but again was criticised for an imbalance of skill and for being unreliable in 'a serious political matter'. A Bolshevik from 1912, he built his reputation by leading Bolsheviks in the Ukraine during the Civil War. His position was consistently on the left, opposing Lenin's views on the non-Russian nationalities and becoming deputy head of Gosplan in 1921 and the Supreme Council in 1922. He was not a member of the Politburo and his inclusion in the Testament may relate to his frequent visits to Lenin during his illness.

Speak like a historian

Why Trotsky failed to secure power

Robert Service's masterful biography of Trotsky highlights some of the key reasons that he failed to secure the power struggle:

If the United Opposition had been created earlier, Stalin would have been helpless against it. Trotsky, Kamenev and Zinoviev would have dominated the Politburo, the Central Committee and Comintern, and Sovnarkom would have been theirs for the taking. Now they faced an uphill struggle. Zinoviev was on record as a critic of Trotsky; he had castigated his 'adventurism' in foreign policy, his excessive inclination towards centralism in political administration and his many clashes with Lenin before and after 1917. Trotsky had replied in kind, denouncing Zinoviev for desertion of Lenin before the October Revolution as well as for his collusion with Stalin and Bukharin in taking the militancy out of the NEP. All such disagreements had been printed in *Pravda* … By aligning themselves with him, Zinoviev and Kamenev called for the democratization of the party and the introduction of restriction of market economics. It was not difficult for Stalin and Bukharin to attribute their alteration of stance to a mere lust for power.

(From Robert Service, *Trotsky: A Biography*, Pan, 2010.)

Discussion points:

1. What does Service mean by 'excessive inclination towards centralism'?
2. What is Service arguing here about the power struggle?
3. What are his criticisms of Trotsky?

Rykov and Tomsky

Alexei Rykov and Mikhail Tomsky were not mentioned in the Testament but were senior figures in the party and would play an important part on the issue of NEP. Rykov was from a peasant family and Tomsky's background was in the trade union movement prior to 1917. They therefore both had impeccable proletarian roots and were long-standing Bolsheviks. Both men became members of the Orgburo in 1921 and the Politburo in 1922. Tomsky had attempted to increase the autonomy of the trade unions but was threatened with dismissal from the Central Committee and then essentially fell in line, becoming chairman of the body that oversaw the newly restrained and conformist trades unions from 1922. Rykov had been Commissar for Internal Affairs (the post rejected by Trotsky) in the first Sovnarkom and went on to be its Deputy Chairman alongside Kamenev during Lenin's illness. On Lenin's death he became Premier of the RSFSR and the USSR, although these posts were not as powerful as the names suggest. Nevertheless, these two members of the Politburo with robust credentials were placed on the right of the party and supported Bukharin in his advocacy of NEP.

ACTIVITY 3.1

ACTIVITY 3.1

Complete the following table to help you assess the relative strengths and weaknesses of the leadership contenders.

	Trotsky	Stalin	Zinoviev	Kamenev	Bukharin
Positions of power					
Policies					
Personality					
Lenin's comments in his Testament					
Overall summary					

Ideological debates and issues in the leadership struggle

The rise of Stalin can be located within the ideological arguments and political positioning that occurred from the beginning of Lenin's decline in 1922. They can be organised into three stages.

- First was the initial opposition to and weakening of Trotsky, which centred round the defeat of the **Left Opposition** at the Twelfth and Thirteenth Congresses (in 1923 and 1924). This involved Zinoviev and Kamenev defending Stalin from the potential damage of the Testament. While focused on NEP and party democracy, this was less of an ideological and more of a political battle against Trotsky.
- Second was the stage from 1925 when Zinoviev and Kamenev began to perceive Stalin as the greater threat and joined with Trotsky in opposing NEP and Stalin's dominance.
- Third was the stage from 1927 when Stalin, once he had defeated those rivals on the Left, began to respond to demands for more rapid industrialisation and turned against the proponents of NEP.

NEP and industrialisation

Trotksy and NEP

While the legalisation of private trade under NEP may well have prevented starvation and total economic collapse, it was not universally popular, particularly among the urban working class. (For details of the workings and success of NEP from 1924 onwards, see *Economic developments*, below.) Despite the defeat

Key term

Left Opposition: This was a general term used to describe those who opposed the Communist leadership in the mid-1920s by calling for more rapid industrialisation and the abandonment of the NEP.

of the Workers' Opposition at the Tenth Congress, there remained a strong scepticism regarding this supposedly tactical retreat towards capitalism. First, it was ideologically unpalatable to many in the party – on its introduction they ripped up their membership cards. Second, and relatedly, there was resentment at signs of a return of 'bourgeois' owners, traders (Nepmen) and the perceived rise of the exploitative peasant class, the kulaks. Trotsky was therefore not alone in his demand for faster industrialisation, to some extent, at the expense of the peasants. This demand would never go away and would eventually be the basis of Stalin's success. As we shall see, however, Trotsky placed this demand to build socialism within the context of the need for worldwide revolution. His vision was almost a continuation of the heroic efforts of the Civil War abroad, but as we have seen the European revolution had failed by 1923, and it was a rival, Zinoviev, who was in charge of the Comintern.

Trotsky essentially misplayed his hand in the years up to 1924. Unlike Stalin, he did not have a party position (let alone three!) and therefore did not have the means to advance what was, in any case, a fairly vague alternative to NEP. He also did not take sufficient advantage of the Testament or simply did not have enough support within the Central Committee. As a result the Testament was not read out at the Twelfth Congress in April 1923. In October he wrote an 'Open Letter' to the Central Committee, but quickly opened himself up to Zinoviev's accusations of factionalism. Stalin, wishing to be perceived as a mediator and moderate, argued against Trotsky's expulsion from the party. He could perhaps already tell that Trotsky was on a path to self-destruction, though Trotsky was not without support. A platform of leading Bolsheviks, the 'Group of 46', which included Pyatakov, signed a declaration supporting Trotsky's view that the party was becoming undemocratic and paralysed by bureaucracy, and therefore losing its revolutionary spirit and its connection to the 'masses'. Trotsky summed these concerns up in a series of articles entitled the *The New Course* in December 1923. He also argued that NEP was not working for the working class, referring to the 'scissors crisis' of that year. Those who took this view in the party were referred to as the 'Left Opposition'.

Bukharin and NEP

Stalin allowed Bukharin to become chief advocate for NEP. In April 1925 a series of measures were introduced that were designed to boost agricultural production and thus enable the state to gain capital to invest in industry by selling grain abroad. This, admitted Bukharin, was 'riding towards socialism on a peasant nag', but he considered it essential, not least because it would maintain the alliance between workers and peasants (the so-called *smychka*). The food tax, introduced in 1924, was reduced, as were the higher taxes on better-off peasants. Peasants could now hire labour and lease out land. Bukharin went further and encouraged peasants to 'enrich themselves' – echoing Guizot, a French bourgeois politician of the previous century whom Marx had condemned. This was a provocation to the Left Opposition. Bukharin was made to withdraw his comment and Stalin stated that 'the slogan "get rich" is not our slogan'. Stalin began to introduce measures that would serve as the basis of faster industrialisation, including more direct planning of the economy by Gosplan.

Stalin, the Left Opposition, and the reading of Lenin's Testament

Early 1924 was a challenging time for Stalin for two reasons. First, he had to deal with the Left Opposition and second, following Lenin's death in January, Krupskaya, Lenin's widow, had demanded that the Testament be read out to the Central Committee. Nevertheless, he dealt adeptly with the situation. After the Testament had been read out, he offered his resignation. Given the threat from Trotsky, Zinoviev and others could not countenance such a blow to their side, and spoke in spirited defence of the General Secretary. The Testament was not read out at the Thirteenth Congress in April, but rather to regional groupings of delegates beforehand. This served to dissipate its effect. Trotsky also found himself outvoted at the Congress. His own past was also against him: his arguments could be labelled as 'Menshevik deviation' and, given his somewhat dictatorial methods during the Civil War, his accusations of tyranny rang hollow. More importantly, at this point he could be accused of being anti-Leninist.

The cult of Lenin

Following his death on 5 January 1924, Lenin was quickly transformed into something of a secular saint or even, as some have suggested, a messianic figure: the saviour of the proletariat and the Soviet Union's founding father. This was physically manifested by having his brain removed and sliced up for study at a specially created institute, and his body embalmed and placed in what would become a permanent mausoleum for public viewing next to the Kremlin in Moscow. (See Figure 3.3) Petrograd was renamed Leningrad and Lenin's works were published for careful study. This led to the coining of a new term, 'Marxist-Leninism', which essentially meant that a new theoretical orthodoxy was created by which all political, academic and cultural thought must justify itself. Any of Lenin's would-be successors had to demonstrate their conformity for fear of being labelled 'anti-Leninist'.

It was in some regards a new religion and cult – a substitute for the Russian Orthodox veneration of saints. Trotsky was disadvantaged in this regard: he failed to attend the funeral (while Stalin was chief mourner); he openly contradicted NEP, which by this point was beginning to bring recovery; and he fell foul of the disciplined party centralism so clearly associated with Lenin's rule. In January 1925, Trotsky was replaced as Commissar of Defence and lost his place in the Politburo the following year.

Figure 3.3: Lenin's body was placed in Red Square in 1924 and has been on display ever since. The original mausoleum was wooden. In 1929 it was discovered that the body could be preserved for much longer so a marble and granite mausoleum was built, and is still there.

'Permanent revolution' versus 'Socialism in One Country'

While Zinoviev and Kamenev had prioritised their struggle against Trotsky, as early as mid-1923 they had considered how to rein in Stalin's growing power. By mid-1925 it was clear that the 'triumvirate' no longer existed, but in their turn against Stalin, Zinoviev and Kamenev focused the criticism on NEP, whose main advocate by this point was Bukharin. In late 1924, Preobrazhenski, on the Left, called for 'primitive socialist accumulation': obtaining grain from the peasantry at a low price in order to export, pay for industrialisation and feed the workers. At the same time, Stalin began to suggest that a period of economic stabilisation was necessary through the continuation of NEP, although he never fully distanced himself from the ongoing calls for faster industrialisation.

The phrase Stalin used to describe this policy was **'Socialism in One Country'**. This was potentially controversial as it suggested that socialism might be built up in the Soviet Union (in one country) without the need for revolution abroad. Given recent foreign trade deals, the failure of revolution in Germany, and perceived stabilisation of the capitalist West, Stalin proposed a period for gathering strength.

At this point, this policy chimed with NEP and as Zinoviev and Kamenev began to dissent from Stalin's view, Bukharin came to the fore to support him and vigorously defend and promote NEP.

Trotsky, though his influence was fading, denounced the idea as wholly un-Marxist. He criticised Socialism in One Country on the basis that it seemed to deny the need for world revolution and involved further concessions to the 'bourgeois' elements and the peasants. He proposed in its place a 'permanent revolution', which essentially appealed for a continuation of the revolutionary struggle abroad and an immediate move towards industrialisation. While it was an openly communist position, rejecting any compromise, much of the new 'Lenin Levy' party intake accepted Stalin's 'Soviet patriotic' view over Trotsky's overly ambitious, vague and unrealistic programme. Although it appealed to younger idealists, 'permanent revolution' allowed neither respite nor security for the Soviet Union. Increasingly, Stalin would make the case that the Soviet Union must be in a state to resist potential 'imperialist intervention' by rejuvenated capitalist powers. Moreover, Stalin could justify his stance in terms of arguments made by Lenin in favour of NEP.

How and why Stalin became party leader and the outcomes for the other contenders

By the time of the Fourteenth Congress in December, Zinoviev began to openly argue against the leadership, thinking that he had a sufficient power base to challenge Stalin. By mid-1926, Zinoviev and Kamenev joined with their old rival Trotsky in a '**United Opposition**'. The arguments rested on the idea that the leadership continued to neglect the workers and bolster the 'kulak threat'. This only served to confirm the view of the majority of the Politburo and of the wider party that Stalin was providing a centrist solution. The opposition's influence quickly waned: Stalin used the Secretariat to replace their supporters with his supporters, and Zinoviev lost his power base in Leningrad (Kirov, Stalin's associate, became Party Secretary in that city). While Bukharin attacked his critics in the press, *Pravda* refused to print opposition views and the **OGPU** (the successor to the Cheka) was used to smash their printing presses.

In July, Zinoviev and Kamenev lost their places on the Politburo. Stalin accused Zinoviev of 'arrogantly preparing a schism'. In November, Bukharin replaced Zinoviev as head of Comintern. In the following year, Zinoviev, Kamenev and Trotsky continued to criticise the leadership (particularly over foreign policy) while claiming to remain loyal to the party. Eventually, at the Fifteenth Congress held in November/December 1927, they were expelled from the party, along with over a hundred of their supporters, accused of a 'factional struggle to create an anti-Leninist party in conjunction with bourgeois intellectuals'. In 1928 Trotsky began his journey into exile, first internally, then abroad. Zinoviev and Kamenev pleaded to be readmitted to the party and renounced opposition.

Even as the United Opposition was in the process of being defeated, Stalin had begun a process of turning against his former ally, Bukharin. Despite the maintenance of NEP, policy had slowly been moving towards faster industrialisation at the expense of the peasantry. In 1925, 'Socialism in One

Key terms

Socialism in One Country: Stalin's theory that the Soviet Union should strengthen itself to resist capitalist encirclement. It followed the defeat of socialist revolutions in Germany and Hungary. The policy was criticised by Trotsky and Zinoviev.

United Opposition: The faction which opposed the policies of Stalin and Bukharin from 1926 and included Zinoviev, Kamenev and Trotsky. Zinoviev and Kamenev had previously been enemies of Trotsky and allies of Stalin.

OGPU: The All-Union State Political Administration was the secret police of the Soviet Union from 1922 until 1934. Felix Dzerzhinsky was the first chief of this state security branch. However, by 1934 it became reincorporated into the NKVD.

Country' had meant, at least for Bukharin who made use of the term, a long-term acceptance of NEP in order to consolidate the position of the Soviet Union. Stalin, despite his undermining of the United Opposition, had not wholly dismissed the calls for state action to drive the expansion of industry. By 1927, Stalin began to see Socialism in One Country more in terms of promoting industrialisation as a means to secure the Soviet Union against foreign aggression. In that year, there was a war scare (encouraged by Stalin) that served to consolidate party support for the new Stalinist line. Stalin had in fact used the fictitious reports of a possible British invasion to discredit the United Opposition as weakening the unity of the Soviet Union at a time of crisis.

Bukharin, unsurprisingly, objected. His slow and steady approach was being cast aside. However, he found himself isolated, and as with the United Opposition, the greater his complaint the more vulnerable he was to being labelled as factionalist. Along with his allies Rykov and Tomsky, his views were described as a 'right-wing deviation' from majority opinion. Stalin now had a clear majority of supporters in the Politburo and in the Central Committee. Bukharin had no such power base. In his role at the head of the Comintern, he had become highly critical of Western social democrats for bolstering capitalism. In so doing he had used the somewhat theoretical terminology of 'social fascism'. Stalin took this rhetoric and simplified it to use against Bukharin and his supporters. Their political defeat had been achieved in April 1929 at the Central Committee plenum. This is the point at which open debate within the party came to an end.

Some historians argue that Bukharin's slow and steady approach meant that the NEP would have worked, but as what followed was so different we cannot know. NEP was a unique economic experiment. It had included many non-communist economists and officials in its design and application. The continuation of NEP was, however, becoming politically less acceptable. The 'grain crisis' in 1927 and the defeat of his Left opponents allowed Stalin to radically alter course. He had previously benefited by stealing his opponents' ideas and he did so again with an economic programme that would have sizeable consequences.

Having attacked the Left Opposition for disunity and disloyalty, Stalin stole their pro-industrialisation position and abandoned NEP and its supporters. For a second time, he rounded on his erstwhile allies. By these two moves against his rivals on the left and then those on the right, Stalin had eliminated the main threats to his monopoly on power. He was then able to unite the party behind a policy of rapid industrialisation; a policy which sat far more comfortably with the broad majority of communists. This became known as the 'Great Turn'.

ACTIVITY 3.2

Complete this diagram, using the key, to demonstrate Stalin's changing alliances and the defeat of each of his rivals.

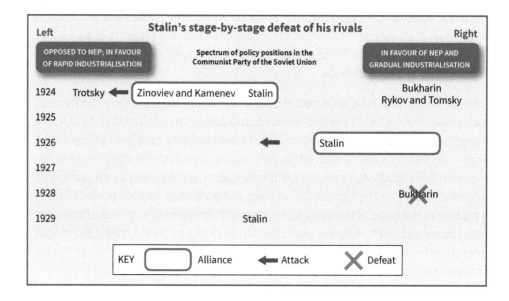

ACTIVITY 3.3

There are several reasons why Stalin emerged as Lenin's successor as leader. Figure 3.4 illustrates some of these factors. Go through your notes and complete the diagram with annotations. You may also refer to the timeline at the end of the chapter.

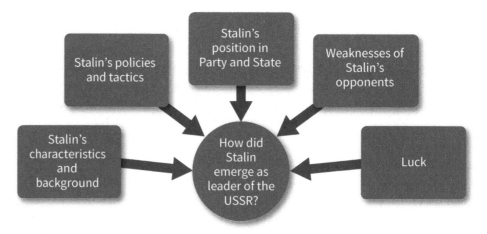

Figure 3.4: Factors in Stalin's emergence as leader of the USSR.

Economic developments

Reasons for and impact of the Great Turn

High NEP

The years 1924 to 1925 have been described as 'High NEP'. The term describes the period when this unique economic experiment was most successful and experienced the highest degree of support, or the least degree of challenge from the Communist Party and regime. By 1924 the currency had been stabilised and apparatuses were in place to balance the budgets of state enterprises. It was a period when private trade flourished and agricultural production recovered as the peasantry had a clear incentive to sell their produce and enjoy the benefits once they had paid their tax to the state. Bolshevik resentment of 'capitalist elements' – the Nepmen and kulaks – never fully diminished and the perceived prospering of these groups as well as 'bourgeois specialists' remained a constant consideration for many in the regime.

Planning

While private trade was legalised, government bodies still played a major part in the economy. As Nove suggests, despite the high degree of state intervention, this was not a command economy.[6] The Supreme Council for the National Economy and its local subordinates acted to control around 400 'trusts', which in turn controlled a number of factories. They did so by providing finance, appointing responsible officials and assisting in planning production.

Gosplan was a separate agency created to work under the Council of Labour and Defence (which itself had been born out of war communism and, like Sovnarkom, had been chaired by Lenin). From the beginning of NEP in 1921 its role had been to create, as far as possible, a single economic plan. By 1923, it was seen as a state planning commission, and the decree that redefined the roles of the various bodies involved acknowledged the need to avoid interference in already functioning arrangements. Control figures were produced for each year, but rather than being rigid targets (like those which would later be used to drive production and provide a political yardstick by which to judge their subjects), these provided a guide for investment priorities. Likewise, price controls for goods from 1922 were approximate, although as we have seen they could have real effects on production and trade.

The influence of government over each sector and industry varied. For example, Glavtextil, the department for textile manufacture, interfered very little in the operations of the syndicate of trusts that organised the wholesale production of textiles. In 1927 it was abolished, being viewed as superfluous. The influence of the central state also depended on the role of provincial and regional economic councils. The proliferation of central agencies also led to the duplication of roles. Dzerzhinsky, head of the Cheka, was put in charge of the Supreme Council in 1924 and complained about the diversity of responsibilities, but made only a little progress in centralising control. This degree of relative autonomy was arguably NEP's strength: decentralisation provided each area with an incentive to work out their own success.

Industry, wages and employment

Heavy industry remained in state hands, but much of the light industry was in the private sector. This meant that private producers had to buy their raw materials from state enterprises. However, price controls in the state sector meant that private manufacturers and traders were able to add a large margin (mark-up in price), as consumer goods remained relatively scarce. By 1926, average industrial wages almost equalled those in 1913. Moreover, those in work enjoyed greater benefits and better working conditions as a result of the social legislation of the new regime.

Matters were different, however, for those without work. Although private sector employment continued to rise between 1924 and 1927, overall unemployment increased between 1924 (1.24 million) and 1929 (1.6 million), with a moderate and short-lived improvement in 1925 (0.95 million). The regime put great store by the cooperative sector, which had arguably been an essential part of recovering from war communism. Nevertheless, cooperatives found it difficult to compete with private traders.

Agriculture and the peasantry

Agricultural cooperatives and collectives were of particular importance to the regime. Lenin had been an enthusiast for them because he hoped, in Figes' words, that they would 'wean the peasants off private traders'[7] and integrate fully with the socialised (publicly owned) sector. With state assistance, cooperatives could provide credit, tools, fertilisers and advice on irrigation and consolidation of strips. They had some success by 1926, as half belonged to cooperatives and agricultural yields were 17% higher than in 1900. The type of collective farm that existed, known as a **TOZ** (an abbreviation for the Association for the Joint Cultivation of Land), was one that struck a balance between common and private ownership. The land was farmed in common, but livestock and tools remained peasants' private property. Membership was voluntary and attracted those who would benefit by combining their meagre strips with those of others, which improved productivity and therefore each peasant's share. This was in stark contrast to what would occur from late 1929.

Concern grew from 1926 onwards that despite relatively rapid growth and recovery to pre-war levels of production, NEP could not provide sufficient capital for investment.

A crisis in the procurement of grain for the cities occurred in 1927. The basic reason behind this was the so-called 'good famine' – a shortage in consumer goods, which encouraged the peasantry to hold onto their grain. Nove puts this down to price controls on state produced goods, which encouraged 'speculators' to buy cheap from the state and sell at a profit to the peasantry; this had begun in 1926.[8] Additionally, the state began to drive down the prices it paid for grain (in 1926 and 1927, by as much as 25%). This was coupled with a poor harvest and led to calls for action. Arguably, the shift away from NEP began while its critics in the United Opposition were being sidelined and condemned. As early as 1926, legislation (Article 107 of the criminal code) was created which promised harsh penalties for those involved in 'speculation'. Stalin only began to make use of it in 1928 but its creation suggests that the tide was already turning against NEP.

Key term

TOZ: A small-scale farm on which land was worked collectively but peasants retained individual ownership of animals and equipment.

This goes some way to explain what seems to be a swift change of policy in 1928. Stalin announced it as 'The Year of the Great Break'. This included a highly ambitious Five-Year Plan to industrialise the Soviet Union at breakneck speed. It would also involve the reintroduction of grain requisitioning and the subsequent forced **collectivisation** of peasant land. All of this was cast in the rhetoric of making a clean break with Russia's underdeveloped past and ridding the socialist state of its remaining capitalist elements.

The economic shift

The slogan 'Socialism in One Country' was now redefined to mean the building up of the Soviet Union's industrial base in order to defend itself against foreign imperialist aggression. This was a simple and popular message within the party and among those, mainly workers, who resented the prospering of Nepmen and kulaks. To what extent a 'kulak class' existed is debatable and depends on definitions of income and ownership. It is fairly clear that there was a section of prosperous peasants, many of whom had contributed to NEP's success. For Stalin, however, perception began to overrule reality. Propaganda and revolutionary fervour became increasingly important determining factors of Soviet life.

Stalin's 'Great Turn' or 'Great Break' or 'breakthrough', announced in 1928, had as its ambition a dramatic and rapid catching up with, and then overtaking of, the industrialised capitalist West within ten years. The transformation was not only to be economic, it was to forge, through heroic efforts, the socialist society which the Bolshevik revolution had taken place to achieve. At the basis of the political and cultural changes, however, would be industrial and agricultural revolution.

This process has been referred to as Stalin's 'revolution from above', but there is much evidence to suggest local initiative and opinion played an important part in its fulfilment. As the '**Right Opposition**' was identified and shunned, Stalin gained genuine allegiance to a utopian vision. This was supported by young activists, who had not experienced the revolution and yearned to play a part in the construction of socialism, having been brought up on the myths of the Communist youth organisation, **Komsomol**.

The first Five-Year Plan and the decision to collectivise

The Five-Year Plan was designed in 1927 by Gosplan, announced in 1928 and revised in 1929. It promised to triple industrial investment, double coal and steel production and quadruple that of pig iron. It involved new projects on a gargantuan scale. They were hugely ambitious and very unlikely to be achieved. This did not matter to Stalin. Their purpose was to drive the workforce as hard as possible. These targets were to be achieved through heroic work and sacrifice.

Perception of what industrial production should be was to drive reality. In 1928 there was a trial of 'industrial specialists' from Shakhty in the Don Basin. It was the prototype of later 'show trials'. Charged with failing to meet industrial targets, the engineers were charged with sabotage, beaten until they confessed to made-up crimes and then publicly denounced. On the face of it, this was an independent investigation. In reality, the result was a foregone conclusion. The aim was to terrorise independent-minded planners, managers and engineers so that they felt

Key terms

Collectivisation: A policy introduced by Stalin in 1928 which aimed to consolidate individual land holdings into collective farms (*kolkhozy*) in the hope of increasing production. The human costs of this policy were enormous.

Right Opposition: A general term used to describe those who opposed the Communist leadership in the late 1920s and early 1930s by opposing the end of NEP and Stalin's programme of rapid industrialisation and collectivisation, as well as the extent of his personal power.

Komsomol: The All-Union Leninist Young Communist League, established in 1918 and a youth division (14–28-year-olds) of the Communist Party. Although membership was voluntary it was almost impossible to pursue higher education without being a member. Younger children could join the Young Pioneers.

bound to follow orders from the party, even if they considered them unrealistic. The trial sent a message that any kind of obstruction to the party's programme would result in personal peril. This was the beginning of Stalin's method of terror: an unpredictable threat hanging over every individual.

The means by which such investment would supposedly be achieved was the full-scale, compulsory collectivisation of the land. Again, there was a real enthusiasm from party activists and 25 000 volunteer workers went out into the countryside to promote and enforce the new policy. The campaign began in earnest in December 1929, but the policy originated in Stalin's trip to Siberia in January 1928. In response to the 'grain crisis', he reintroduced requisitioning to obtain grain for the cities. At the time these were labelled 'extraordinary' and 'temporary' measures, but this 'Urals-Siberian method' was to be extended across the Soviet Union. At the heart of collectivisation, the process of peasants combining, and thus losing, all but their basic household possessions was Stalin's stated ambition to 'liquidate the kulaks as a class'. From a communist perspective this meant ending the exploitative practices and unfair advantages of the rich peasants. In reality, it was a means of finally gaining control over the headstrong peasantry.

ACTIVITY 3.4

Reread the sections on NEP in this and the previous chapter and compile evidence in a table like this.

	Successes	Failures	Your overall judgement
Industry			
Agriculture			
Trade			
Employment			
Political stability			

Create a graph to display the success of each of these aspects from 1921 to 1928.

Government, propaganda and the beginning of the Stalinist cult

By 1929, the basis of what would be referred to as the 'Stalinist model' was in place. Power had been left in the hands of the 'nomenklatura system': the grouping of the key jobs in the party and state appointed by the Secretariat, with Stalin at its apex. The campaigns for rapid industrialisation and collectivisation had begun as a result of the so-called Great Turn. These campaigns involved the hallmark methods of Stalinism: propaganda and coercion. In addition, Stalin began to be more and more associated with these policies, not only as an advocate and organiser (as in the Urals-Siberian method) but also as the symbolic leader. In other words, there was a shift towards Stalin as the great leader of the

Soviet Union, no longer merely Lenin's disciple and chief guardian of his legacy, but heroic leader of the Soviet Union, and indeed Lenin's equal.

It is very important, however, not to overstate the extent to which this shift had occurred before 1929. Stalin had built his power base on the reputation of humility. His priority during the 1920s was to build up power and influence subtly. By expelling and marginalising his main rivals in the Politburo and Comintern, he had no need to be anything else than General Secretary. Indeed, he did not chair Politburo meetings and increasingly relied on telephone conversation with individuals, which avoided the possibility of collective opposition to his desired policy.

The launch of the Five-Year Plan and forced collectivisation was accompanied by posters, news reports and speeches encouraging the population to strive to build socialism through superhuman effort and to regard any critic of this effort as a traitor, spy and saboteur. As will be shown, xenophobia (fear of foreign influence) became a major part of Soviet propaganda. The first years of rapid industrialisation saw the use of modernist montages of industry and an emphasis on the image of the heroic working class. As the personality cult of Stalin developed throughout the 1930s, images of heroic workers were superseded by

 Voices from the past

Stalin

A letter by Stalin in response to one by Deputy Commissar of Finance, M.I. Frumkin, on collectivisation.[9]

19 November 1928

Are there spokesmen of the Right deviation among our Party members? There certainly are … I think that in this respect the palm should go to Frumkin. (Laughter) I am referring to his first letter (June 1928) and then to his second letter, which was distributed here to the members of the CC and CCC (November 1928) …

Let us take the 'basic propositions' of the first letter.

1. 'The sentiment in the countryside, apart from a small section of the poor peasants, is opposed to us.' Is that true? It is obviously untrue. If it were true, the bond would not even be a memory. But since June (the letter was written in June) nearly six months have passed, yet anyone, unless he is blind, can see that the bond between the working class and the main mass of the peasantry continues and is growing stronger. Why does Frumkin write such nonsense? In order to scare the Party and make it give way to the Right deviation.

2. 'We must return to the XIV and XV Congresses.' That the XV Congress has simply been tacked on here without rhyme or reason, of that there can be no doubt. The crux here is not in the XV Congress, but in the slogan: Back to the XIV Congress. And what does that mean? It means renouncing 'intensification of the offensive against the Kulak' (see XV Congress resolution) … [I]n calling for a return to the XIV Congress, Frumkin in rejecting the step forward which the Party made between the XIV and XV Congresses, and, in rejecting it, he is trying to pull the Party back.

Now gather all these propositions of Frumkin's together, and you get a bouquet characteristic of the Right deviation.

Discussion points:

1. Who or what is the 'Right deviation'?
2. The tone of the speech is revealing about Stalin's position at the time. How would you describe the tone and what it suggests about Stalin?
3. How valuable is this source to the historian studying Stalin's rise to power?

images of Stalin as the mastermind and leader of the Soviet Union's triumphant march towards socialism.

Stalin's attitude to foreign powers

The Soviet Union's position with regard to foreign governments remained purposefully paradoxical. On the one hand, with the turn towards NEP, the creation of the constitution and agreements with Britain and Germany the Commissariat for Foreign Affairs claimed to respect the legitimacy, sovereignty and diplomatic rights of foreign powers. On the other hand, the Comintern's avowed role was to promote the interests of the worldwide proletariat, which meant promoting subversive and revolutionary activity and organisation in all countries – particularly the capitalist West. Those governments that recognised the Soviet Union were perfectly aware of its dual strategy. The very nature of the Soviet regime meant that there was a close link between foreign policy and internal party politics, and Stalin, his rivals and allies did not hesitate to use it to their own political ends.

China

The Chinese Communist Party had formed in 1921 but was a comparatively weaker force than the emergent Chinese Nationalist Party, or 'Kuomintang', headed from 1925 by General Chiang Kai-shek. Under the instruction of Comintern, the Chinese communists allied themselves with the Nationalists in a struggle against the warlords, who had been competing for power since the disintegration of the Chinese state in 1915 and 1916. The Soviet Union provided support to both groups in the hope of gaining a newly unified China as an eastern ally. In 1927, however, Chang Kai-shek became sufficiently confident in the strength of his forces to turn on his erstwhile allies. The Comintern then ordered the communists to undertake a revolution in Shanghai in April. It failed and a nationalist campaign of 'purification' followed, in which thousands of trades unionists and communists were killed. In a further step, however, Stalin then insisted that the communists continue to work with the Kuomintang, as he viewed them as the stronger power, and more likely to succeed. Trotsky and Zinoviev ridiculed the policy as both a betrayal of their Chinese comrades and as an un-Marxist cooperation with the 'bourgeois' nationalists. The episode was damaging and embarrassing for Bukharin as head of Comintern, but it indicated Stalin's ideological flexibility. He would soon compel Comintern to shift its policy once again to suit his new internal agenda.

Germany and the Treaty of Berlin

The relationship with Weimar Germany following the Rapallo Treaty of 1922 was an important feature of Soviet policy. Their shared status as nations marginalised by the victorious allies had brought them together in mutual interest, particularly in terms of military development and trade. From 1924 this friendship began to be threatened by allied overtures to Germany. A conference in London that year resulted in the Dawes Plan, which amended Germany's reparations schedule and began a reconciliation with their former enemies. The previous year, 1923, had been one of tumult in Germany, including the Ruhr Crisis, and this prompted the Allies to stabilise relations. The Locarno Treaties in 1925 meant that Germany

Speak like a historian

Social democracy

Social democracy is a political ideology that seeks to create a universal welfare state and establish trade unions as bargaining tools for workers, within a capitalist system. It can also represent a view that seeks to build socialism within a state, but using gradual or reformist methods.

When Bukharin succeeded Zinoviev in 1926, he gained many supporters within the Comintern abroad. He advanced arguments against social democracy, but he also encouraged the German Communist Party, for example, to concentrate their attacks on Hitler's Nazi Party. Stalin, having brought Zinoviev to heel, now began to undermine Bukharin. Shortly before the Sixth Congress of the Comintern in July 1928, he denounced anti-communist socialists as the greatest threat to socialism. He deployed the rhetoric of 'social fascism' against them and called for an end to the 'united front'. With the war scare of the previous year and the announcement of the 'Great Turn', he declared that the revolutionary struggle was entering a 'Third Period' as capitalism entered a new crisis. This was mainly rhetoric meant to match the newly heroic tone of the Five-Year Plan and collectivisation. It also served to undermine Bukharin and his supporters and enabled Stalin to purge Comintern of those who objected to the change of policy.

recognised the redrawn map of Europe. In 1926, Germany was admitted to the League of Nations – an acknowledgement of its acceptance back into the fold.

For Chicherin, Commissar of Foreign Affairs, this was alarming and a demonstration of how the Soviet policy of seeking revolution in middle Europe had failed. Nevertheless, the two powers still shared a mistrust of Piłsudski's intentions in Poland and in April 1926 there was a further agreement between the Soviet Union and Germany, the Treaty of Berlin, which renewed their secret military and trade agreements and in which the parties promised neither to attack each other nor to join any other party engaged in hostilities against either country. The maintenance of relations with Germany remained a key consideration for Soviet security, even with the rise of Hitler, whose stated aim was to destroy Bolshevism.

Changes in Comintern in the 1920s

As has been suggested, in setting up Comintern the intention of the Soviet regime was to promote revolution abroad while maintaining a diplomatic façade through the Commissariat of Foreign Affairs. The reason why this dual and contradictory approach was maintained is arguably down to the fact that while the diplomacy and trade deals of the mid-1920s were comparatively beneficial to the Soviet Union, the Comintern's attempt to export revolution was not. Initial hopes for the natural spread of the revolution to the West faded. Mussolini's right-wing fascists dominated Italy from 1922, and Germany was reconciling with its former foes by 1924.

The Communist parties of Europe had formed as breakaways from the broader socialist movement with the encouragement of Comintern following the Second Congress (see *Comintern* in Chapter 2). They were brought further into line with Moscow by 1924, when they were instructed to act as part of a 'united labour front' in the West. The reality of this was, however, not to compromise with moderate socialism, but to infiltrate and radicalise it. This involved, for example in Britain,

Use your notes and the timeline below to highlight when you think Stalin's leadership of the party was secured.

The dates for these Congresses are in the Gregorian calendar used by western European nations. The Bolshevik government adopted the Gregorian calendar at the beginning of February 1918. All dates given prior to this are in the 'Old Style' Julian calendar. On 1 February 1918 (Old Style) the date was converted to 14 February and then the calendar continued day by day.[10]

dual membership of the Communist Party and the Labour Party, and was labelled 'entryism'. The Labour Party dealt with this in 1925 by banning anyone who was a Communist Party member. The 'united labour front' was an admission that the Communist Parties of the Comintern were not sufficiently influential on their own. Furthermore, Comintern policy and rhetoric remained hostile to social democracy and increased the division of the left.

Timeline 1921–1929

Year	Congress	Events, policies and associated personalities
1921	Tenth 8–16 March	March: Defeat of the Kronstadt Rebellion and Workers' Opposition. Introduction of NEP under Lenin. Ban on factions. December: Lenin ordered to take a six-week vacation.
1922	Eleventh 27 March – 2 April	April: Stalin made General Secretary of the Party Secretariat. 25 May: Lenin's first stroke. Emergence of the triumvirate of Stalin, Kamenev and Zinoviev (against Trotsky). Lenin asked Trotsky to join him in a 'bloc against bureaucracy'. 15 December: Lenin's second stroke. Lenin dictated papers for Twelfth Congress, which became known as his Testament.
1923	Twelfth 17–25 April	8 March: Lenin's third stroke. April: Congress – Testament not read out. October: Trotsky's 'Open Letter to the Central Committee'. 'Group of 46' leading Bolsheviks form Left Opposition: they oppose NEP and demand the spread of revolution abroad.
1924	Thirteenth 23–31 May	5 Jan: Lenin's death – Krupskaya demanded his Testament should be read out to Central Committee. Stalin offered his resignation, but it was refused. Testament read out to regional delegations but not discussed at Congress. Bukharin defended a long-term NEP against Preobrazhenski, who argued for greater state planning and faster industrialisation. Trotsky denounced as a 'factionalist' by Zinoviev and Kamenev. Stalin supported the policy of Socialism in One Country.

Year	Congress	Events, policies and associated personalities
1925	Fourteenth 18–31 Dec	January: Trotsky removed from the Politburo. 'The high point of NEP'.
1926		United Opposition formed, including Trotsky, Zinoviev and Kamenev.
1927	Fifteenth 2–19 Dec	12 December: Trotsky and supporters expelled from the party. Zinoviev and Kamenev recanted their opposition. Stalin used a 'war scare' to justify a new 'revolution from above' to prepare the USSR for war against capitalist enemies. A new grain crisis developed as a result of newly lowered prices.
1928		Trotsky sent to internal exile. Stalin reintroduced grain requisitioning as a 'temporary' measure: known as the Urals-Siberian method. Bukharin, Rykhov and Tomsky, pro-NEP 'Rightists' opposed by Stalinist pro-industrialisation supporters. First Five-Year Plan (1928–1932) launched focusing on heavy industry. Renewed rhetoric against the 'kulaks' as an exploiting class.
1929		Trotsky sent to foreign exile. December: Collectivisation began in earnest.

Further reading

For an in-depth consideration of NEP, Alec Nove's *An Economic History of the USSR* (Pelican, 1989) (second edition) remains one of the most useful and readable. For a clear overview of institutional change during this period, Mark Sandle's *A Short History of Soviet Socialism* (UCL, 1999) provides a helpful reference. For deeper research into the lives of the two main contenders for power, Robert Service's *Stalin: A Biography* and *Trotsky: A Biography* (both Pan, 2010) are highly valuable.

Practice essay questions

1. 'Stalin's rise to power was a result of his popularity within the party.' Explain why you agree or disagree with this view.
2. 'Lenin must shoulder the greatest responsibility for the eventual success of Stalin by 1929.' Assess the validity of this view.
3. 'NEP was an economic success but a political failure.' Assess the validity of this statement.
4. With reference to the sources below and your understanding of the historical context, assess the value of the three sources to a historian studying why Trotsky failed to win the power struggle.

Source A

Adapted from Lenin's Last Testament written in 1922 (www.marxists.org).

Comrade Stalin, having become Secretary-General, has unlimited authority concentrated in his hands, and I am not sure whether he will always be capable of using that authority with sufficient caution. Comrade Trotsky, on the other hand is distinguished not only by outstanding ability, but also he is personally perhaps the most capable man in the present Central Committee, but he has displayed excessive self-assurance and shown excessive preoccupation with the purely administrative side of the work. These two qualities of the two outstanding leaders of the present Central Committee might inadvertently lead to a split, and if our Party does not take steps to avert this, the split may come unexpectedly.

Source B

Adapted from Victor Serge's book *From Lenin to Stalin*, written in 1937 (www.marxists. org).

Lenin was good-natured, unassuming, ordinary in appearance; an outsider would scarcely have noticed him. Trotsky, on the other hand, would nowhere have passed unnoticed, with his shock of hair, the erect carriage of his head, the intensity of his blue-grey eyes. He had about him something authoritative and compelling. On the platform his voice had a metallic ring, and each sentence was like a sharp thrust. He was to become the superior orator of this revolution. His written style was consummately skilful. But the main thing was that the hour which had struck was the hour he had awaited, foreseen, and desired all his life.

Source C

From a document written by Bukharin with Lenin's sister Mariya in 1926 (in Acton, E. and Stableford, T., *The Soviet Union, Volume 1*, p. 203).

In view of the systematic attacks on comrade Stalin by the opposition minority in the CC and the ceaseless assertions that Lenin had virtually completely broken with Stalin, I feel duty-bound to say a few words about Lenin's attitude to Stalin, because throughout the last stages of V.I.'s life I was with him.

Vladimir Il'ich had an extraordinarily high opinion of Stalin, to such an extent that at the time of both the first and second strokes V.I. gave the most intimate jobs to Stalin, emphasizing that it was to Stalin that he was speaking.

At the worst of times of his illness V.I. did not summon any member of the CC or want to see anybody – he called only Stalin. So the speculation that V.I.'s relations with Stalin were worse than those with other people is the direct opposite of the truth.

Chapter summary

Having studied this chapter you should be able to:

- assess the leadership contenders' relative strengths and weaknesses
- define the range of opinion in the Communist Party
- give reasons for, and trace, the change in economic policy
- give reasons for Stalin's rise to power and identify his methods of control
- assess the strength of the Soviet Union's international position.

End notes

1 Sandle, M., *A Short History of Soviet Socialism*, p. 118.

2 Pipes, R., *A Concise History of the Russian Revolution*.

3 Taken from Lenin's notes, part of his Testament, 24 December 1922 (www.marxists.org/archive/lenin/works/1922/dec/testamnt/congress.htm).

4 From Lenin *Collected Works*, Volume 36, pp. 593–611 (www.marxists.org/archive/lenin/works/1922/dec/testamnt/congress.htm).

5 From Lenin *Collected Works* (www.marxists.org/archive/lenin/works/1922/dec/testamnt/congress.htm).

6 Nove, A., *An Economic History of the USSR*, p.86.

7 Figes, O., *Revolutionary Russia, 1891–1991*, p. 193.

8 Nove, *An Economic History of the USSR*, p. 130.

9 Cited in Acton, E. and Stableford, T., *The Soviet Union: A Documentary History, Volume 1, 1917–1940*, document 143, p. 268.

10 This information comes from *A Political Chronology of Europe*, 2001, London, Europa.

PART 2 STALIN'S RULE, 1929–1953
4 Economy and society, 1929–1941

In this section we will investigate the economic and social change brought about by Stalin's so-called 'revolution from above'. This includes:

- agricultural and social developments in the countryside: voluntary and forced collectivisation; state farms and mechanisation; the impact of collectivisation on the kulaks and other peasants; the famine of 1932–1933 and 'neo-NEP'; the success of collectivisation

- industrial and social developments in towns and cities: Gosplan; the organisation, aims and results of the first three Five-Year Plans; new industrial centres and projects; the involvement of foreign companies; the working and living conditions of managers, workers and women; Stakhanovites; the success of the Five-Year Plans

- the development of the Stalin cult: literature, the arts and other propaganda

- the social and economic condition of the Soviet Union by 1941: strengths and weaknesses.

Introduction

Sometimes referred to as the 'revolution from above',[1] Stalin's project to transform the Soviet Union from an agriculturally and industrially 'backward' country – he used the term 'backward' a great deal to justify the manic pace of change – to an industrial superpower ready for total war was achieved both through repression and suffering, as well as through the genuine enthusiasm and voluntary sacrifice of the Russian people. Robert Service states, 'Industrialisation and collectivisation were two sides of the same coin.'[2] These two great processes took place within the context of a political programme and ideology. They were undertaken not merely for material gain but also for the purpose of greater political control. For Stalin, building socialism in the Soviet Union depended on a constant process of removing its 'enemies', both internal and external. In a sense, this was merely the extension of a Bolshevik logic forged in the Civil War. Nevertheless, it involved a new cult of leadership, both by Stalin and by a heroic Soviet elite, which might be seen as rather alien to the early Bolsheviks and, arguably, to Lenin.

Agricultural and social developments in the countryside

Introduction to collectivisation

It is important to realise that the provision to the state of more efficiently produced crops was not the sole aim of collectivisation of agriculture. This was, of course, an important aim: it was Stalin's solution to the debate of the 1920s to raise sufficient capital to drive rapid industrialisation. However, bound up with the 'peasant problem' – in communist minds – was the role of the peasantry as a counter-revolutionary force, or at least foot-draggers on the path to socialism. NEP had been conceived to maintain the *smychka* – the alliance of the workers and the peasantry, and as such it had drawn criticism from its inception (beginning). Many communists saw the peasantry, or at least the agricultural sector as it stood, at best as a hindrance and at worst as ridden with class enemies.

Lenin had already identified such enemies during the Civil War, when he founded 'committees of the poor' to denounce and work against their better-off neighbours, who were held responsible for the hoarding of grain (see *War communism* in Chapter 2). Lenin's aim here was similar to Stalin's – to procure grain at low prices. However, this linked to a political aim inherent in the policy: to rid Soviet society of, as they saw it, an exploitative class of peasants – the *kulaks*, those who had benefited most from NEP. Collectivisation would also end large-scale private ownership of land, which despite the land seizures of the early years had not disappeared. It was ideologically more fitting for a socialist society, and it also enabled greater political control. Collectivisation could be seen as Stalin bringing to heel what was the majority of the Soviet people: if the 1920s had seen the defeat of the workers, then the 1930s was the defeat of the peasantry (if one takes this paradoxical view of a Workers' and Peasants' State).

Voluntary and forced collectivisation

As described in Chapter 3, forced collectivisation of farming began in December 1929 and coincided with the promotion of Stalin's cult of personality. The process had, however, begun in early 1928, when Stalin, on a visit to the east, undertook

Speak like a historian

Collectivisation

When historians speak of 'collectivisation' they are referring to the policy in the Soviet Union of ending private land ownership and cultivation into 'collective' or state-run farms. This was on the assumption that larger farms would be able to increase output; however, the underlying motives were to destroy the *mir* (the peasant commune), which had remained a source of power in rural areas that had avoided Bolshevik interference thus far. This would also enable the party to assert its authority over the peasants.

the 'Urals-Siberian method', which was essentially the reintroduction of grain requisitioning. On his return to Moscow he proposed it as a means of solving the grain crisis, which had developed the previous year.

Collectivisation, though heavily promoted by the '25 000-ers' (groups of young activists who went into the countryside to promote it) was at first voluntary. To some extent, the collective farm, ***kolkhoz***, was simply the next evolutionary step from that already in existence, the TOZ, which was associated with the cooperative movement, and which Lenin had hoped might prove the basis for future Soviet agriculture. The kolkhoz was a corporate body run by a committee that rented its land from the state and delivered a fixed quota of the harvest. Its workers were paid according to the number of days they worked on the farm (as opposed to a small personal plot they were allowed to retain). A second type was the state-owned farm, ***sovkhoz***, whose workers were employed to work the land in the same manner as those hired to work in factories. Once the process became compulsory and peasants were required to hand over virtually all they owned to the farm, there was little practical difference between the two.

State farms and mechanisation

Progress towards the collectivisation of all agriculture varied by region but was basically complete by 1933, by which time there were approximately 250 000 collective farms. The 1917 revolution had strengthened the role of the commune or *mir*. The peasantry had reverted to a traditional, conservative and arguably agriculturally inefficient institution as a result of socialist revolution. This was a challenge to their way of life far greater than that posed by Stolypin from 1906. The efficacy of collectivisation can be debated; however, it did involve the mechanisation of Soviet agriculture through the setting up of **machine-tractor stations (MTS)**. There was, on average, one MTS for every 30 collective farms. Such technology meant a substantial break with what in many places remained a medieval form of agriculture. This would perhaps suggest that increased productivity would follow swiftly, but the relatively modest gains made by the end of the decade relate to the means by which collectivisation was enforced.

The impact of collectivisation on the kulaks and other peasants

Dekulakisation

In December 1929, Stalin called for a 'resolute offensive against the kulaks' in order to 'eliminate them as a class'. In January 1930 this policy, which combined economic and political aims, was agreed by the Politburo. As Stalin put it, '**dekulakisation** is an integral part of the creation and development of collective farms'. It involved excluding or expelling those classed as 'kulaks' from the collective farms and confiscating their land. There was no clear objective definition of who a kulak was. This meant that anyone who fell foul of the party or was denounced by neighbours was liable for deportation or worse.

Dekulakisation took place within the context of the early show trials, which began with the prosecution of 'bourgeois specialists' in Shakhty in 1928. The trials were designed to create an atmosphere of terror: to intimidate those who considered opposing the regime. Fictitious parties were made up, denounced and used to remove opponents. These included the 'industrial party' and the 'labouring peasant party', which were cited as dangers to the state in November and December 1930. At the same time as dekulakisation, there was an anti-religious campaign, which attacked the authority, property and personnel of the Orthodox Church in the villages as well as the towns. Churches were closed and their bells melted down. In 1930 the *mir* was abolished.

This assault on the peasants' traditional way of life was unsurprisingly met with opposition, but opponents left themselves open to accusations of counter-revolution. By July 1930, 320 000 households had fallen victim to dekulakisation. Some 1.8 million individuals were deported to other areas of the Soviet Union; 400 000 were moved to another part of their own district; 390 000 were sent to a newly established network of labour camps; and 21 000 were shot. Dekulakisation was the scapegoating of a fairly ill-defined minority for the purposes of persuading others to conform to the policy of collectivisation. It was also the exorcising of a ghost that had haunted the Communist Party since it had seized power: the headstrong and backward peasants who by definition did not fit an ideology based on the industrial proletariat.

Reaction, respite and reprise: 1930–1931

Collectivisation was not easily achieved. Stalin is reputed to have later told Churchill that his confrontation with the peasantry had been a greater challenge than his confrontation with Nazi Germany. Peasant uprisings recorded by the Soviet government grew in number: in 1929 there were around 1300; in 1930 there were ten times as many. The reaction is perhaps unsurprising: the pace of collectivisation was rapid and the process was confused, chaotic and hugely disruptive. By the beginning of March 1930, 55% of the peasantry were in collectives – this had been achieved in two months. From January to March, there was a concerted campaign to socialise all livestock and close down peasant markets. In a reaction that was to repeat itself, peasants slaughtered their animals (including those used for ploughing) rather than allow them to be handed over to the collectives. This resulted in a bout of feasting on meat day after day. It was an enormously wasteful process and seems particularly tragic given the later famine.

Key terms

Kolkhoz is the Russian term for collective farms, established after the October revolution of 1917. They were set up spontaneously, and voluntarily in many cases, until 1928 when Stalin decided to force the collectivisation of all individual holdings.

Sovkhoz were state-owned collective farms entirely owned and run by the state. Farm workers were employees of the state like factory workers in state-owned factories.

Machine-tractor stations (MTS) provided collective farms with machinery to help mechanise Soviet agriculture from 1928 onwards.

Dekulakisation was a policy that developed as part of collectivisation. It involved liquidating the richer peasants or those who fought against collectivisation. Under this policy at least 1.8 million peasants were deported and up to 5 million more shot. (Figures from the time are unreliable and historians still debate the numbers involved.)

When criticisms of the 'excesses' appeared in the Soviet press, Stalin responded on 2 March, in typical manner, by blaming others: he accused local officials in an often-cited article in *Pravda* of being 'dizzy with success'. This created even greater confusion but resulted in a (temporary) mass exodus from the collectives: by June the number had dropped to 23%. This allowed the harvest of 1930 to be sown and reaped: it was at 83.5 million tonnes of grain compared to 71.7 million tonnes the previous year. This reprieve was, however, short-lived, and peasants again began to be brought back into the collectives by persuasive or coercive means.

Stalin made it clear in July 1930 that it was imperative to export as much grain as possible in order to finance rapid industrialisation. Again, in February 1931, he warned against allowing the tempo to slacken. Occasional tactical let-ups were followed by renewed campaigns. It became increasingly the case that those who remained outside the collectives were allocated the worst-quality land and were taxed more heavily. Many joined before they were forced to do so. By 1932, 61.5% of peasant households had been collectivised and 77.6 % of the crop area; by 1935 these figures had risen to 83.2% of households and 94.1% of crop area. Before that point, however, rural society was to undergo another serious disaster.

The famine of 1932–1933 and 'neo-NEP'

The apparent aim of collectivisation was to increase the production and export of grain in order to fund industrialisation. The crisis that occurred in the winter of 1932–1933 seems to demonstrate how counter-productive the programme was, if one discounts Stalin's possibly more important aim of 'defeating' the peasantry.

Voices from the past

Stalin

Stalin's speech of 27 December 1929, attacking the kulaks:[3]

To launch an offensive against the kulaks means that we must smash the Kulaks, eliminate them as a class. Unless we set ourselves these aims, an offensive would be mere declamation, pinpricks, phrase-mongering, anything but a real Bolshevik offensive. To launch an offensive against the kulaks means that we must prepare for it and then strike at the kulaks, strike so hard as to prevent them from rising to their feet again. That is what Bolsheviks call a real offensive. Could we have undertaken some five years or three years ago with any prospect of success? No we could not …

But today? What is the position now? Today, we have an adequate material base for us to strike back at the kulaks, to break their resistance, to eliminate them as a class, and to replace their output by the output of the collective farms and state farms. You know that in 1929 the grain produced on the collective farms and state farms has amounted to not less than 400 000 000 pudy (200 000 000 pudy less than the gross output of the kulak farms in 1927). You also know that in 1930 the gross output of the collective farms and state farms have supplied more than 130 000 000 pudy of marketable grain (i.e. far more than the kulaks in 1927).

That is how matters stand with us now, comrades.

There you have the change that has taken place in the economy of our country.

Discussion points:

1. What is Stalin arguing here?
2. Stalin celebrated his 50th birthday just six days before this speech. The timing is significant because he was now undisputed leader of the Communist Party. Is this confidence evident in his speech?
3. What treatment of the kulaks does Stalin advocate?

Central policy of 1932 suggests that the Soviet government was not unaware of the strain placed on the peasantry and the dangers this entailed. In May 1932 the 'collective farm market' was legalised. This is sometimes referred to as 'neo-NEP', as it had a similar function: once peasants had handed over what they were compelled to, they were permitted to sell the remainder at free-market prices. This became an important part of peasant income. This was, however, a far more constrained form of trade and was not matched by any kind of legalised trading class (although the black market remained operative). In addition, reductions were made in the delivery quotas set for each region: in the Ukraine quotas were reduced by 14% in the summer of 1932.

Yet this was insufficient to prevent disaster. The harvest of 1932 was poor and failed to meet even the reduced quotas. The regime reacted, not with greater leniency, but by enforcing the quotas, confiscating seed grain – both that required for livestock as well as for the peasants themselves. The result was famine, which struck most fully in the Ukraine, the North Caucasus, the Volga region and Kazakhstan.

Figures of those who died as a result of the famine of 1932–1933 are difficult to calculate, partly based on the difference between estimated expected rise in population and the recorded rising population over the years concerned. They must also be distinguished from those who were subject to dekulakisation and forced labour. Those who died as a result of starvation are estimated to have numbered between 5 and 7 million. There is a question as to whether the famine was in some way allowed to occur, if not deliberately created. Robert Conquest suggests that collectivisation was in part a war on remaining nationalist elements, particularly in the Ukraine.[4] While there may be insufficient evidence for such a claim, it is true that relief to famine-struck areas was limited; possibly simply in order to 'contain' the lack of food and prevent the spread of discontent, but more certainly to ensure a continued export of grain abroad.

Was collectivisation a success?

If Stalin's aims were primarily political and social, that is to say, if he undertook collectivisation to consolidate the Communist regime's control over rural society, to end the threat of peasant revolt and the need for a compromise with the peasantry that was distasteful in Bolshevik eyes, then it is difficult to argue that he failed. It might be more difficult to say that he had 'won over' the peasantry to communist ideology. There is a greater degree of debate over collectivisation's economic success. Stalin's economic aim had been to use collectivisation as a means of facilitating rapid industrial development. Given his expectations, a 10% increase in production over the decade is arguably modest. Added to this are the facts that dekulakisation removed many of the most successful and able cultivators from the soil; and harsh treatment of the peasantry, particularly through unrealistic grain quotas, led to the waste and tragedy of famine.

This said, the percentage of the harvest that was delivered to the state increased from 14.7% in 1928 to 39% in 1940. Less reliance on imported agricultural products allowed for greater investment in foreign machinery. Chaos and misfortune in the countryside drove much of the rural population into the towns, providing labour

ACTIVITY 4.1

Historians have debated the relative success of Stalin's policies towards the peasants. Go through your notes and organise them into a table to help you reach a judgement on the successes and failures of each of these aims:

- Collectivisation
- Feeding the people
- Mechanisation of farms.

for industry. Finally, the agricultural sector was used to absorb shocks (such as a poor harvest), so that the effect was not felt by industry. None of these suggest a particular improvement for agriculture, but do suggest a benefit to industry. As Stalin made clear, change in the countryside was closely and deliberately linked to the process of rapid industrialisation that took place at the same time.

Industrial and social developments in towns and cities

Gosplan and the beginnings of industrialisation

While Stalin's 'Great Turn' against NEP did not take full effect until 1928, the apparatus for achieving a planned economy had been gradually developed during the 1920s, with an eye towards more rapid industrialisation. Indeed, some of the major projects of Soviet industrialisation (the Volga-Don Canal, the Dnieper hydroelectric dam and the Turksib railway link between Siberia and Turkestan) were already underway in 1926. With the defeat of the United Opposition in 1926, Stalin was in a position to appropriate the 'super-industrialisation' agenda – previously advocated by Trotsky and Preobrazhenski – for himself, which would bring him into conflict with Bukharin and the 'Right Opposition' by 1928. In fact, 1927 was the decisive year for a swing away from NEP, and this was closely linked to the war scare of that year, triggered in part by Britain breaking off diplomatic relations in May, and stirred up by Stalin, who emphasised the need for the Soviet Union to be in a position to meet a foreign threat. As previously suggested, the underlying desire in the party for rapid industrialisation had never gone away.

A separate State Planning Commission, better known as Gosplan, was set up in February 1921 under the authority of the Council of Labour and Defence – which Alec Nove describes as the 'effective economic-military cabinet' – and was originally chaired by Lenin. Founded just before the implementation of NEP, Gosplan's role was to 'work out a single general state economic plan' and its main purpose was coordination.[5]

Both the Supreme Council and Gosplan underwent a degree of evolution throughout the NEP years. The departments of the Supreme Council were serially reorganised and most significantly, the separate Supreme Councils of the republics were established under the All-Union Supreme Council in 1923, which became the Government Commissariat. Similarly, Gosplan was 'strengthened' in 1927 as the State Commissions of the different Soviet republics were brought under its authority. Unsurprisingly, there was a degree of duplication of roles by the two bodies. This was especially the case as the party moved away from mere 'control figures' towards the agenda of a mid-term economic plan whose purpose was rapid industrialisation. Demands for such a plan began in the midst of 'High' NEP. It was perhaps economic recovery that gave the party confidence to assert greater control. In 1926, the party called for 'economic hegemony of large-scale socialist industry over the entire economy' and rival drafts began to be produced, both by Gosplan and by the Supreme Council. In December 1927, nearly a quarter of the sessions of the 15th Party Congress were given over to the consideration of these plans.

'Teleologists' versus 'geneticists'

Nove suggests that the mid-1920s was a time of genuinely innovative economic thinking in the Soviet Union.[6] Particularly among the ranks of Gosplan, Mensheviks and other non-party economists were involved in developing soviet economic policy. As party policy moved towards more direct planning, the divide emerged between those (arguably more in favour of NEP) whose main focus was on the methods required to achieve industrialisation – the so-called 'geneticists' – and those who focused primarily on setting targets for outcomes – the so-called 'teleologists'. As the mood of the party began to shift towards renewed revolutionary zeal, manifested in the desire for a heroic effort to industrialise within a relatively minimal historical period, the 'teleological' approach found greater favour. Ambitious targets could be set and then raised yet further – any difficulty in meeting these could be met, according to Stalin's rhetoric, by idealistic energy and graft. To object to such target-setting on the grounds of realism became a dangerous counter-revolutionary act.

As a result, Gosplan and the Supreme Council jointly put together a Five-Year Plan, due to begin in October 1928, which had two versions: the 'initial variant' and the 'optimal variant'. The 'initial variant' gave highly optimistic targets for increased investment and production: overall investment was to rise by 153%, electricity production by 236% and pig iron production by 142%. The 'optimal variant' went even further: investment up by 237%, electricity by 335% and pig iron by 203%. Plan targets ceased to reflect rational calculations about economic possibilities and came to represent purely the preferences of the political leadership. The targets certainly served a political purpose, but they also served as a crude economic incentive: to fail to strive towards them was proof of disloyalty. This was of course made clear in the early show trials, beginning with Shakhty in 1928, and with the dismissal of Bukharin, who wrote a dissenting article, 'Notes of an economist', in *Pravda* in September 1928.

ACTIVITY 4.2

Examine Table 4.1 to answer these questions:

1. How does production of 1927–1928 compare with the actual production by 1932?

2. How do the 'initial' and 'optimal' targets compare with the actual production by 1932?

3. What do these figures suggest about the efficacy of ambitious targets on Soviet production?

Product (Millions of tons)	1927–1928 Actual production	1932–1933 Initial target	1932–1933 Optimal target	1932 Amended target	1932 Actual production
Coal	35.4	68	75	95–105	64
Oil	11.7	19	21.7	40–55	21.4
Iron ore	5.7	15	20.2	24–32	12.1
Pig iron	3.3	8	10	15–16	6.2

Table 4.1: Targets and actual production during the first Five-Year Plan.[7]

Organisation, aims and results of the first three Five-Year Plans

Aims and context

The Five-Year Plan (and its variants) was to become the standard means by which communist states around the world organised their 'command economies'. The three plans, which ran from Stalin's rise to power in 1928 to the outbreak of hostilities between Nazi Germany and the Soviet Union in 1941, therefore have a broader significance. Their importance in this context, however, relates to the broad aims for which Stalin imposed them. Apart from the aims of social transformation and political control, Stalin's objective can be summed up as the following: to build an industrialised infrastructure and economy equal to, or surpassing, that of the capitalist West in order to withstand and defeat a major military threat to the Soviet Union. The military imperative seems to have been a consistent consideration during the pre-war period, but became increasingly apparent from 1937 onwards.

The three Five-Year Plans coincided, not by chance, with three distinct political and social phases.

- 1928–1932: The first phase was that of fanatical enthusiasm closely linked to the process of forced collectivisation and dekulakisation, which ended with the famine and crisis of late 1932 to early 1933. Despite the chaotic nature of this 'plan' and the human suffering involved, much was achieved by 1933.
- 1933–1937: The second phase was one of consolidation. It saw the completion of many projects begun under the first plan and the reintroduction of wage differentials (different levels of pay for different levels of responsibility and pay incentives for improved performance) and a greater emphasis on technical expertise and the value of specialists. It dispensed with ideas such as the disappearance of money as had been imagined by the idealists of the first years. Some communists had hoped that money would become completely unnecessary within an economic system based on state planning. The steady success of these so-called 'three good years' relied on a stable currency and traditional pay incentives.
- 1938–1941: 1938 brought with it the third plan and a crisis partially induced by Stalin himself. As well as an increased emphasis on meeting the growing

 Hidden voices

Commissar Frumkin

The dismissal of Bukharin largely arose because of a letter written by the Deputy Commissar of Finance, M.J. Frumkin, who had complained that the party was alienating the peasantry and stifling criticism within the party. Stalin and Bukharin disagreed over how to respond to the letter to such an extent that they stopped speaking, which surely signalled the end for Bukharin. This is an extract from Frumkin's letter:[8]

5 June 1928

… The deterioration in our domestic situation is primarily connected with the countryside, with the position of agriculture. We must not close our eyes to the fact that the sentiment in the countryside, apart from a small section of the poor peasants, is opposed to us, and

that this mood is already beginning to spread into urban areas … in ascribing exceptional importance to the role of the countryside in the present crisis, I consider it my duty to direct the Politburo's attention to those matters which are uppermost in the minds of hundreds and thousands of party members and about which they talk at every opportunity. I hardly need to point out that our current difficulties do not stem solely, or even mainly, from our mistakes in planning the economy …

Discussion points:

1. What does Frumkin mean by 'current difficulties'?
2. Why was Frumkin so anxious about the economic and agricultural policies pursued by the party?
3. Bukharin shared many of Frumkin's anxieties. Why do you think Stalin was dismissive of them?

military threat from Japan and Germany, the plan had to deal with a crisis of over-accumulation (from an overly successful Second Five-Year Plan) and Stalin's hugely disruptive mass arrests of economic officials in a bout of paranoia that also seriously undermined the officer corps. On 22 June 1941, Hitler launched Operation Barbarossa, invading the Soviet Union's western borders, at which point the economy became entirely focused on the needs of the military.

The first Five-Year Plan, 1928–1932

Although the first plan was underway by October 1928, it was not formally approved until April 1929, when the Party adopted the 'optimal' variant (see 'Teleologists' versus 'geneticists', above). The targets would be raised repeatedly thereafter. In late 1929 the Politburo decided that the plan was to be fulfilled in four years rather than five. This became Stalin's slogan from June 1930, and yet higher targets were agreed for the key industries in July of that year. In the same month, Ordzhonikidze was appointed head of the Supreme Council and spoke in favour of Soviet autarky – that is, making the Soviet Union self-reliant. Coal production was to be tripled rather than doubled. Pig iron production was to go up five times rather than three times. Oil production, rather than doubling, was to increase by four or five times its 1928 level. In February 1931, Stalin stated in a speech: 'It is sometimes asked whether it is possible to slow down the tempo somewhat, to put a check on the movement. No, comrades, it is not possible. The tempo must not be reduced! On the contrary, we must increase it.'[9]

This was economic policy based on propaganda, but, as Nove suggests, it was undertaken in an atmosphere of high optimism as well as self-deception.[10] There was a clear incentive for officials to fabricate results and this in turn fed the regime with data that encouraged it to push for more. The nature of dictatorship made even well-intentioned criticism dangerous for the person providing it. One-man management was comprehensively re-established in September 1929, enforcing labour discipline and a pressure on the individual concerned to pay greater attention to perception than reality. There were huge costs and inefficiencies to this headlong rush, but such belief in superhuman achievement was partly based in the staggering progress which, though falling short of the revised targets, came very close in some areas to the 1929 'optimal variant'. In this sense, exhortation worked.

Major industrial projects

In one sense, the propaganda could be justified. Some of the better-known and most prestigious projects of Soviet industrialisation had already been begun. Still, ground was broken on previously undeveloped sites and areas of underexploited natural resources. These included expanding the network of hydroelectric power stations on the Dnieper river in Ukraine, the development of oilfields in Baku (Azerbaijan) and Grozny (Georgia), the mining of coal in the Donbass region and of various minerals in the Urals, Siberia and Central Asia. Centres for iron, steel and other metallurgical manufacture were established at Sverdlovsk, formerly Ekaterinburg, in the Urals and Zaporozhye on the Dnieper. Sverdlovsk was also the centre of the Urals Machine Building Plant (Uralmash), established in 1926. Tractor factories were built from scratch in Stalingrad (until 1925, Volgograd), Rostov on the Don and Kharkov in the north-east of Ukraine. These served as the bases for the later development of armament production. It was at this time that Soviet technical expertise was developed, with an important contribution from thousands of foreign engineers, many of them American and German, who were searching for employment following the devastating effects of the Great Depression triggered by the Wall Street Crash of 1929.

One enterprise that embodied this early stage of Stalinist industrialisation was Magnitogorsk in the very south of the Urals. The creation of an iron and steel works (and the consequent expansion of the city) brought together all the relevant elements: the exploitation of hitherto relatively untouched natural resources, an army of idealistic volunteers and a major contribution by foreign experts. The city of Magnitogorsk took its name from the Magnitnaya Mountain, which – fairly uniquely – was entirely composed of iron ore. This made it an obvious target for Soviet industrial efforts. Coal was provided by mines and the newly established industrial city of Stalinsk (Novokuznetsk), which was located along the Trans-Siberian Railway in western Siberia, south-east of Novosibirsk.

'Shock work' and 'socialist emulation'

Political interference and propaganda were a major part of the early stage of industrialisation. One of the most disruptive aspects of the continually inflated targets were so-called 'shock-constructions' carried out by specially formed brigades, which suddenly diverted resources towards prestigious projects in an effort to complete them quickly and to the detriment of lesser projects. The reality of a 'plan' that was constantly revised and interfered with inevitably resulted in logistical chaos. Despite this, Nove suggests that the broader element of 'socialist competition' or 'socialist emulation' did have a noticeable effect in improving productivity and technical expertise, reducing costs and increasing output. This was a means of motivating workers to continually strive to exceed their quotas by the means of 'counter-plans'.[11]

This, to some extent, took the place of capitalism's incentives for increased wages (though these were reintroduced at a later stage) and the threat of unemployment. Out of this grew the **Stakhanovite movement** (see below).

Costs and crises

The scale and pace of the first Five-Year Plan, as well as countless unplanned interventions, put enormous strains on Soviet society. The movement of peasants into towns and industrial projects was dramatic: the average town's population expanded by 50 000 every week. The result was inadequate housing provision and inexperienced factory hands without training in how to use machinery. In rushed production, working conditions were hazardous and the quality of work could be poor. Coordination on such a large scale and with constant political interference proved almost impossible. Increased production targets took no account of the railway's maximum capacity to transport such a quantity of goods and raw materials. Bottlenecks were a constant problem. The costs of the projects ran far beyond what had been planned. Building plants and cities in 'the middle of nowhere' was both expensive and time-consuming. Matters were further complicated by the actions of local officials and managers. The culture of target-setting from above led to the falsification of production figures, which distorted the accuracy of information available to a centralised system that was already

Key term

Stakhanovite movement: A movement formed by workers who followed the example of Alexei Stakhanov, who over-achieved targets set for him (mining 102 tons of coals in under 6 hours). In 1935, under the second Five-Year-Plan, some workers tried to emulate or compete with his achievements.

unwieldy in its scope and burdened by an ever-expanding bureaucratic class. Unreliable supply led to competition between enterprises, as well as theft and semi-legitimate and illegitimate markets. Before the end of wage egalitarianism, there was no economic incentive to produce more efficiently.

As before, in the early years of the Civil War, the all-out effort, in this case for industrialisation rather than military victory, resulted in the uncontrolled printing of money and soaring inflation. The eventual solution was to backtrack, with the legalisation of the 'collective farm market' and 'neo-NEP' – although this was no retreat from state ownership. Consumer goods production had been very heavily hit by the emphasis on heavy industry. Greater financial discipline was introduced from 1931 as the new head of Gosplan, Kuibyshev, began to formulate the second Five-Year Plan. As part of this, the egalitarianism of the early years was abandoned in favour of tighter managerial control and the reintroduction of pay incentives.

One of the major difficulties this caused was labour mobility. Workers, unhappy in one place, would move on to new sites in search of better pay and conditions. This was countered through greater labour discipline and restrictions on movement. A new sales tax, introduced to increase much-needed revenue, was an additional burden. It is difficult to separate the process of industrialisation under the first Five-Year Plan from the process of collectivisation and dekulakisation taking place in the countryside at the same time. Both had set in train the fundamental transformation of the Soviet economy and society. Both were messy, chaotic and cruel, but laid a foundation for later progress. For idealists, who were not victims of persecution, these were heady days of socialist endeavour.

 Hidden voices

'Shock worker' Shidek

The following extract is from a recollection of a 'shock worker', V. Ya Shidek, who was involved in construction in the Kuznetsk Basin.[12]

They set us a quota of 500 bricks, but we pushed that up to 1000. We tried to work fast and so didn't stop for a smoke. You needed a couple of minutes to roll your own with makhlorka – and that was dozens of bricks' worth. So we smoked only papirosy and that was on the job …

When we were trying to finish the first battery as a gift to the XVI Party Conference, I didn't leave the kiln for four days and didn't go home. A rail served as a pillow for my rest, although to make it softer, I covered it with canvased gloves.

Just before this my wife fell ill, so I sent her off to Tomsk, leaving our 3-year-old and 7-year-old at home. Then, on my second day after I'd gone, my youngest son fell ill and died suddenly. Under the pressure of work I had

forgotten about the kids. I went home on the fifth day and found that my youngest son had died, while the oldest was wandering around the site looking for me, but couldn't find me … the little corpse was starting to smell. I had no choice but to bury him, and afterwards had to go and get drunk. I drank to victory and grief.

Discussion points:
1. How credible is this account?
2. The tone of the piece is in line with a wealth of testimony collected at the time about 'shock workers'. Describe in your own words what these workers were like.
3. Why weren't these shock brigades as successful as the party hoped?

The second Five-Year Plan, 1933–1937

As with the first Five-Year Plan, the draft of the second was not officially passed until January 1934. Its formulation had begun in May 1931 under Kuibyshev and some of its defining aspects, such as the end of wage egalitarianism, began to take effect from that point. Following the crisis of late 1932, the initial proposals were radically altered during 1933.

The second Five-Year Plan was essentially to be one of stabilisation and consolidation. This meant retaining a money system, and a shift in tone regarding 'bourgeois' specialists. As part of consolidation there was a renewed emphasis on hierarchy (now of course within the context of Soviet meritocracy rather than inherited privilege or capitalist exploitation).

The mid-1930s saw the lionisation of the technical expert. This is perhaps understandable, as specialists, many from working-class backgrounds and the product of one- or two-year courses in the quickly expanding higher-education sector, began to join or replace their foreign colleagues. This was in a sense beginning to fulfil Stalin's vision of a self-reliant Socialism in One Country. Kuibyshev proclaimed as much when he took the reins at Gosplan. According to Chris Ward, Kuibyshev intended to begin to elaborate a 'fully socialist economic system'.[13] The priorities of the second Five-Year Plan were therefore:

- the completion of the myriad projects begun but not finished in the enthusiasm of the first Five-Year Plan
- investment in an overworked and inadequate transport infrastructure
- an attempt to improve living standards through more substantial investment in consumer goods and an end to rationing in 1935.

Although more modest, the second Five-Year Plan was not a retreat as such. Whereas the first Five-Year Plan had led to the completion of 150 new industrial projects, by the end of 1936, 4500 were complete and the machine-tool and metallurgy industries of the Soviet Union had achieved self-sufficiency.

Industrial slowdown from 1937

In 1937 there was a serious setback in industrial performance, one that was almost entirely the result of deliberate and wasteful policy. Despite the consolidation of the so-called 'three good years' of 1933–1936, industry had begun to experience a slowdown as a result of the emphasis on completing projects rather than constructing new ones. Overall investments since the end of the first Five-Year Plan

 Hidden voices

Valerian Kuibyshev

Kuibyshev had joined the Bolsheviks in 1904 and had performed various subversive activities for them after being expelled from a military academy for his political ideals. He chaired the Revolutionary Committee of Samara during the Civil War after the Bolsheviks seized power and by 1926 became the Chair of the Supreme Council of the National Economy, and then directed Gosplan until 1934. He was a hugely influential member of the Communist Party and was one of the few members of the Politburo to die of natural causes (he died of heart failure in 1935).

reached their peak in 1936 and remained at a reduced level until the outbreak of war in Europe in 1939. The construction industry contracted, especially as priorities began to shift towards the armaments industry.

Stalin's reaction to the slowdown (inasmuch as it was an economic rather than a political decision) was to denounce 'wreckers' and 'saboteurs' within industry who, he claimed, were responsible for any failings. This he did at the 'February–March' party plenum in 1937. What followed was a large-scale purge of the party, but more importantly of a great range of qualified personnel: 'army officers, civil servants, managers, technicians, statisticians, planners, even foremen'.[14] Economically, the 'great purge' organised by Nikolai Yezhov (see *The Yezhovshchina: The Great Terror* in Chapter 5) was completely counter-productive. Not only were the necessary experts removed from industry, but the atmosphere of terror stifled innovation and initiative and promoted a bureaucratic conservatism. Given that Stalin had undertaken an arguably comparable process with the peasantry through collectivisation and dekulakisation, it is perhaps not surprising that he was prepared to sacrifice economic gain in favour of what he perceived to be greater political security. On the face of it, this was a catastrophic way of preparing for war, but from Stalin's perspective (which is difficult to fully understand) he was ridding the Soviet Union of unreliable elements. Even if he did not believe that spies beset the country, as with collectivisation, terror proved an effective means of political control, which seems to have been his overriding concern.

The third Five-Year Plan, 1938–1941

As with the previous Five-Year Plans, aspects of the third began to take effect prior to its beginning point in January 1938 and its official adoption at the 18th Party Congress in 1939. The drafting process was, of course, very seriously affected by the purges, as Gosplan functionaries were removed from their offices. Vosnesensky, who replaced Kuibyshev as the head of Gosplan in January 1938, set about reconstructing the organisation. In addition to the man-made problems of 1937, the winter had been particularly harsh and investment had shifted away from consumer goods. This marked the beginning of a renewed downward turn for the Soviet population towards the privations of the wartime economy.

Molotov claimed, at the adoption of the third Five-Year Plan in March 1939, that the Soviet Union was now placed to make the final step towards socialism's ultimate goal. However, economic and foreign policy developments suggest that these were empty words from a regime in which propagandist rhetoric was an essential part of reality. In fact, before the German invasion interrupted it, production in the underlying strategic industries was well below what had been intended. By 1940, steel production had reached only 5.8% of what was planned, and rolled metal only 1.4%. Oil – possibly the fundamental strategic industry – hardly expanded. Nove suggests, as an explanation, the ongoing effects of the purges and the deployment of thousands of the Soviet Union's specialist engineers as forced labour in prison camps.[15] It must also be stated that the third Five-Year Plan was again very optimistic in its target-setting. There was, however, dramatic growth in the armaments industry (up by 250%) and the successful conversion of the great tractor plants to tank production. Much of industry had been strategically developed to the east of the Ural Mountains in anticipation of invasion from the

ACTIVITY 4.3

The chronology of events is very important in understanding the connections between the purges, collectivisation, mounting foreign pressure and industrialisation. Part of this timeline has been completed. Go back through the chapter and add to it.

west. The armed forces grew from 1.5 million personnel in 1937 to 5 million by June 1941. The increases in defence expenditure drove up collective farm free-market prices. Official retail prices were increased as a result, and the working day was lengthened.

Timeline 1929–1941

Year	Industry	Agriculture
1928	First Five-Year Plan	Forced collectivisation begins
1929		
1930		
1931		
1932		
1933	Second Five-Year Plan	Collectivisation complete
1934		
1935	Stakhanov	
1936		
1937		
1938	Third Five-Year Plan	
1939		
1940		
1941		

New industrial centres and projects

Some of the better-known and most prestigious projects of Soviet industrialisation were begun prior to the first Five-Year Plan. Nevertheless, ground was broken on previously undeveloped sites and areas of under-exploited natural resources. These included the expansion of the network of hydroelectric power stations on the river Dnieper in Ukraine; the development of oilfields in Baku (Azerbaijan) and Grozny (Georgia); the mining of coal in the Donbass region and in the new industrial city Stalinsk in western Siberia, and of various minerals in the Urals, Siberia and Central Asia. Additionally, centres for iron, steel and other metallurgical manufacture were established at Sverdlovsk, formerly Ekaterinburg, and Magnitogorsk in the Urals and Zaporozhye on the Dnieper. Sverdlovsk was also the centre of the Urals Machine Building Plant (Uralmash), established in 1926. Tractor factories were built from scratch in Stalingrad (until 1925, Volgograd), Rostov on the Don and Kharkov in north-east Ukraine. These served as the bases for the later development of armament production.

The involvement of foreign companies

It was at this time that Soviet technical expertise was developed, with an important contribution from thousands of foreign engineers, many of them

American and German, who were in search of employment following the devastating effects of the Great Depression triggered by the Wall Street Crash of 1929. In 1928 the American company Arthur G. McKee was commissioned to assist the replication of a US-style steel mill at Magnitogorsk. The company was serially frustrated by unrealistic demands and incompetent peasant labour, but various foreign specialists, including German architects, acted to direct construction.

Social change: working and living conditions of managers, workers and women

To fully assess life in the Soviet Union during the 1930s it is necessary to account for broader aspects of culture and propaganda, political control and terror. Nevertheless, there are some important economically grounded trends and themes which defined the experience of Soviet citizens. The social disadvantages of collectivisation and industrialisation are perhaps obvious. Dekulakisation and similar terror within industry drove the creation of forced labour camps. Conditions of forced labour involved disregard for the workers' safety and health. Those who could not bear the strain were allowed to work to their deaths. The collectivisation programme itself was, as discussed, highly disruptive and led to a very high degree of migration to towns. Between 1926 and 1939 the urban population grew from 18% to 33%, that is, from 26 million to 56 million. This placed a huge strain on transport and accommodation. Housing construction could not keep up, and across the same period average floor space per individual shrank from 8.3 m^2 to 6.7 m^2.

For the early idealistic pioneers involved in the great projects such as Magnitogorsk, simple living was possibly part of the romance, but poor accommodation was matched by dangerous working conditions as a result of rushed and under-mechanised construction methods. Wages did rise across the period, but in response to rising prices, particularly following the ending of rationing in 1935. Wage differentials were one means whereby the government attempted to limit the overall cost. Basic industries were also subsidised, so that the price for products such as coal were kept low, although this was amended in 1936. In the three years running up to war, wages rose by 35%, but free-market prices rose by 200%.

Despite these privations and burdens, some advantages were gained. First among these was the end of unemployment. During the third Five-Year Plan there was an increasing labour shortage. The demand for workers coupled with socialist ideology brought many women into the workplace: in 1928, 24% of women were wage earners; by 1940 this had risen to 39%. While this was a perceived social advance for women, it must be noted that many retained their social role as keepers of the household and therefore took on a double burden. With the rise in prices it was also necessary to have more than one income per household. There was also substantial spending on health and education. The number of children at school rose from 12 million in 1928 to 35 million in 1941. In addition there were mass literacy campaigns. Higher education, especially that geared towards technical training, expanded rapidly. It was this infrastructure that allowed the hasty replacement of those removed by the purges. This, alongside the initial expansion of industry, had resulted in an undeniable degree of social mobility.

A poor peasant might well rise to a managerial position in a few years. The social security system founded in the 1920s was retained. As will be discussed, economic changes did allow for the creation of a moderately prosperous technical class who, in material terms, could be grateful to Stalin (see *Education and social mobility* in Chapter 5).

Each Five-Year Plan had slightly different aims. Go through your notes and use this table to evaluate the success of Stalin's industrialisation programme.

Five-Year Plan	Priorities	Context	Successes	Failures
First: 1928–1933	Heavy industry; major industrial projects (e.g. Magnitogorsk)	Forced collectivisation 1929–1933; propaganda of heroic working class		
Second: 1933–1937	Completion of projects begun in previous plan; stabilisation of economy; reintroduction of wage differentials	Recovery: 'neo-NEP'; 1934 interlude; Kirov's murder; greater social conservatism; propaganda focused on experts and leaders		
Third: 1937–1941	Shift towards armament production	Show trials of Zinoviev, Kamenev and Bukharin; purges of party, military and NKVD		

The Stakhanovite movement

One factor in the improved productivity of these years was the Stakhanovite movement. This was essentially a 'cult of productivity' based on the achievement of Aleksei Stakhanov, a coal miner in the Donbass region, who in September 1935 had managed to drill fourteen times his allotted quota of coal. His record was subsequently beaten, but formed the basis of an effort for greater efficiency: his achievement had also been due to the intelligent use of unskilled labour. This resulted in the party insisting on more ambitious 'work norms' – the expected level of productivity per worker – from early 1936. Some of these proved unrealistic and 'Stakhanovite' workers received threats as a result of being favourably treated by ambitious managers. It also led, again, to the erratic diversion of resources in some cases. However, Nove states that, alongside fines for absenteeism and the introduction of new technology, this led to greater productivity.[16] Within the context of propaganda, it reconciled personal aspiration with Soviet collectivism by providing a role model: a 'hero-worker' (see Figure 4.1). It also functioned as a way of removing excuses from those accused of failing, who would be labelled 'wreckers' and 'saboteurs', as had those at Shakhty in 1928.

The success of the Five-Year Plans

As a simple measure of success, the aim of industrialising the Soviet Union up to a level comparable with the United States was achieved. The fact that this occurred in little over a decade surely marks it out as a heroic feat of human endeavour. Between 1928 and 1940 there was an average growth rate of 10% each year and overall industrial output was trebled. Much of this had been achieved as part of the first Five-Year Plan. Between 1928 and 1933 national income had doubled and the output of capital goods (such as fuel) had nearly trebled. The labour force had more than doubled. There had of course been two major moments of setback and crisis, one in 1932–1933 and another in 1937–1938, and both were to some extent caused by seemingly counter-productive political repression. The control of foreign trade (particularly in grain) enabled a high level of investment in machinery, but a reduction after 1935 led to cutbacks in investment and slower technological development.

It is difficult to ascertain whether the culture of over-optimistic plans, 'socialist emulation' and forced labour acted as an overall boost to production, or whether the consequent lack of coordination, compromise on quality and strain on infrastructure and society meant that more realistic plans would have, in the end, been more productive. This was an era of self-induced crisis (both in the positive and negative senses) and was arguably the outworking of a political imperative that was essential to Bolshevik ideology – that socialism must be built through revolutionary struggle. It might be fair to ask whether the NEP would have yielded the same results over the same period and prepared the Soviet Union for war.

The development of the Stalin cult

The 'cult of personality', which played an essential part in Soviet culture and politics, is generally recognised as having developed from December 1929 on the occasion of Stalin's 50th birthday. The cult manifested itself mainly in the form of posters, paintings and other works of art, the official reporting of news and Soviet achievement and history. Stalin was often portrayed as a central figure, sometimes as a 'Sun-Man', but often among groups of proletarians, peoples of the Soviet Union and smiling children (as in Figure 4.2). His image, as Graeme Gill notes, came to dominate this symbolic universe.[17]

The emphasis was not on Stalin's private life, which was hardly referred to, but on his public persona. Historians suggest that he was dependent on adulation and it made up part of his dictatorial psyche. Nevertheless, his image was crafted to be that of a leader closely connected with the party, the Soviet people, the legacy of Lenin and the broad historical forces behind socialism.

It is reported that Stalin refused to allow Moscow to be renamed Stalinodar, although this did not prevent Tsaritsyn (later known as Volgograd) being renamed Stalingrad and the great mining town of western Siberia as Stalinsk. Moreover, Stalin insisted that references to himself in the film *The Great Citizen* (1937) be replaced by 'the Central Committee of the Party'. It is suggested that such modesty

Figure 4.1: Propaganda posters such as this one were produced as early as 1931 to inspire workers to meet the extraordinarily high targets for output set by the party.

Figure 4.2: This 1937 Soviet Union poster shows children thanking the party and 'Dear Stalin' for a 'Happy, Joyful Childhood'.

99

was studied and a conscious attempt to mimic Lenin's diffidence to fame. Stalin appeared in worker- or military-type clothing, among his people. At a time when the Soviet Union was in the throes of social dislocation, a paternal figure to the various peoples of the Union was there to unify and reassure.

The slogan 'Stalin is the Lenin of today' became widely used, evoking the cult of Lenin itself. One play portrayed Lenin as the sun, Stalin as light and Trotsky as the dark villain. The mere symbolic power gave him a hold over his colleagues. While rejecting references to 'the teachings of Lenin and Stalin', he had the final word on what was doctrinally acceptable and what was not. By associating himself with broader historical forces and the achievements of the state, he reduced the ability of party members to act together to influence him, even at the highest level. Stalin was also aware that the Russian people had traditionally responded to an all-powerful leader and encouraged his association with such historical figures. He thereby provided, says Kevin McDermott, 'a direct populist link between the leader and the masses'.[18] The pervasive presence of Stalin's image within Soviet culture very simply conveyed the message that he was to be loved and feared.

Figure 4.3: A painting of 1939, 'Lenin and Stalin in Gorki near Moscow'.

Literature, the arts and other propaganda

In a similar manner to education, literature and art were subject to the enthusiasms of 'socialist construction' during the early part of the first Five-Year Plan. The body that led the way was the Russian Association of Proletarian Writers (RAPP) created in 1928, which intended to praise the great economic advances. This resulted in works such as *The Struggle for the Promfinplan in the Third Year of the Piatletka* (Five-Year Plan).

Such earnest attempts were seen as inadequate and the RAPP was replaced by the Union of Writers in 1932. The figure who led this organisation was Maxim Gorky, who was close to Stalin and who shared the view that the best aspects of the past must be used to create a new form of art that served to encourage the people in their building of socialism. The RAPP had attacked so-called 'fellow-travellers' – artists and intellectuals who were not party members but who sympathised with the regime. At a meeting at Gorky's town house in October 1932, Stalin and senior members of the Politburo met with a group of around 50 writers. While there was to be clear party involvement, including Stalin's own personal intervention in censoring and approving works, this 'strong nucleus' would have around it, says Evan Mawdsley, 'a wide strata of non-party writers'.[19] This was an acknowledgement that Russia had a rich cultural past from which to draw, not least through depictions of its ancient military heroes. These could be used for building socialism. As Stalin put it in October 1932, writers were 'engineers of human souls' who were to 'show our life truthfully, on its way to socialism'.[20] From this meeting emerged the dominant artistic doctrine in Soviet culture known as **Socialist Realism**.

Socialist Realism

In August 1934 the Union of Writers held a conference to elaborate on the notion of Socialist Realism. The figure who would help define and police the party's cultural line and the tone of Soviet culture was Andrei Zhdanov. He was a close ally of Stalin and replaced Kirov as party leader in Leningrad following his death in 1934. He would have a more direct influence over culture after the Second World War (as we will see in *Zhdanovism and the cultural purge* in Chapter 6), but was instrumental in outlining the basis of the new doctrine in 1934. Above all, Socialist Realism was a rejection of decadent Western (capitalist) culture and thus a tool to fashion the new Soviet man.

In literature, it found its expression in works such as Mikhail Sholokhov's *And Quiet Flows the Don* (published in four volumes between 1928 and 1940), which portrayed everyday life in the Cossack south and subtly conformed to the party's message. The reintegration of pre-Revolutionary Russian cultural figures was most obvious through the celebration of the centenary of Alexander Pushkin's death in 1937. As with other areas of culture, the watchword was 'accessibilty' to the masses.[21]

In music, the traditional Russian folk song was adapted for the purposes of propaganda, not least for the young, whose organisations taught them songs extolling the virtues of the party and Stalin, and their destiny in life to strive towards the construction of a utopian future. The composer Dmitri Shostakovich trod a fine line throughout his career. His music is unmistakably modern and frequently discordant. At points he gained approval and had to second-guess Stalin's likely response. In January 1936, *Pravda* condemned his most recent work as 'cacophony, not music'.[22] Like the experimental work of artists of the 1920s, he was subject to the charge of 'formalism' (defined broadly by Mawdsley) as 'non-accessible, non-realistic, non-socialist'.[23] The year 1936 saw a turn towards an era of a more conservative, tamer form of art, but one that still served a political purpose. While no longer experimental, it was definitively not 'bourgeois' (of a traditional musical style associated with pre-revolutionary culture) – indeed, this was still a label to be scrupulously avoided.

Key term

Socialist Realism: A style of realistic art that developed to further Socialism in One Country. It glorified the working class.

ACTIVITY 4.5

Referring to Figures 4.2 and 4.3, consider these two questions:

1. What are their propaganda messages and how are they portrayed?

2. In what sense do these paintings reflect the conservative style of socialist realism?

With the onset of the great terror under Yezhov, to be defined as culturally 'deviationist' was as dangerous as being identified as a spy, traitor or saboteur, especially as what constituted 'deviation' was arguably a matter of taste. In 1937, around 1500 writers were subject to the purges. Painting and other works of art produced at this time fitted this mould. They were realistic and arguably fairly dull portrayals of proletarian (working) life. Scenes from Stalin's career, showing him to be a leader, teacher and father of the people, were also commonplace.

It might be argued that in such a cultural atmosphere, originality and experimentation were almost impossible. This could lead to an inaccurate portrayal of 'dullness'. In fact, for many Soviet citizens this was a very exciting time. The aim of Soviet cultural propaganda was to promote the regime's objectives: 'economic activity, socialist utopia, national defence and the leader himself'.[24] Mawdsley makes an essential point: while this was an attempt to use culture as part of totalitarian control, it was closely related to the technological change being experienced in all industrialising countries: communist, fascist and capitalist. He writes: 'The appearance of mass culture – popular fiction, cinema, radio, spectator sports – went hand in hand with twentieth century urbanisation.'[25]

The urban environment was in fact one of the main means by which to inculcate and enthuse the population with the idea that they were involved in 'building socialism'. Sheila Fitzpatrick points to accounts of young individuals who believed that a utopian urban landscape was just around the corner. Its aesthetic was modern, clean, scientific, rational – as reflected in the shining concrete constructions of industry and the new 'Stalin Gothic' skyscrapers of Moscow University. Plans for constructions were themselves part of propaganda.[26] The model for the new 'Palace of the Soviets', intended to be built on the site of the recently demolished (in 1931) Church of Christ the Saviour in Moscow, was superimposed on the actual photography of the film *New Moscow* released in 1939. Another major demonstration of Stalinist grandeur was the mosaic-, mural- and chandelier-filled Moscow Metro, opened in 1935. Gorky himself was responsible for the publication *Our Achievements*, which throughout the 1930s publicised the great industrial projects.

As buildings acted to literally construct the future, so films acted to edify the population. Film had been a rare commodity during the leaner years of the 1920s. In the 1930s, cinema became one of the most popular means of tying the Soviet people to the state. Aviators and polar explorers were heralded as the heroes of the new Soviet age. They were depicted in films such as *Seven of the Brave* (1936) and *Tales of Aviation Heroes* (1938). The aspiration to the new social mobility were vaunted in *Member of the Government* (1939), which told the tale of a woman who worked her way through the ranks from peasant to the Supreme Soviet. The mixing of Russian nationalism and Soviet patriotism was well underway before the outbreak of war, in films such as *The Fatherland Calls* (1936). Recreational culture, including film, was of course one of the best means by which to engender optimism and hope for the socialist future and blend it with the promotion of duty and sacrifice.

The social and economic condition of the Soviet Union by 1941

Strengths and weaknesses

In his speech of February 1931, Stalin stated: 'We have fallen behind the advanced countries by fifty to a hundred years. We must close that gap in ten years. Either we do this or we'll be crushed.'[27] Stalin cannot have known that his prediction would have proved so accurate. It is very clear that the fear of foreign military intervention crushing the Soviet regime was a dominant motivation for Stalin. At this point, it is useful to consider the condition of the Soviet Union on the eve of war, with a particular emphasis on how well placed the 'socialist motherland' was to engage in large-scale conflict.

Industry and trade

In basic terms, the three Five-Year Plans had achieved an enormous and rapid expansion of productive capacity in materials and heavy industry, and in transport. In this respect, the 'gap' of which Stalin spoke should be regarded as having been very significantly narrowed, though possibly not closed. The make-up of the Soviet industrial base was significantly altered by wartime developments (see *The Soviet economy* and *Mobilisation and evacuation of industry* in Chapter 6), but the fact that the Soviet Union was able to manufacture the majority of its armaments during the war (and was mainly dependent on its allies for communications technology and raw materials such as aluminium) suggests a successful transformation of Soviet industry over the decade.

As discussed, the Third Five-Year Plan began to be increasingly geared and adapted towards war. Nove suggests that while machinery and engineering output increased by a claimed 59%, increases in production of steel, rolled metal, cement and oil (essential for war) were relatively insignificant and fell well short of plan targets.[28] There were two major weaknesses in Soviet industry. First, despite rapid urbanisation (the proportion of those living in urban centres rose from 18% in 1926 to 33% in 1939), the supply of labour remained insufficient for the required expansion. In June 1940, a million school leavers were conscripted into 'labour reserve schools' because the crisis was so acute. Second, the wave of mass terror in the late 1930s saw the imprisonment or execution of thousands of trained technical experts and experienced managers who were removed at a critical time.

Finally, it is important to note both the positive and negative effects of developments between 1939 and 1941 when the Soviet Union made a short-lived agreement with Nazi Germany as it undertook the invasion of Poland, much of Scandinavia and western Europe. First, there was increased trade with Hitler's regime, somewhat paradoxically given that it had been so badly affected by Hitler's anti-Communist attitude during the 1930s. Second, Stalin's invasion of the Baltic states of Latvia, Lithuania and Estonia significantly increased Soviet industrial capacity for the two years before war between the Soviet Union and Nazi Germany began. Third, the Soviet–Finnish War of 1940 prevented the delivery of coal to Leningrad's industry. The Soviet industrial system successfully began its conversion to armament production before 1941, though at a cost to the labour force and an uneven industrial base.

Agriculture

As with the urban workforce, pressures on the collective farms grew, and measures were taken to 'squeeze' the peasantry. In 1939, 2.5 million hectares of small private plots were confiscated and collectivised. Delivery quotas for livestock products and crops were increased and, although this led to larger state grain reserves, it also had, in some cases, counter-productive effects (as had been previously experienced). Between 1932 and 1940, the area sown with grain increased by only 1%. Inadequate to the task of supporting a growing population, this also demonstrated that the Soviet government's approach to agriculture and rural society was burdensome and neglectful.

Living and working conditions

The shift of the economy towards war production meant that the availability of consumer goods quickly reduced. Unofficial rationing began, and the improvement of living standards that some people had experienced during the 1930s ended. While average wages continued to rise (by 35% between 1937 and 1940), 'free market' prices of goods in special shops rose by 75%. Working conditions and labour discipline became far more restrictive, mainly due to the lack of manpower. Working hours increased, absenteeism became a crime and workers required permission to leave their job. In addition, the generous social benefits of the 1930s were reduced from 1938, including maternity leave and free education.

ACTIVITY 4.6

Use the information from this chapter to complete the table.

Factor	Strengths	Weaknesses	Overall judgement: How ready for war was the Soviet Union by 1941?
Industry			
Agriculture			
Morale			
Military			
Political control			

For a full appreciation of the Soviet Union's situation by 1941, revisit this table once you have read Chapter 5. Add information regarding the effects of political developments, the Terror, social and cultural change and international relations.

Summary of key events

- Stalin aimed to transform agriculture through collectivisation:
  - This mainly took place between 1929 and 1931.
  - Stalin's aim was to make agriculture more efficient to increase production.
  - He hoped to fund industrialisation by selling the extra grain produced.

- The process was chaotic and was responsible for creating a famine in 1932.
- Despite the suffering it created, Stalin managed to enforce collectivisation.
- Stalin aimed to transform industry through Five-Year Plans:
  - There were three Five-Year Plans before 1941.
  - Stalin was responding to Communist Party demands for faster industrialisation in order to build socialism and end the use of capitalist-like methods.
  - Soviet industry was massively expanded within a decade through enormous efforts and human sacrifice.
  - Stalin was mainly concerned to make the Soviet Union ready to defend itself in a large-scale war.
- Stalin became central to Soviet culture and propaganda:
  - A 'cult of personality' grew up around the Soviet leader.
  - Soviet society became culturally more conservative: artists were keen to please Stalin and appear as loyal communists.

Further reading

For an in-depth account of economic change, Alec Nove's *An Economic History of the USSR* (Pelican, 1989) remains indispensable, although R.W. Davies' *Soviet Economic Development from Lenin to Khrushchev* (Cambridge University Press, 1998) provides a concise and detailed account. Davies, Harrison and Wheatcroft's *The Economic Transformation of the Soviet Union, 1913–1945* (Cambridge University Press, 1993) provides a series of very informative themed essays. Sheila Fitzpatrick's *Everyday Stalinism* (Oxford University Press, 2000) is a very rich collection of people's experiences under Stalin. Orlando Figes', *The Whisperers: Private Life in Stalin's Russia* (Penguin, 2008) is similarly wide-ranging and evocative. It is well worth reading these to extend and deepen your understanding of this era.

Practice essay questions

1. How successful was the Communist regime in modernising Russian agriculture in the years 1928 to 1941?
2. 'The main aim of collectivisation was to gain full control over the peasantry.' Assess the validity of this view.
3. To what extent were the three Five-Year Plans (1928–1941) effective in preparing the Soviet Union for war by 1941?
4. With reference to the sources below and your understanding of the historical context, assess the value of the three sources to a historian studying the purpose of 'shock workers' in Soviet industry.

Source A

Christian Rakovsky, a member of the Trotskyite opposition, summer 1930 (in Boobbyer, P., *The Stalin Era*, pp. 50–51).

Today they increase the programme for coal and iron to make it possible to fulfil the programme for machine building; tomorrow it will be necessary to expand the programme from machine building to make it possible to fulfil the enlarged programme for coal and iron; later they will again find it necessary to increase the programme for coal and iron in order to guarantee the new programme for machine building. In the midst of this spiral it suddenly turns out that it is posing tasks the transport will not be able to cope with unless the latter receives an appropriate supply of iron and steel – and so the programme for coal and iron is boosted again and the circle begins anew.

Source B

Manya Gordon, a Soviet historian, writing in 1941 (in Boobbyer, P., *The Stalin Era*, p. 53).

Under the leadership of the party, the trade unions have now removed their bankrupt leaders and have begun a determined fight against the elements of 'trade unionism 'and opportunism in the trade union movement. Today the basic factor in energising and improving the entire work of the trade unions must be socialist competition and its offspring, the shock brigades. Socialist competition and the shock brigades must become the primary concern of all the constructive activities of the unions.

Source C

Extract from *I Chose Freedom* (1947), the memoirs of Viktor Kravchenko, a Soviet engineer and party member in Ukraine during the 1930s who later defected to the West (in Boobbyer, P., *The Stalin Era*, p. 57).

At eleven o'clock one evening, with reporters and photographers present, the 'Stakhanovite' shift got underway. As expected, it 'overfulfilled' the normal quota by 8% … Congratulations arrived from officials in the capitals … But this 'victory' on the industrial front merely left me heartsick. It was, at bottom, fraudulent and must boomerang. The other two shifts, deprived of the best personnel and their best tools, lost more than the favoured group had won.

Chapter summary

Having studied this chapter you should be able to:

- identify Stalin's reasons for the collectivisation of agriculture and industrialisation by means of the Five-Year Plans
- trace the development of collectivisation and industrialisation
- assess the economic and social impacts of economic change
- identify aspects of the Stalin cult and associated cultural change
- comment upon the condition of the USSR prior to its entry into the Second World War.

End notes

1   Gill, G., *Stalinism*, p. 17.
2   Service, R., *Stalin: A Biography*, p. 272.
3   From Stalin, *Works, Volume XII*, 1955, cited in Acton, E. and Stableford, T., *The Soviet Union: A Documentary History, Volume 1, 1917–1940.*
4   Conquest, R., *The Great Terror: A Reassessment*, p. 20.
5   Nove, A., *An Economic History of the USSR*, p. 90.
6   Ibid, p. 124.
7   Figures taken from Nove, *An Economic History of the USSR*, pp. 137 and 180.
8   *Literaturnaya gazeta,* 26 December 1928, cited in Acton and Stableford, *The Soviet Union, Volume 1*, pp. 264–266.
9   Nove, *An Economic History of the USSR*, p. 180.
10 Ibid, p. 183.
11 Ibid, p. 224.
12 Taken from *Kuznetskstroy v vospominanyakh*. Novosibirsk, 1934, pp. 93–97, cited in Acton and Stableford, *The Soviet Union, Volume 1*, pp. 311–314.
13 Ward, C., *Stalin's Russia*, p. 48.
14 Nove, *An Economic History of the USSR*, p. 227.
15 Ibid, p. 248.
16 Ibid, pp. 224–225.
17 Gill, *Stalinism*, p. 25.
18 McDermott, K., *Stalin*, p. 115.
19 Mawdsley, E., *The Stalin Years: The Soviet Union 1929–1953*, p. 54.
20 Cited in McDermott, *Stalin*, p. 77.
21 Mawdsley, *The Stalin Years*, p. 55.
22 Cited in McDermott, *Stalin*, p. 86.
23 Mawdsley, *The Stalin Years*, p. 56.
24 Ibid, p. 58.
25 Ibid, p. 58.
26 Fitzpatrick, S., *Everyday Stalinism*, p. 69
27 Cited in Service, *Stalin*, p. 273.
28 Nove, *An Economic History of the USSR*, p. 247.

5 Stalinism, politics and control, 1929–1941

In this section we will investigate the methods and institutions involved in Stalin's dictatorship and the internal state of Soviet society and position of the USSR in the world prior to the outbreak of the Second World War. This includes:

- dictatorship and Stalinism: the machinery of state terror; the NKVD; the early purges; Kirov's murder; the show trials; the Stalin constitution

- the Yezhovshchina: mass terror and repression at central and local levels; treatment of national minorities; the gulags; the end of the purges; the death of Trotsky; responsibility for and impact of the Terror and purges

- culture and society; church; women, young people and working men; urban and rural differences; 'Socialist man' and cultural changes; similarities and differences between Lenin's and Stalin's USSR

- Stalin and international relations: cooperation with Germany; entry into the League of Nations; pacts with France, Britain and Czechoslovakia; intervention in the Spanish Civil War; reaction to Western appeasement and Japanese aggression; the Nazi-Soviet Pact and its outcome.

Introduction

The 'personal dictatorship' created by Stalin by 1941 has served as a template for understanding subsequent 'totalitarian' dictatorships of the 20th century, many of which deliberately followed his model. This classic understanding of the **totalitarian** model, while being generally accurate, can cloud our analysis of Stalin's control over the Soviet Union during the 1930s.

While the above aspects undoubtedly apply, Stalin was not in complete control until the outbreak of the Second World War in 1939. His paranoia must count as one of the foremost reasons behind the extent of the Terror. Stalin's power was reliant on a close group of senior Bolsheviks, who failed – through ambition, caution or conviction – to challenge his certainty that he was right. At times his position was shaky. It had always rested on his ability to play his colleagues off against one another and to maintain them in a state of insecurity. With the constant rhetoric of enemies, without and within, any form of dissent, direct or indirect, real, perceived or entirely fictitious, became a matter of treachery, not only to Stalin but to the whole Soviet Union.

Key term

Totalitarian: A political system where the state retains complete control over society and all aspects of citizens' lives.

Dictatorship and Stalinism

The machinery of state terror

The birth of terror

Robert Service states that 'the Great Terror of 1937–8 was not a thunderclap in a cloudless sky but the worsening of the storm that was already raging'.[1] The Shakhty trials of 1928, where 5 of the 53 accused were executed, were the beginning of successive waves of repression against so-called 'wreckers'. (See the coverage of the July 1929 'industrial party' and the November 1930 'labouring peasant party' in Chapter 4.) Some of these 'wreckers' were ill-trained peasants while others were non-party technocrats (being employed for their expertise rather than for their political loyalty to the party). In August 1930, Stalin wrote to Molotov demanding that two leading economists, Kondratiev and Groman, be shot along with 'a whole group' of others, including 'several dozen common cashiers'.[2] This approach was not at all new to Stalin. The idea of making an example of a selected quota of victims was rooted in the practices of the Civil War; Stalin had carried out atrocities in Georgia and elsewhere during that time. Lenin had encouraged such tactics. Dekulakisation, taking place at this time, was of course a major example of this method. Violence, however, was mainly restricted to this context of driving economic achievement and attacking 'bourgeois' elements.

Stalin was not operating with the mindset of an all-powerful dictator, but one of a central director constantly frustrated by his inability to control the localities and the lethargy of communist bureaucracy. This is what lay behind the 'Urals-Siberian method' of early 1928 – this was an example of his previously established practice of directly intervening in person to 'knock heads together' or, as it was put in September 1930, 'inspecting and checking up by punching people in the face'[3] His constant refrain was that party and state officials were sleeping on the job. He criticised 'departmental interests' within the Soviet bureaucracy and linked to these to 'Menshevik attitudes'.

These criticisms were partly based in reality: the increase in bureaucracies to run the planned economy encouraged some inter-departmental rivalry and empire building. What is more, those economic experts who objected to unrealistic targets immediately identified themselves as politically disloyal. Stalin had, of course, been using his position within the party since 1922 to appoint those loyal to himself, but his ability to control was limited. Moshe Lewin put it this way: 'Each "little Stalin" could be destroyed but was immediately replaced'[4] As late as June 1937, Stalin complained: 'No, the centre doesn't see everything ... only a part and the rest is seen in the localities. It sends people, but doesn't know these people 100% and you must check up on them.'[5]

The NKVD

The infrastructure of repression was increasingly linked to Stalin's ability to dominate his colleagues. The creation of the **NKVD** was at first taken as a sign of the weakening of the state's arbitrary power. It absorbed the OGPU, which had been responsible for the Gulag, the network of prison and labour camps, and which had assumed the powers and role of the Cheka (see Figure 5.1). Genrikh Yagoda, who had been chief of OGPU and assisted Stalin in the purges of preceding years, was now made head of the NKVD. It has been suggested by Graeme Gill that he was anxious to prove the indispensability of the security apparatus following the 'moderation of domestic policy in 1933 to 1934'.[6] Subsequent events would support the idea that Yagoda had something to prove. Far from weakening the machinery of terror, 1934 set in train a process that made the NKVD's secret police increasingly accountable to wider Soviet government and to the party.

Stalin did not trust his colleagues, the party, the bureaucracy or even the OGPU, responsible for Gulag, the labour camp system, and the implementation of collectivisation. He had his own personal secretariat headed by Poskrebyshev, who maintained links with the NKVD. It has also been suggested that this office was fused with the Central Committee's 'special' section or 'Secret Department', which was also headed by Poskrebyshev. Stalin's personal assistants had held positions within such bodies since 1922 and it is possible that he had a network of men whom he had placed in various parts of the party, communication and security apparatus, providing him with his own intelligence network that enabled him to gain advantage against his rivals and to check on the implementation of policies. It demonstrates both his power and his weakness that he required such intelligence. It also speaks to his personal hold over particular individuals.

Key term

NKVD: The People's Commissariat for Internal Affairs – the NKVD – contained the regular police force (including traffic police and firefighting and border guards). It became infamous for running the gulag system after 1934 where it conducted executions, as well as keeping harsh conditions within the camps.

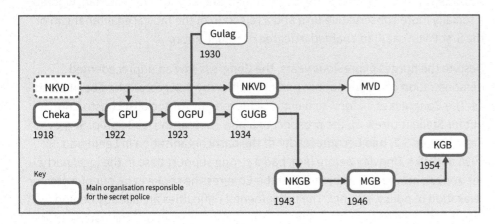

Figure 5.1: The development of Soviet state repression and control through security institutions.

The early purges

Although Stalin had rid the Politburo of his major rivals by 1930, those at the top of the party continued to challenge his leadership. His management of collectivisation in late 1929 and early 1930 drew criticism – thus his attempt to divert blame to local officials, guilty of becoming 'dizzy with success'. Criticism was manifested in what Gill refers to as 'three shadowy opposition groups'[7] of the early 1930s: the Syrtsov–Lominadze group in 1930, the Eismont–Tolmachev–Smirnov group of 1932 and *The Ryutin Platform* of the same year. The last of these was the most open and prominent. Martemyan Ryutin created a 200-page indictment of Stalin's policy, calling for lower capital investment, an end to forced collectivisation, the rehabilitation of oppositionists and Stalin's dismissal. The comparably minor price to be paid at this point was expulsion from the Central Committee, along with Kamenev, Zinoviev and 17 others.

Yet criticism was more guarded than it had been. Zinoviev and others demoted or sidelined in the struggles of the 1920s were keen to demonstrate their commitment to party unity. Nevertheless, senior Bolsheviks questioned Stalin's judgement. The crisis of late 1932 and early 1933 saw a shift away from what Kevin McDermott calls the 'semi-collegial atmosphere' of the leadership. In 1933 there was another purge of the party, which involved the expulsion of 854 300 members. This process was undertaken at the same time as, following Kaganovich's advice, Stalin used the reform of the Commissariats to gain greater control over the local parties.[8] Grigory (Sergo) Ordzhonikidze (shown in Figure 5.2) had previously complained of local party interference in factory management. Stalin trusted neither Commissariats nor local party organisation. Such behaviour did not endear Stalin to the membership and he would face the consequences at the 17th Congress in 1934.

Kirov's murder

The 16th Congress had taken place in June 1930. This was during the summer of respite from collectivisation before its return later that year. Similarly, the 17th Congress took place during a relatively more liberal phase that followed the

1932–1933 crisis. This was at the beginning of the second Five-Year Plan, whereby a socially more conservative turn and a rejection of the radical egalitarianism of the first Five-Year Plan enabled a degree of stabilisation.

Despite the purges of previous years, the Congress saw an unprecedented demonstration of independence and opposition by delegates. It had been billed as 'The Congress of Victors', to hail the achievements of socialist construction, but for Stalin it threw up the prospect of a new rival for the leadership. Sergey Kirov (Figure 5.2) had become leader of the party organisation in Leningrad in 1926 and, like Zinoviev before him, had a strong support base in the local party. His appeal, however, was broader. At the Congress he spoke in favour of a greater relaxation of policy, stating: 'The fundamental difficulties are already behind us.'[9] This, of course, contrasted with Stalin's constant complaints of the party and state institutions sleeping on the job. Kirov remained loyal to Stalin, praising him in his speech and resisting his own promotion. Nevertheless, he was a figure around whom Stalin's critics could rally.

While the machinations of the Congress are less than transparent to historians, it is clear that Stalin was being challenged. First, the most obvious challenge was a vote to abolish the post of General Secretary. This was successful and, in theory, made Stalin equal with his colleagues. Second, it is quite possible that many delegates asked Kirov to stand against Stalin for the General Secretaryship before it was abolished. If so, then Kirov evidently refused. Finally, evidence suggests that in the elections to the Central Committee, Stalin fared very poorly and Kirov very well. It is suggested that up to 300 delegates voted against Stalin, in contrast to 3 votes against Kirov. The results were not published and it is possible that Stalin's accomplices subverted the process. Kirov remained a popular figure, and despite his loyalty he spoke in favour of a more moderate tempo and an end to forced collectivisation of the peasantry.

On 1 December, a young communist by the name of Leonid Nikolayev shot Kirov dead in his office in Leningrad. The assassin was immediately arrested and executed without trial, as were – with time – all those involved in his arrest and execution. Even if Stalin had not planned the murder of Kirov (there is some suggestion that Nikolayev had been ordered to undertake the assassination) then this turn of events was enormously convenient for him. No longer a threat, Kirov was extolled as a Soviet hero and Stalin used his death to initiate an attack on both the Leningrad party and on his major rivals, who though politically humiliated remained, in his eyes, a potential threat to his power. They were accused of being involved in Kirov's murder.

Following Kirov's murder, Stalin introduced an 'extraordinary law' that removed party immunity and gave the security police (now under the newly established People's Commissariat for Internal Affairs – the NKVD) the power to arrest party members without first seeking permission. Investigations were brief and were swiftly followed by execution. McDermott states that this was the point at which purges of the party 'became physical rather than simply administrative'.[10] While there are several points from which to trace the beginning of Robert Service's 'raging storm'[11] of terror, December 1934 is clearly one of them.

Figure 5.2: Sergey Kirov (left) and Sergo Ordzhonikidze (right) were key allies of Stalin. However, their deaths, in 1934 and 1937 respectively, proved to be convenient for his consolidation of power.

The response to Kirov's murder was a continuation of Stalin's method of identifying plots centred on individuals or regions. In this case it involved the suppression of the supposed 13-strong 'Leningrad centre', of which Nikolayev was supposed to be a member. Another 98 officials were shot for preparing 'terrorist acts'.[12] The witch-hunt spread further, however. The Central Committee demanded that local organisations identify 'Trotskyites' and 'Zinovievites' in their midsts, which led to thousands of arrests. Eventually, out of the 1996 delegates and the 17th Party Congress, 1108 were arrested and 848 were executed.

Included in the list of those arrested were Kamenev and Zinoviev. These, along with 16 others, were accused in January 1935 of being part of a 'Moscow centre' and were put on trial, though not in public, for being 'morally and politically responsible' for Kirov's death. Zinoviev had, of course, previously begged for readmission to the party in 1929. His reaction was to accept 'moral responsibility' but he did not confess in full. Vyshinsky, Stalin's chief prosecutor, was able to convict them, but they were spared the death penalty. Twelve important members of the Leningrad NKVD were imprisoned alongside Stalin's one-time collaborators. They were further disgraced with their works, along with those of Trotsky, being removed from all Soviet libraries.

The show trials

Stabilisation notwithstanding, Stalin continued his campaign against his long-standing rivals. From late 1936 to early 1938 three sets of high-profile 'show trials' were held in Moscow. They involved Vyshinsky presenting mainly fictitious evidence, much of which had been confessed to after torture. His speeches were full of colourful denunciations of the accused that were intended not to persuade the judges (conviction was a foregone conclusion) but to serve as propaganda for broader consumption. The process was intended not only to physically destroy Stalin's rivals once and for all but to destroy their reputation and complete their humiliation prior to their demise. This often involved not only their own confessions but also their denouncing each other.

The first such trial began in August 1936. Chris Ward notes that it was against the 'Trotskyite-Zinovievite Counter-Revolutionary Bloc'.[13] As outlined above, Zinoviev, Kamenev and 16 others associated with the opposition of the early 1930s were accused of organising Kirov's murder and plotting to kill Stalin and six other members of the Central Committee. In addition, they were accused of being in collusion with Trotsky in 1932. Zinoviev and 13 others confessed and in so doing accused Smirnov of not coming clean. They were shot on 24 August.

Behind the initial document accusing those condemned was Nikolai Yezhov. This careerist, who had served as Yagoda's deputy in the NKVD, replaced his boss on 26 September on Stalin's order. Yagoda had been accused of allowing the OGPU to 'lag behind by four years'. This was a reference to his failure to deal with those now being tried, back in 1932. This was the beginning of Yezhov's rise to infamy.

Part of the process of the first trial was the implication of others, including Bukharin, Rykov and Tomsky, their old rivals on the Right. Tomsky heard of this and committed suicide. In January 1937 a second show trial took place. Among those accused of forming the 'Anti-Soviet Trotskyite Centre' were Pyatakov, mentioned in Lenin's 'Testament' and Ordzhonikidze's deputy, and Radek, who had also helped frame the new constitution. Again, the long list of charges included wrecking, planning assassinations, espionage and contacts with Trotsky and the governments of Japan and Germany. Thirteen individuals, including Pyatakov, were given the death penalty. Having pleaded with Stalin for his deputy's life, Ordzhonikidze died a few days later, reportedly of a heart attack. This was yet another convenient death for Stalin. Despite his previous criticism of Stalin, the fellow Georgian was given a funeral with full honours, early in 1937, just prior to the decisive February-March plenum (assembly) (see *The Yezhovshchina: the Great Terror*, below).

This meeting was to have enormous consequences and began a process of terror. In the midst of this campaign, the third show trial of March 1938 was held. In this trial Stalin removed the remaining veterans of the revolution and his other one-time accomplices including Bukharin, Rykov and Yagoda and 17 others. The list of accusations was similar to that of before: wrecking, conspiracy with all types of enemy, internal and external, and plotted assassinations of various leaders: Bukharin was accused of attempting to kill Lenin and Stalin; Yagoda was accused of trying to kill Yezhov. In contrast to Zinoviev and Kamenev, Bukharin did not confess to all charges, although reportedly pleaded that his family be left alone. Everyone else eventually confessed. Seventeen of the twenty were shot shortly after the verdict. Bukharin was reportedly defiant to the end. Vyshinsky pronounced: 'Over the road cleared of the last scum and filth of the past, we … With our beloved leader and teacher, the great Stalin, at our head, will march … towards Communism!'[14]

The Stalin constitution of 1936

In February 1935, Molotov announced that Soviet society, now transformed by the 'cleansing' processes of the early 1930s, required a new constitutional basis. Despite the fallout from Kirov's murder, there was some hope that this 'further democratisation of the electoral system' would allow for a greater securing of Soviet citizens' rights against the arbitrary power of the state. Bukharin was included in the process and, alongside Stalin, drew up a new constitution that guaranteed a host of economic rights: sexual equality, welfare, education, housing and work. In addition, and more surprisingly, the constitution also promised freedom of speech, publication and assembly, privacy, and religious belief. It also involved the creation of direct elections to the soviets but retained the ban on all parties other than the Communist Party (which by definition represented the proletariat). There was a broad process of consultation and the so-called 'Stalin Constitution' was ratified by a special Soviet congress in December 1936. Given what followed, this may appear as a collection of false promises that had little to do with reality. This, however, fails to recognise the intention of Stalin and leading communists to stabilise that part of Soviet society which they regarded as purged and transformed. As described below, while many suffered, others were experiencing social benefits by the mid-1930s.

The Yezhovshchina: The Great Terror

'To the final destruction of all enemies!'

The above quotation[15] was Stalin's toast on 7 November 1937. It is a neat summary of the purpose of what came to be known as the 'Great Terror' overseen by Yezhov as head of the NKVD. It would subsequently be known as the '**Yezhovshchina**', as in its conclusion in November 1938, Stalin and his colleagues began to distance themselves from such 'excesses'.

The process began at the February-March plenum (assembly of members of the party) at the beginning of 1937. Debate was apparently extensive and centred around the implications of the new constitution and the need to properly 'democratise' the party. However, in the atmosphere of the time, one in which fears of foreign enemies and their subversive agents within the Soviet Union was foremost in the leadership's mind, 'democratisation' meant the ability of local party organisations to criticise and purge their leaders. This suited Stalin, who saw the need for yet another set of purges – to weaken established provincial leaders, to further terrorise the party into obedience and to create spaces for the promotion of young and obedient careerists.

Mass terror and repression at central and local levels

Purges of the party, the military and the people

It should be noted that some people approved of, and took advantage of, the Terror. It gave some the opportunity to denounce their enemy or rival, even for petty reasons. It allowed yet another wave of younger Stalinists to progress to higher office. Some, if they were not affected and did not approve of the party, were glad to see it devouring itself.

Alongside the show trials, another set of purges (or *chistki*, as they were known) took place. Stalin continued to root out and settle scores with those who had opposed him in the party, particularly at the 17th Congress of 1934. Of the 139 Central Committee members elected at the Congress, 98 were eventually killed. More broadly, thousands more were removed from their posts. At the 18th Party Congress, held in March 1939, Stalin stated that 500 000 new recruits had taken up party and state posts. This indicates to some extent the number of positions that had been recently vacated. This has been referred to as 'the destruction of the Bolshevik party' – those original party members and veterans of the Civil War who remembered Stalin as an equal.

Apart from the party, Stalin also purged the military. A few figures had been implicated during the first show trial and faced charges at the second in 1937, including Muralov. Most prominent among the victims was Marshal Tuchachevski, Chief of the General Staff, who was openly critical of Stalin's military strategy, which he argued should be more ambitious. He had been a highly successful professional soldier and had built his reputation during the Civil War. Even though he had been a party member since 1918, his insistence on professional independence (characteristic of ex-tsarist officers leading the Red Army) did not fit well with Stalin. He was arrested, along with a number of other senior military men, in May 1937 and accused of Trotskyism and treason against the Red Army.

Key term

Yezhovshchina was the systematic campaign of mass terror organised by Nikolai Yezhov, head of the NKVD in 1937–1938.

They were shot in June. Further arrests and executions followed. The effect on the military command was dramatic: by December 1938, three of the five Marshals of the Soviet Union were dead, as were nearly all commanders, a handful of senior naval staff, around 60% of corps commanders and divisional commanders and half of brigade commanders.

The treatment of national minorities

Stalin began from the premise that nationalism was 'bourgeois' and ran counter to solidarity with the Soviet state. This is what had motivated him to act with such determination against his own countrymen in Georgia at the end of the Civil War. Lavrentiy Beria's eventual promotion to head of the NKVD also had some basis in his ruthless treatment of the Georgians (again his own countrymen) as chief of the OGPU, where he acted against nationalist dissent. Other notable national victims of Stalin were the Ukrainians and the Kazakhs. There was certainly a degree of resentment in Bolshevik circles against the Ukraine from Civil War days, but there is some doubt as to whether Stalin was actually engaged in 'genocide' as Hitler clearly was against the Jews. Ukranians suffered disproportionately through collectivisation, but mainly because of the concentration of good agricultural land targeted. It is also true that relief was withheld from the region during the famine of 1932–1933, but possibly only to (heartlessly) concentrate the shortages there to avoid a wider deficit of grain.

Stalin was also concerned with the Ukrainian communists themselves. In August 1932, he wrote that 'rotten elements will waste no time opening the front inside and outside the party'.[16] Kazakh nomads were forced to cultivate the soil in their region, even though this had never been their practice. This resulted in up to 1.8 million deaths. This suggests that while particular nationalities were affected by Stalin's policy, it is likely to have been in pursuit of an economic rather than ethnic goals.

From the summer of 1937, the Great Terror took on an ethnic aspect in the 'national sweeps' against East Europeans, Germans, Finns, Poles and those from the Baltic States. They were seen as potential spies of hostile powers to the west. Similarly, Koreans, Chinese and Afghans were also targeted as representing threats from the east. By February 1938, the 'national' campaigns constituted the majority of the NKVD's operations. How far intentional anti-Semitism played a role is debatable, but given the high representation of Jews at senior levels within Soviet organisations and those associated with foreign communist parties, a disproportionate number suffered.

Methods and extent of repression

The basic functioning of the Terror was identification of suspects, swift sentencing with no appeal and a fate which involved, in the main, deportation to a labour or prison camp or execution. A key aspect of generalised terror was the quotas sent out to each region. Stalin and Yezhov would simply declare that there was a general threat and then order the arrest of a certain number of individuals in each locality. This, of course, meant that the local NKVD was required to arrest this number, irrespective of any real threat. In practice, what often occurred was a request from local leaders to extend these quotas. This may have resulted from a desire to demonstrate loyalty or from the fact that they could easily identify a number of social 'undesirables' who could conveniently be removed. Denunciation was a very effective means of expanding the list of suspects. Those at particular risk were the acquaintances of professionals who owned card indexes (for example doctors). These provided ready lists for further arrests. Torture or 'physical methods' were part and parcel of the so-called 'meat grinder' – the conveyor-like system established by the NKVD that went from arrest to torture to confession to sentencing in one methodical process. Those responsible for sentencing were the *troiki*, three-man panels whose membership was confirmed by Stalin himself. Stalin played an essential role in the Terror, but a number of historians have emphasised the collusion and initiative of more junior officials.

The gulags

As explained, the network of prison camps established by the Cheka from 1918 were taken under the control of the Main Camp Administration (Gulag) in 1930. The term 'gulag' came to refer to any prison camp.

Putting a number on the victims of the Terror remains difficult. Documentary evidence suggests that up to 800 000 people were convicted under Order Number 00447 until it was rescinded in November 1938. Of these, 75 950 were put into 'category one' and executed, while 193 000 were put into 'category two' and given 8- to 10-year sentences. There is evidence that Stalin made a personal decision over categorisation for many of these.[17] Archives opened in the 1980s give a figure of 681 692 executions carried out during 1937 and 1938, which makes up over 85% of those executed under Stalin (1930–1953). The reality of these figures could be substantially higher given that there are no recorded results of local initiatives. This does not account for all deaths as a result of the Terror. Between 3.5 and 4 million people were officially recorded as being sent to labour camps, prison camps or into exile, but the figure may, in reality, have been much higher. The statistics of course do not account for the broader social disruption involved in mass terror.

The end of the purges and the fall of Yezhov

The 'Yezhovshchina' was a self-perpetuating process in which denunciation led to further denunciations. It was also a process through which perpetrators became victims. As early as October 1937, Stalin began to criticise the effect of mass arrests on industrial management. At the January plenum in 1938, the leadership condemned the 'heartless and bureaucratic attitude' of some and praised those officials who had reversed some convictions.[18] Order Number 00477 was, however, not rescinded until September 1938. Yezhov was removed from his post in December 1938 and reassigned to head the Commissariat for Water Transport. Beria took his place and began to build his own 'empire' within the NKVD apparatus. In April 1939, having whiled away his time ineffectually since his demotion, Yezhov was arrested and accused of framing innocent people, plotting to kill Stalin and being a British spy. He confessed quickly and denounced others, including members of his own family, and was shot in February 1940. (See also Figures 5.3a and 5.3b.) It is an unsurprising irony that the Terror consumed its prime administrator.

Figures 5.3a and 5.3b: The original photograph (top) shows Yezhov to the right of Stalin. In the doctored version (above) his proximity to Stalin has been wiped from the record.

The death of Trotsky

What could be regarded as the final episode in Stalin's elimination of all his living rivals was the NKVD's successful attempt to kill Trotsky in August 1940. Following his exile from the Soviet Union in 1929, Trotsky attempted to gain followers for his 'Fourth International', founded in 1938. Before settling in Mexico, he had lived briefly in Turkey and Norway. He drew some followers, mainly among the Western left. He published his anti-Stalinist arguments in his *Bulletin of the Opposition*. Despite his own record of inhumanity, he became a rallying figure for those on the left who rejected Stalinism and its 'bureaucratic' nature. His influence within the Soviet Union was, however, completely negligible.

There was nevertheless a whole department dedicated to assassinating Trotsky. Leonid Eitingon, whose assumed name in America was Leonov, headed the operation on the ground. The first attempt on Trotsky's life was in January 1938. The second was on 23 May 1940, by a group from the Mexican Communist Party, who successfully broke into Trotsky's villa and sprayed it with machine-gun fire, but Trotsky was only injured. The next attempt was successful: Ramón Mercader, a newly recruited agent, deliberately entered into a relationship with an American Trotskyite, Sylvia Ageloff, a trusted friend of the Trotsky household. Over a number of months Mercader gained Trotsky's confidence. On 20 August, on the premise of wanting Trotsky to look over an article he had written, Mercader took an ice pick from his coat pocket and plunged it into Trotsky's head. Mercader was arrested on the spot; Trotsky died the next day. The Kremlin denied all knowledge of Mercader, who was tried and jailed for the killing.

Responsibility for and impact of the Terror and purges

Who was responsible for the Terror? The main individuals involved are obviously the heads of the NKVD and Yezhov in particular, staff at various levels of the security apparatus, those Soviet citizens who engaged in denouncing their friends, family and strangers and, of course, Stalin himself, who enforced a climate of fear from the very top, as well as setting random targets for arrests which his subordinates were compelled to fulfil. The question of responsibility can of course be understood on the institutional as well as individual level. Within a totalitarian state, there was no guarantee of an individual's security and therefore the most likely human reaction was to avoid personal misfortune by inflicting it or diverting it to others.

There are a number of possible reasons why Stalin undertook the Terror and other associated repressive measures. Most of these can be boiled down to his need for personal and political control of the Soviet Union. They can perhaps be categorised in the following ways:

* gaining personal control
* transforming Soviet society
* ensuring the security of the Soviet regime.

Personal control

It seems fairly clear that paranoia played a major part in Stalin's thinking. He was methodical in removing those who had been his major political rivals and ultimately ensured that they were condemned to death. It also enabled him to divert blame on to others for economic failures and 'excesses' for which he bore ultimate responsibility. By co-opting a number of senior party colleagues into the prosecution of Terror, Stalin bound them to him. He could even test their loyalty by persecuting their relatives. Stalin held his closest colleagues to him by

The Terror is a complicated phenomenon to study because the nature of the purges appeared to change as time wore on. Go through your notes and make a list of who was purged, when they were purged, why they were purged and which element of society they formed a part of.

Should you wish to carry out extra research on the purges, a good place to start is *Life and Terror in Stalin's Russia, 1934–1941* (Yale University Press, 1996) by Robert W. Thurston.

fear, but more broadly ensured the conformity of the entire Soviet population by the exercise of arbitrary power. Propaganda and his personality cult clearly also played a role in achieving such despotism. Possibly the most obvious way in which he maintained control during these years was through attacking what he regarded as 'comfortable cliques' and swiftly promoting a new layer of young and obedient officials. As demonstrated, adulation and loyalty could result in temporary reward and promotion but be followed by scapegoating and elimination. In sum, Stalin manipulated and incriminated his colleagues – not even the most loyal were safe.

Transforming Soviet society

Apart from control, Stalin wished to transform Soviet society, both economically and socially. The Terror played a part in this. As well as ensuring conformity, it encouraged the mass of people to invest in an ideology that involved both optimistic idealism and what McDermott refers to as 'anti-bureaucratic, pseudo-populist campaigns of denunciation'.[19] In addition, by removing those elements he regarded as 'bourgeois', 'capitalist', 'fascist', 'intellectual' and 'Trotskyite', he may well have had the broad intention of making way for more trustworthy proletarian elements. As will be discussed, there is evidence to suggest that successive purges acted in some sense to advance social mobility. Finally, in his pursuit of creating 'socialist man', Stalin clearly believed, and indeed explicitly stated, that society was being 'cleansed' of those who were politically and socially undesirable. This, of course, invites parallels with National Socialism.

Securing the Soviet regime and state

Bound up with the above factors is the consideration of national security. Given the damage the purges did both to the Soviet Union's economic advance (in particular the crises of 1932–1933 and 1937–1938) and its military personnel, quite apart from the administrative difficulties created, the argument that Stalin undertook Terror in order to protect the country might seem surprising. There was, however, a constant theme in Stalin's rhetoric of protecting the Soviet Union from both foreign and internal threats. Particularly prominent was the threat that combined both in the spectre of the 'fifth column' or the 'enemy within'. The extent to which this was a genuine fear, rather than a useful and deliberately concocted illusion, is debatable. Nevertheless, it is reasonably clear that the threat of foreign intervention drove the industrialisation programme and motivated Stalin in his efforts. It became abundantly clear towards the end of the 1930s that the Soviet Union was prone to attack both from the West and the East. McDermott sees this clearly demonstrated during the 'February–March' plenum of 1937, where Stalin interjected in Yezhov's speech on the threat of wreckers: 'and he will save up his strength until the moment of war, when he will really do us a lot of harm'.[20]

Culture and society

The Church and religion

The Orthodox Church had been an integral part of Russian and Slavic identity. It had been responsible for primary education and the church calendar was closely intertwined with the agricultural year and changes in the seasons. Parish priests, portrayed in Soviet propaganda, along with rabbis and mullahs, as parasites living on the backs of the poor, were in fact often as poor as their neighbours. Bolshevik ideology defined religion as a means by which the old forces of tsarism and the bourgeois distracted, confused and controlled the proletariat. Rejecting the 'superstition' of religion was a necessary step for socialist 'enlightenment', which was supposedly based on scientific rationalism.

The League of the Militant Godless was an officially sanctioned organisation of atheists intent on destroying the influence of religion. They encouraged the destruction of church buildings, most famously the Church of Christ the Saviour in Moscow, or their conversion to non-religious uses such as for storing grain. In the early stages of collectivisation 'brigades' of volunteers turned up in villages and confiscated holy icons and burned them in bonfires before the horrified population. Church bells were broken up and sent off as raw material for industry. The theory was that without the church, or mosque or synagogue, villages would be less resistant to joining the collective and breaking with their former pattern of life. The Acting Patriarch of the Russian Orthodox Church, Sergei, who had assumed his responsibilities on the death of Tikhon in 1925, remained in constant fear of arrest although he acted to demonstrate the Church's loyalty to the Soviet state. He would eventually be made Patriarch of Moscow in 1943 when Stalin looked to the Church to help in maintaining the cohesion of a war-ravaged society.

Women, young people and working men

Industrialisation and communist ideology had a major impact on social structure and customs, but not as had been imagined by some early radicals. The early decrees of the Bolshevik regime had proclaimed women's equality with men, made divorce straightforward and immediately obtainable, and had legalised abortion. These constituted an assault on deeply entrenched traditional beliefs that had been challenged by (mainly urban) revolution. They could also be seen as part of the social rupture that occurred as a result of the Civil War. The industrialisation and collectivisation campaigns of 1928 onwards had a similar effect. The low wages of men and the communist rhetoric of sexual equality combined to drive many women into the labour force. In 1929, there were 3.3 million women employed in various sectors of the national economy; by 1935, there were 8 million. This can be viewed as the liberation of women (as suggested by the propaganda of strong female workers) only to a certain extent.

In 1931, in reaction to the social instability caused by economic policy, Stalin's 'Six Conditions' speech not only reintroduced a more traditional approach to education but also rowed back on the social liberalism of the 1920s. As part of the rejection of the egalitarianism of the early years of the first Five-Year Plan, abortion was to be restricted to cases where the mother's life was in danger, divorce was made more difficult to obtain, and a there was to be a renewed emphasis on the family as a basic social unit. The law of 1936 that banned abortions also introduced generous state allowances for each child and set about tripling the number of kindergartens by 1939. This was completely at odds with the thinking of the early to mid-1920s adopted by some radical communists. They had viewed the destruction of the family unit as a basic precursor to transition to communism.

The reality, it could be argued, was that Stalin accepted that a more conservative social model would enable both survival and stabilisation. A *Pravda* article of

9 June 1936 stated, 'The Soviet marriage … is not built on private property. Nor is it simply a legal formality for satisfying sexual desires. [It] opens up the truly spiritual side of marriage, its moral beauty, which is beyond the reach of capitalist society… To strengthen and develop the Soviet family is one of the main tasks of democracy.'[21] Women arguably suffered as a result: they were expected both to perform their duties as mother and housewife and to go out to work (where they faced sexual harassment and lower wages); the so-called 'dual burden'. All this said, women had access to the professions as well as the factory floor, and some made progress within the administrative hierarchy. Following Russian tradition, women were an integral, if minor, part of the Soviet infantry and other military services during the Second World War.

Working men

In comparison with women's dual burden, the life of a working man under Stalin might be regarded as easier. The reassertion of a more traditional, family-centred outlook meant that chauvinistic attitudes regarding women's work and men's leisure retained their place within Soviet society. This was an era of full employment, although it is important to note that much of the rapid construction work was undertaken by a class of mobile labourers, part of the movement from countryside to town, who would work on one project and move to the next. In addition, despite the abundance of work, its context was one of fanatical Stakhanovism on the one hand and disillusion as a result of unrealistic targets and consequent waste on the other. As trades unions were merely there to enforce the will of the party, there was no official way to air grievances. The growing stratification of Soviet society and the promotion of technical experts and managers meant that the early image of the heroic working man stood alongside a reality of the subservient labourer who kept his head down.

Young people

Besides the reforms to education, the young were specifically targeted by the Soviet regime to be a generation raised with no memory of capitalism and thus placed to be the vanguard, advancing towards communism and the creation of a new 'socialist man'. Chief organisations created to achieve this were the Pioneers, for children aged 7 to 13, and the Komsomol (the Young Communist League), for those in their teens and early 20s. All-Union versions of these organisations had been established in 1922. The clearest parallel in the West was the scouting movement. Their activities and rituals were comparable: military-style uniforms and ceremonies (see Figure 5.4, for example), solemn oaths of loyalty, outdoor pursuits and services to the community. In this respect they were used to idealistically further the aims of the party, including assistance with collectivisation. Membership was not compulsory, but was clearly a means to advancement, particularly into higher education. As previously mentioned, the idealism of youth was made use of in the great industrial projects. These provided adventure and freedom for young men and women, despite long hours and dangerous working conditions.

Figure 5.4: Commissar Kliment Voroshilov meeting Komsomol members in 1935.

Control through culture

If Soviet society was transformed by industrialisation, collectivisation and terror, then an integral part of all these processes was propaganda. As with other 'totalitarian' regimes, there was an expectation that the party's ideology would be suffused into all aspects of life, economic, political and cultural. This was primarily about social control, but for communist ideologues, it was also about recreating humanity. The extent to which Stalin really succeeded in creating a new 'socialist man' is highly questionable, but it is arguably the case that Soviet society was changed by the 1930s. Early propaganda and Soviet cultural movements were associated with the avant-garde and modernism. Some of this 'revolutionary' imagery remained, particularly in the promotion of the Five-Year Plans. The most striking aspect of Stalin's direction of culture, however, is the swing towards a cultural and social conservatism that coincided with the abandonment of the classlessness of the first Five-Year Plan. This was viewed by anti-communist critics as the 'Great Retreat'. Its origins are traced back to a speech given by Stalin in June 1931, known as the 'Six Conditions' speech, which attacked the experimentalism of cultural revolution during the preceding years.

Education and social mobility

As with the arts, early Soviet ideologues looked to abolish institutions and customs that represented and instilled bourgeois ways of thinking. The People's Commissariat for Enlightenment, under Lunacharsky since 1917, had promoted a culture that was distinctly modern and broke with the bourgeois past. Bubnov replaced Lunacharsky in September 1929; he looked to abandon formal schooling in favour of learning through 'productive labour'. This was in step with the spirit of the first Five-Year Plan, with its attack on unreliable 'bourgeois specialists' and its promotion of proletarian (working-class) culture. This opposition to formal schooling was, however, short-lived. Investment in education was substantial: in 1927 there were 1.8 million pupils at secondary schools; by 1934, there were 5.9 million; and by 1939, there were 12 million. By 1941 there were 199 000 secondary schools.

In 1932, technical training was reorganised and there was a greater emphasis on theory and examinations. Degrees were reintroduced in 1934 and fees were introduced for secondary education, which put a check on social mobility and favoured the promotion of the sons and daughters of the administrative class. With the turn towards hierarchy and authority, schooling became traditional in style but served the purpose of promoting Soviet ideology. The history curriculum, for example, emphasised great Russian leaders of the past, such as Ivan the Terrible and Peter the Great, and emphasised chronology, most especially dates in the official Stalinist version of Soviet history.

The most notable and irrefutable advance made under Stalin was a dramatic improvement of literacy. This was an essential part of communicating the party's message. The party's newspapers *Pravda* and *Izvestiya* were cheaply available, as were many works of literature. The promotion of reading and writing was at the heart of Soviet ideology. It was one of the main methods by which 'Old Russia' would be modernised and a new way of thinking established. Mass literacy campaigns were undertaken so that by 1939, 94% of males between the ages of 9 and 49 were able to read and write. This was more than double the figure at the beginning of the 20th century.

Urban and rural differences

The gradual recovery of industry under NEP and the subsequent rushed industrialisation saw a process of migration opposite to that which had happened under 'war communism' during the Civil War. Even before collectivisation and industrialisation there is evidence of millions of peasants migrating to urban centres. From 1928, rapid industrialisation became the foremost 'pull factor' bringing inexperienced peasants onto construction sites and into factories for work. From late 1929, collectivisation, fixed state prices for grain and dekulakisation became decisive 'push factors' swelling migration from countryside to industrial centres.

Rural life underwent renewed crisis. As Wheatcroft and Davies put it, 'Soviet peasantry was at one and the same moment hurled into a much more mechanised agriculture and into a social system analogous with serfdom'.[22] Quite apart from the hunger and poverty created through this initially chaotic process, centuries-old forms of agriculture were overturned and the highly prized self-reliance (and the means for independent survival) of the Russian peasant was seriously disrupted. The enforced resettlement of millions of 'kulaks' and consequent loss of experience and expertise, the pre-emptive slaughter of cattle, the reluctance to sow a crop which would only be confiscated and the forced settlement of nomad peoples resulted in famine by 1933.

The connection between this period of rural chaos and increased urban settlement is noticeable. In 1933 internal passports were introduced in an attempt to stem the flow and rural to urban migration dropped by over two-thirds. Yet in the following years the rate returned to approximately 2.5 million a year. In all, between 1926 and 1939, the urban population more than doubled (from 26.3 to 56.1 million). About a fifth of this came from natural growth, and another fifth from reclassification of rural land. However, the remainder had come from the countryside. Despite the promise of higher pay, existence for many migrant workers was precarious. Many former peasants ended up as migrant workers, moving from project to project rather than settling in one place.

It is important to note that some, especially the new official government class, enjoyed an improved quality of life during the 1930s. Whatever the political restrictions, and despite a failure to improve the majority of housing stock, those living an urban life, particularly in prestigious centres, could afford a more comfortable existence than would have existed for the majority prior to the revolution. Even the collective farms, once the process had stabilised, provided a greater range of facilities than had existed in the old commune.

'Socialist man' and the impact of cultural change

As stated, the 1930s saw a transformation of Soviet society. The ideological principles behind the intended change were modernisation of a 'backward' society and the formation of a new 'socialist person'. The ideal is described deftly by McDermott as 'modern', 'clean living' and 'cultured' in outlook, rational in deed, untainted by 'bourgeois' egotistical motivations or religious sentiments and, above all, 'collectivist in spirit and dedicated to state goals'.[23] One can question the extent to which this was achieved throughout the population. Peasants remained overwhelmingly negative about Stalin following collectivisation. Many national groups were attacked and their cultures to some extent subsumed by a Russo-centric Kremlin. Traditional religious life was certainly diminished. Women's roles changed but not necessarily wholly to their benefit. It can be argued that the young, who had known nothing else, were most fully converted. Industrialisation and collectivisation had fundamentally altered the balance of urban to rural life.

National cultures

What is true is that Russian culture did generally become more dominant across the Soviet Union during the 1920s. With the sending out of officials and volunteers to the peripheries, Russians had a greater presence in each of the Soviet republics than had previously been the case. The Russian language became compulsory as a taught subject. Urbanisation and the promotion of literacy also led to an acquaintance with, or adoption of, Russian. Although local languages were not banned, the lingua franca in the centralised state was Russian and the Uzbek language, for example, was no longer to be written in Arabic script but in a Cyrillic version. Despite occasional propaganda that portrayed Stalin as a father to a multitude of united peoples, the new 'Soviet' identity was firmly based in Russian culture and past examples, at a suitable historical distance from Nicholas II, were held up as totems of Russian resistance with the onset of war.

Similarities and differences between Lenin's and Stalin's USSR

The debate around the possible comparison of the Soviet Union under Lenin and Stalin centres on whether the seeds of the dictatorship that Stalin had created by

ACTIVITY 5.2

Historians have much debated the key similarities and differences between life under Lenin's rule and Stalin's over the years. Go through the notes you have made so far and draw a table to help organise your thoughts. Compare each of these points for Lenin and Stalin:

- Economic conditions in towns
- Economic conditions in the countryside
- Political freedoms and restrictions
- Social freedoms and restrictions.

1941 were sown under Lenin's regime. This was particularly important in historical scholarship at moments of reform within the Soviet Union and improved relations with the Western powers. Soviet propaganda under *glasnost*, for example, certainly suggested that reform could be based on a return to Lenin's original vision.

There is evidence to suggest that Lenin simply would not have considered Stalin's methods as acceptable, not least the way in which Stalin dealt with his senior comrades and the party as a whole. While Lenin was clearly responsible for instigating methods of terror against the population, it is questionable whether he would have accepted the same method within the party. Arguably, he would not have allowed a normalisation of terror to the degree that Stalin did. Lenin's modus operandi within the party was to argue, often bitterly, with his colleagues to get his way, but it was not to murder them. This stated, it was he who urged the ban on factions in 1921, which served as the basis for subsequent expulsions and purges.

It is also questionable whether Lenin would have accepted the degree of social conservatism and hierarchy that formed the basis of Stalinism – this is, however, more a matter of speculation. Lenin certainly placed the survival of the Communist regime above every other consideration. Stalin converted this into the survival of his own personal power and was prepared to face serious economic reverses and own-goals to maintain it (such as the purging of the military's High Command, and of crucial economic agents such as specialists and experienced farmers). Despite this, the Soviet Union was transformed, economically and socially, by 1941. McDermott describes what Stalin created as a 'militarised étatist [statist] "barracks socialism" that bore few similarities to the more libertarian … and egalitarian tenets of Marx, even Lenin'.[24]

To emphasise the obvious, Lenin departed the scene with very many matters unresolved, particularly the questions of party democracy, the position of the peasantry within a workers' state and rapid versus gradual industrialisation. Stalin's solution to these questions was brutal but arguably decisive. By 1941, despite the very many weaknesses and social fractures that existed, the Soviet Union had consolidated its position. Its industry and technology could match that of the capitalist West and its society was literate and motivated by a founding myth and practical ideology. In 1924, the Soviet Union was sufficiently weak to be ignored. By the end of the 1930s, despite the catastrophe that lay ahead, it was a major player within international diplomacy and had established the foundations necessary to counter a real, rather than imagined, foreign threat.

Stalin and international relations: Soviet foreign policy

The international situation in 1928

By the mid-1920s, the Soviet Union could be regarded as having been internationally isolated. In 1927, Baldwin's Conservative government in Britain annulled the Anglo-Soviet trade agreement and broke off diplomatic relations. The French government remained hostile. Mussolini had established a fascist government in Italy. The Locarno Treaties, negotiated in October 1925, made between the victors of the First World War and the states of eastern and central Europe (including Germany), had defined Europe's new borders and paved the way for Germany's admission to the League of Nations. The Weimar regime in Germany had by this point regained a measure of stability and sought integration into the new international system established by the Western Allies. Germany's reconciliation with the West and agreements with the Soviet Union's western neighbours led Stalin to fear the formation of an anti-Soviet coalition led by Britain and France.

Cooperation with Germany

In simple terms, the 1930s can be characterised, with hindsight, as a time of complacency and a drift towards another Europe-based global conflict. Central to this idea is the failure of Britain and France to recognise the threat posed by Hitler and the weakness demonstrated by the League of Nations in failing to check the expansionist ambitions of Germany, Japan and Italy (who would become to be known as the Axis powers). Russia's responsibility for the growing crisis is mixed. On the one hand, Litvinov pursued a policy of 'collective security' against Germany and was in favour of upholding the Treaty of Versailles. To this end, the Soviet Union made several new non-aggression pacts, similar to those made in 1926, with Finland, Latvia, Estonia and Poland in early 1932 and with France in November of that year. Despite these agreements with the likely enemies of Germany, the Soviet Union maintained its relationship of military and trade cooperation with the Weimar regime (as Germany had been referred to since the establishment of its post-First World War republic). This included a trade agreement in June 1931 which extended the Treaty of Berlin of 1926. Stalin, however, remained cautious and became wary of the attitude of Chancellor Franz von Papen, whom he suspected of making overtures to the French at the Lausanne Conference in June 1932. The appointment of Hitler as Chancellor on 30 January 1933 led to the suppression of the German Communist Party (KPD) and Germany's withdrawal from the League of Nations in October.

Entry into the League of Nations

In September 1934, the Soviet Union belatedly joined the League of Nations. This was part of Litvinov's shift towards 'collective security', mainly against the threat from Nazi Germany. He had started this before Hitler's rise to power, but began to look to integrate the Soviet Union more fully into the international diplomatic system. In November 1933, Litvinov visited the recently elected President Roosevelt in Washington. At this point it was clear that the international system was under pressure. Capitalism itself had suffered a major blow to its standing because of the Wall Street crash and the consequent Depression (which had resulted in Roosevelt's election in late 1932). The credibility of the League was being undermined by its inability to deal with challenges from Japan (in Manchuria), Germany and eventually Italy in Abyssinia. Collective security fitted with the Comintern's developing strategy of the 'Popular Front' of left parties against fascism. While the Politburo backed Litvinov, Stalin remained quietly wary, always wishing to keep his options open. Another military deal was made with Germany in 1934. Stalin retained his suspicion of Britain and France.

Speak like a historian

The Anglo-Soviet trade agreement

The Anglo-Soviet trade agreement was signed in 1921. It was significant in that it gave the Russian Soviet Federative Socialist Republic (RSFSR) recognition by one of the most powerful capitalist countries at the time. By 1924 Britain was seeking to distance itself, however, after the British press had published a letter supposedly from Communist International (Comintern) (Grigori Zinoviev, no less) calling for communist revolution in Britain.

Pacts with France, Britain and Czechoslovakia

The Soviet Union's attempt to create an 'Eastern Locarno' (similar in ambition to the Locarno Treaty of 1925 which sought to provide stability in Western Europe) of non-aggression pacts against Germany was only partially successful, particularly as Britain and France remained lukewarm in this regard. Litvinov made some progress in May 1935 when he succeeded in making an alliance with France and, two weeks later, with Czechoslovakia. However, these arrangements did not include substantial military agreements. One of the reasons the French had agreed to an alliance was Hitler's increasingly obvious disregard for the Treaty of Versailles, including rearmament and conscription, which were specifically forbidden under the terms of the treaty.

Allegations of 'appeasement' are easily levelled at Britain and France. Both powers courted Mussolini rather than Stalin in order to guard against Hitler. This was ultimately unsuccessful and did not prevent Hitler's remilitarisation of the Rhineland in March 1936, which broke the Locarno Treaty. Much of British political opinion by this point viewed the Treaty of Versailles as having been too harsh. Hitler's anti-communist regime was even seen as a safeguard against Soviet communism. Léon Blum's 'popular front' socialist government in France was more sympathetic to Moscow, but broke apart as a result of internal disagreements over involvement in the Spanish Civil War.

Intervention in the Spanish Civil War

In July 1936, Nationalist officers, led by Francisco Franco, rebelled against the newly formed centre-left Republican coalition government in Madrid. They received support from much of the army and from the conservative Roman Catholic Church in Spain. The result was a Civil War that reflected the division in global politics during the 1930s of far left and far right. It became the international crucible of the struggle between socialism and fascism. As a result, the two sides received military assistance from their respective ideological counterparts. Hitler and Mussolini provided substantial aid to the Nationalists, most notoriously bombing the civilian population of Guernica in April 1937. The Soviet Union's aid to the Republic did not match that of the fascist powers to Franco, but it did provide tanks, aircraft, armoured vehicles, guns and ammunition as well as food and military advisers to the tune of £88 million.[25] Alongside this, it sponsored

Comintern

Comintern (the abbreviation for the organisation 'Communist International') was founded in 1919 in Moscow, against the backdrop of the Russian Civil War. Lenin had dominated the organisation even though Grigori Zinoviev had been Chair until 1926. Its aim was, by all available means including armed force, to overthrow the international bourgeoisie and create an international Soviet republic as a transition stage to the complete abolition of the state. Stalin dissolved it in June 1943 because he recognised that his allies suspected him of trying to bring about revolution in Europe.

the anti-fascist International Brigades made up of volunteer socialists and communists from around the world.

The British and French governments steadfastly refused to assist the Spanish Republican government against Franco and his fascist allies. Indeed, Britain had made a naval agreement with Nazi Germany in 1935 to allow it to expand its navy to 35% of the size of the British fleet. This suggests a greater unease about the progress of Soviet allies in Europe. The Soviet Union support for the socialist cause in Spain was, however, less than steadfast. Not only did they charge the Republican government for their assistance, but they made their aid to the communist-dominated government dependent on their opposing Trotskyist and anarchist elements, who made up a substantial part of the forces ranged against Franco. This resulted in fighting between pro-Stalinist government forces and Trotskyist anarchists in Barcelona in 1937, in which the latter were defeated. This internal struggle between forces on the left, promoted by Stalin, weakened the effort against Franco's Nationalists. Apart from wishing to counter the anti-Stalinist left at the expense of socialist victory, Stalin was also anxious to moderate the Republican government in order to prevent Britain and France doing a deal with Hitler. Given their seemingly relaxed attitude to Hitler's contravention of the Treaty of Versailles, this is perhaps understandable.

Reaction to Western appeasement and Japanese aggression

The Chinese province of Manchuria was situated directly west of Japan, north of Beijing and the Korean Peninsula, south of Siberia and east of Mongolia. The final leg of the Trans-Siberian Railway ran over the top of Manchuria and then headed south to Vladivostok, the Soviet Union's easternmost port. The Eastern Railway had been built through the middle of Manchuria, making the diversion over its 'top' unnecessary. The Soviet Union had a complicated and poorly managed relationship with the rival Chinese Nationalist Kuomintang under Chiang Kai-shek and the Chinese Communist Party.

In the spring of 1929, Zhang Xueliang, an ally of Chiang Kai-shek, seized the Eastern Railway, which had been under joint Chinese-Soviet control. This prompted the Soviet Union to intervene with a Far Eastern Army in August. Both sides eventually agreed to talks in October 1930. This prompted Japan, which sought influence in the region, to invade Manchuria in September 1931. It set up its own government of 'Manchukou', as it referred to the province. The Soviet Union reacted by looking to restore its links with the Kuomintang, having failed to create a non-aggression pact with the Japanese. Chiang Kai-shek did not prove a reliable ally of the Soviet Union, refusing to act against the Japanese in Manchuria and instead fighting against the Chinese communists.

The Soviet Union attempted to revive the nationalist-communist coalition of the 1920s while seeking to appease the Japanese, selling the Eastern Railway to Manchukuo in March 1935. This was, however, ineffective, as Japan signed the 'Anti-Comintern Pact' with Germany in November 1936. The Soviet Union was faced with the prospect of a war on two fronts. In July 1937, Japan launched a full-scale invasion of China, which resulted in renewed cooperation between the Soviets and the Chinese Nationalists. The Red Army defeated Manchukuo forces in August 1939, but the Imperial Japanese forces constituted a continuing threat as they expanded further in the next few years (see Figure 5.5, for example).

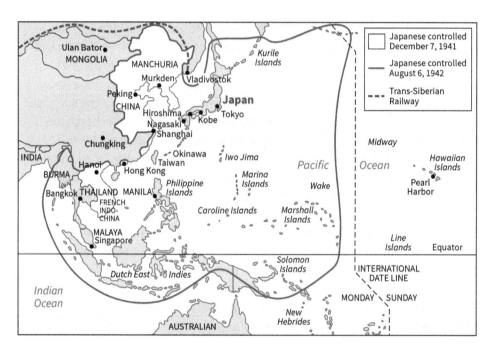

Figure 5.5: Japanese expansion 1941–1942.

The British and French attempts to check Hitler's expansionist ambitions were ineffective. Following the remilitarisation of the Rhineland in 1936, they acquiesced in the *Anschluss* (joining) of Austria with Germany in March 1938 and Hitler was therefore encouraged in his ambition of incorporating the ethnically German Sudetenland, part of Czechoslovakia, into his expanding Reich. Litvinov offered to activate the Franco-Czech-Soviet treaty and guarantee Czechoslovak independence, but Poland refused to allow the Red Army through its territory. Suspicious of their supposed saviour, the Polish preferred to fight alone rather than risk Soviet occupation. At the Munich Conference in September the British and French governments permitted Hitler to occupy the Sudetenland, on the understanding that he would claim no more territory. In March 1939, Hitler broke this promise and occupied the remainder of Czechoslovakia. Britain then made a military alliance with Poland to guarantee its independence from Germany.

The following months saw talks between Britain, France and the Soviet Union regarding Poland's security. The British and French were aware that any realistic plan to defend Poland would have to involve the Soviet Union. In April, the Soviet Union offered such an alliance which would involve defending the sovereignty of all the states that lay between Germany and the Soviet Union, from the Baltic to the Mediterranean. The British and French remained cautious. First, the Polish would have nothing to do with an agreement with the Soviet Union. Second, the British and French did not believe Soviet forces capable of carrying out such a guarantee. While the negotiations took place over the summer, the above factors prevented agreement.

The Nazi-Soviet Pact of 1939 and its outcome

Litvinov's attempt at 'collective security' had failed, and Molotov replaced him on 3 May 1939. Believing France and Britain to be unreliable, Stalin kept his options open regarding Germany and Italy. His overwhelming concern, given that European war seemed very likely, was to ensure the security of the Soviet border. Germany had begun to signal to the Soviet Union from April that a deal might be possible to achieve this goal. Molotov's appointment was seen as somewhat of a positive response. Litvinov's policy had been clearly aimed at winning over Britain and France to oppose Germany. In addition, he was Jewish. Molotov, on the other hand, was seen as reliably close to Stalin. The Soviet Union was experiencing pressure from Japanese forces on its eastern border.

Following the break-up of talks with Britain and France, Stalin turned to a radical solution to relieve the threat in the west. On 23 August 1939, it was announced that Molotov had negotiated a non-aggression pact with Ribbentrop, Germany's Foreign Minister. The 'Nazi-Soviet Pact' not only meant that neither power would fight each other, but also secretly agreed to the partition of Eastern Europe (see Figure 5.6). Germany would be allowed to occupy Lithuania and western Poland and the Soviet Union would be allowed to occupy eastern Poland, Estonia, Finland, Latvia and the north-east of Romania, known as Bessarabia. An agreement between two parties so clearly ideologically opposed might seem surprising. It is perhaps best understood as a temporary solution for both Nazi Germany and the Soviet Union. Stalin was desperate to secure his western border. Hitler was anxious to prevent an effective alliance between the Soviet Union, Britain and France, and to gain a free hand in Poland. The deal probably had no bearing on Hitler's long-term ambition to invade the Soviet Union and destroy Bolshevism. It is difficult to see how Stalin could have expected the deal to last. Conscious of the likelihood of eventual hostilities and the outbreak of more general conflict, the Nazi-Soviet Pact is most simply understood as a temporary convenience for both sides.

On 1 September 1939 Hitler invaded Poland. Britain and France, though unable to give any real assistance to Poland, declared war on Germany two days later. On 17 September, the Soviet Union invaded eastern Poland, capturing 200 000 Polish troops and ending resistance by the end of the month. The Soviet Union then

ACTIVITY 5.3

Go back to Activity 4.6 and add new information from this chapter to the table.

fought a bitter campaign against Finland from November 1939 to March 1940, in order to secure Leningrad and Murmansk against a possible invasion. This 'Winter War' was very costly and demonstrated the damage that had been done to the Soviet military by the purges. The Red Army then proceeded to occupy Estonia, Latvia and Lithuania by June 1940, as German forces moved north and west into Scandinavia and France. The three Baltic states were made into Soviet Socialist Republics and Romanian territory was shared between the Ukrainian SSR and a newly created Moldavian SSR.

Figure 5.6: Soviet annexations following the Nazi-Soviet Pact of 1939.

Further reading

Robert Conquest deals with mass repression in great detail in *The Great Terror: A Reassessment* (Pimlico, 2008), as does Robert W. Thurston's *Life and Terror in Stalin's Russia, 1934–1941* (Yale University Press, 1998). Simon Sebag Montefiore's *Stalin: The Court of the Red Tsar* (Weidenfeld & Nicolson, 2010) is an enjoyable and highly readable biography of Stalin and all aspects of his regime. The international context of the 1930s is covered effectively in Robert Service's *Comrades: Communism: A World History* (Pan, 2008).

Practice essay questions

1. 'Stalin's main reason for undertaking the purges and the Great Terror was the defence of the Soviet Union.' Assess the validity of this view.
2. 'Comintern failed to achieve its objectives because it was too tied to the needs of the Soviet Union.' Assess the validity of this view.
3. 'By the end of the 1930s, Stalin had remade Soviet society in his own image.' Assess the validity of this view.
4. With reference to the sources below and your understanding of the historical context, assess the value of the three sources to a historian studying the Great Terror.

Source A

Vyacheslav Molotov, member of the Politburo, writing in his memoirs (a conversation with Felix Chuev) (in Boobbyer, P., *The Stalin Era*, p. 75).

Let us assume [Stalin] made mistakes. But name someone who made fewer mistakes. Of all the people involved in historic events, who held the most correct position? Given all the shortcomings of the leadership of that time, [Stalin] alone coped with the tasks then confronting the country … 1937 was necessary. Bear in mind that after the revolution we slashed right and left; we scored victories but tattered enemies of various stripes survived, and as we were faced by the growing danger of fascist aggression, they might have united.

Source B

A request sent by the Irkutsk (Siberia) party leadership to Stalin and Yezhov on 25 August 1938 (in Boobbyer, P., *The Stalin Era*, p. 77).

In view of the as yet unfinished purge of the oblast [region] of right-Trotskyite white-guardist panmongol, counter-revolutionary hostile elements, residents of Kharbin, SRs, kulaks of the first category, we request the TsKVKP [Central Committee of the Communist Party] to extend by the limit by 5 thousand people in the first category for the Irkutsk oblast.

Source C

A communication of the Central Committee of the Communist Party to regional party organisations, January 1938 (in Boobbyer, P., *The Stalin Era*, pp. 77–78).

There have been many instances of party organisations, without any verification and thus without any basis, expelling Communists from the party, depriving them of their jobs, frequently even declaring them enemies of the people without any foundation, acting flawlessly and arbitrarily toward party members.

Taking it further

Having reviewed your study of the Soviet Union during the 1930s, consider how you might qualify, change or extend this short paragraph:

Stalin's method of rule was self-defeating. His political priorities were completely at odds with his economic ones. While claiming to want to build a strong socialist fatherland, he failed to prepare it for war because of poor diplomacy and mismanagement.

 Chapter summary

Having studied this chapter you should be able to:

- establish the reasons for terror and dictatorship
- trace the development of the methods of totalitarian control
- define the impact of totalitarianism on Soviet society and culture
- identify the key principles of Soviet foreign policy and the reasons for going to war.

End notes

1 Service, R., *The Penguin History of Modern Russia: From Tsarism to the Twenty-First Century*, p. 210.

2 McDermott, K., *Stalin*, p. 96.

3 Ibid, p. 96.

4 Ibid, p. 110.

5 Ibid, pp. 109–110.

6 Gill, G., *Stalinism*, p. 31.

7 Ibid, p. 30.

8 McDermott, *Stalin*.

9 Service, *The Penguin History of Modern Russia*, p. 212.

10 McDermott, *Stalin*, p. 98.

11 Service, *Penguin History of Modern Russia*, p. 210.

12 Ward, C., *Stalin's Russia*, p. 110.

13 Ibid, p. 112.

14 Ibid, p. 116.

15 Cited in McDermott, *Stalin,* p. 88.

16 McDermott, *Stalin,* p. 83.

17 Ibid*,* p. 102.

18 Ward, *Stalin's Russia*, pp. 118–119.

19 McDermott, *Stalin*, p. 108.

20 Ibid, p. 105.

21 Cited in Boobbyer, P., *The Stalin Era*, p. 157.

22 Davies, R.W., Harrison, M. and Wheatcroft, S.G., *The Economic Transformation of The Soviet Union 1913-1945*, p. 68.

23 McDermott, *Stalin*, p. 80.

24 Ibid, p. 76.

25 Ward, *Stalin's Russia*, p. 164.

6 The Great Patriotic War and Stalin's dictatorship, 1941–1953

In this section we will investigate how the Soviet Union experienced the Second World War and explore its legacy. This involves consideration of:

- the impact of war on the Soviet Union: Operation Barbarossa and the Stalinist reaction; the course of the war; the USSR under occupation and the fight-back; the Soviet economy; mobilisation and evacuation of industry; foreign aid

- the defeat of Germany: reasons and results; post-war reconstruction; industry and agriculture

- High Stalinism: dictatorship and totalitarianism; renewed terror; the NKVD under Beria; Zhdanovism and the cultural purge; Stalin's cult of personality; the Leningrad affair; purges and the Doctors' Plot

- the transformation of the Soviet Union's international position: the emergence of a 'superpower'; the formation of the Soviet Bloc; conflict with the United States and the capitalist West; Stalin's death and his legacy at home and abroad.

Introduction

In some senses, the Soviet Union was more prepared for war than many of the other combatants. It had a centralised command and propaganda structure, both political and economic, which enabled it to react quickly to the necessities of war and mobilise and deploy its population, three times the size of that of the German Reich, for those purposes. The Soviet Union's industrial capacity was also much greater and the third Five-Year Plan had been adapted in favour of armaments production. On the other hand, the purging of the officer corps, Stalin's conviction that Hitler would not attack in 1941 and the consequent failure to prepare meant that when Hitler did attack on 22 June 1941 the Soviet Union experienced dramatic early losses of men, industry and territory. Twenty million Soviet citizens, soldiers and civilians, were killed in what became known as the Great Patriotic War.

Needless to say, the war had a major impact on Soviet society, but in the main acted to consolidate Stalin's position and, indeed, promote his image as its indisputable and indispensable leader. Some hoped that the limited degree of political, economic and cultural tolerance that had existed out of necessity during the war would lead to a moderated form of control; however, it became quickly apparent that this was not to be. Following the war, Stalin re-imposed peacetime terror and cultural conformity. Although Stalin was 67 years old by 1945 and died only eight years later, the post-war years were critical in defining international politics and the geopolitical balance for the remainder of the 20th century.

The impact of the war on the Soviet Union

Operation Barbarossa and the Stalinist reaction

It would be entirely inaccurate to state that Stalin did not expect invasion from the West. The great motivating factor behind his actions and policies during the 1930s was a fear of foreign threats to the Soviet Union. Stalin felt isolated within European diplomacy and was, perhaps with reason, highly sceptical of French and British motives. For this reason, even up to early 1941, when it was clear that Western Europe was defeated, he continued supplying Germany with essential materiel for its war. Kevin McDermott has suggested that Stalin did not think Hitler would strike east until he had defeated or reached an agreement with Great Britain.[1] There was seemingly an expectation that fighting, when it broke out, would follow some form of diplomatic crisis (such as that which preceded the invasion of Poland in 1939) and that the Red Army would be able to quickly push back any invading force and fight on enemy territory.

By early June 1941, it seemed as though Stalin believed Hitler's attack would not come that year. Stalin was keen to avoid provocation and possibly for this reason made little protest about German reconnaissance flights over Soviet territory. Nevertheless, Stalin received intelligence both from the NKVD and from Britain informing him that the Germans were preparing an invasion. Stalin remained distrustful of the British. Perhaps he did not change his mind because his policy was not focused on preparing for imminent war; for instance, earthworks and fortresses had not been built and armaments factories had not been moved to the

Key term

State Committee for Defence: This body was created in June 1941 following the German invasion of the Soviet Union and put in overall charge of the Soviet war effort with Stalin at its head.

safety of the east. The army was in the middle of redeploying its forces and the frontiers were relatively lightly manned. It was these circumstances, as well as his awareness of a purged officer corps, which made Hitler so keen to act. The name of the invasion, 'Operation Barbarossa', referred to Friedrich Barbarossa, the 12th-century Germanic Holy Roman Emperor.

The German invasion begins: catastrophe

In the early morning of 22 June 1941, 150 divisions of the Wehrmacht supported by 5000 aircraft invaded the Soviet Union along the entirety of its western border. This was 'blitzkrieg' on the largest scale yet. It involved a rapid advance of armoured divisions, supported by air attack, which was then consolidated by the slower-moving infantry. Stalin apparently could not believe the news and for a while continued to believe this was merely 'provocation'. This meant the German forces proceeded without resistance until he gave the order to fight back at 6.30 a.m., a full three hours after he had learned of the attack. So unprepared were the four divisions that many soldiers had not been issued with ammunition.

During the following week Stalin became furiously busy, attempting to organise some kind of response. A main headquarters was established, as had occurred at the outbreak of the First World War. Stalin insisted that German forces should be immediately repulsed through attacks that had no hope of succeeding. Soviet forces lacked effective communications, and commanders in the field found themselves unable to speak either to headquarters or to the front line.

The Soviet Air Force was thinly spread and reserve squadrons stood lined up, without camouflage, conveniently arranged for destruction by the Luftwaffe. After five days of what Richard Overy calls his 'personal battle with reality',[2] Stalin retreated to his dacha (country house) on the outskirts of Moscow. By this point, Minsk in Belarus had already fallen. When members of the Politburo came to see Stalin on 30 June, he responded in a way that suggested he thought they might arrest him. Quite to the contrary, they had decided on establishing a **State Committee for Defence** to run the war and requested that he should become its chief. The following day Stalin returned to Moscow and on 3 July he addressed the Soviet people on the radio, calling on them to undertake a total war on the treacherous Germans and leave them nothing but a 'wasteland' to conquer. In characteristic fashion, he declared war on Russia's enemies, both external and internal. His rhetoric was purposefully nationalistic. *Pravda* had already referred to the conflict as 'the Fatherland war'.

Stalin did not wish to be popularly associated with the ongoing military failure. This perhaps explains why Molotov was given the task of announcing the German invasion himself, several days before Stalin made his address. His approach remained true to form: blaming his commanders for their failure to stem the enemy's advance, and demoting, arresting or shooting them for betrayal. The NKVD took the declaration of war to be a licence for renewed terror and inhumanity. In hasty retreats, prisoners were summarily executed and, somewhat less explicably, tortured and mutilated. Dual political and military control of fighting units was reintroduced (which meant that every unit had a political officer to enforce loyalty to the party), the western Soviet Union was declared to be under martial law and labour conscription was introduced.

Speak like a historian

The Nazi-Soviet Pact

The Nazi-Soviet Pact (sometimes referred to as the Molotov-Ribbentrop Pact, from the names of the ministers responsible) was signed between Germany and the Soviet Union on 23 August 1939. Under the terms of the pact both countries promised neutrality, should the other side become involved in a war. The pact included a secret protocol that divided the territories of Estonia, Finland, Lithuania, Latvia, Poland and Romania into German and Soviet 'spheres of influence', which anticipated the carving up of these countries later.

In the first month of the war, 319 units were sent into battle and nearly all of them were destroyed. Retreats were forbidden but inevitable. In August, Order Number 270 defined those who surrendered or were captured as 'traitors of the motherland'. It could be argued that the first few months of the war were the playing out of the Stalinist logic of impossible objectives, heroic efforts and wasteful persecution. By the end of September, the three main prongs of the German attack had reached the main objectives: in the north, Leningrad; in the centre, Moscow; in the south, the Black Sea.

The course of the war

The siege of Leningrad

In the north, German forces had swept through the Baltic States. As in Ukraine, many viewed them as liberators from the recently established Soviet rule. Leningrad sat at the easternmost point of the gulf of Finland, its route out into the Baltic Sea. By 25 September the German Army Group North had cut off the land route to Leningrad from the rest of the Soviet Union and blockaded the port. This began a siege that would last 900 days. The fact that the city had not fallen was primarily the result of the intervention by General Zhukov. As a relatively young member of the General Staff, aged 43, Zhukov had made his name with Stalin by arguing against his demands for counter-offensives during the first stages of the invasion. Although this got him demoted to head of the Reserve Front, his subsequent defence of Smolensk, on the route to Moscow, marked him out as a problem-solver.

On 8 September, Zhukov made his first visit to Leningrad. There he replaced Voroshilov who had been sent in August. With the Leningrad party leader, Andrei Zhdanov, he organised the defence of the city. First, he evacuated over half a million civilians before the land route was cut off. Another half million he had planned to move became trapped in the city. The city was turned into a defensive camp. A workers' militia of 36 000 was organised and the streets were barricaded. The suburbs were converted into a complex of defences, mined and filled with layer upon layer of obstacles. Air-raid shelters were built, but life was to continue as normally as possible. By this time, Stalin was aware that Hitler intended to besiege the city rather than expend forces taking it. His logic ran that, once cut off, the city would starve.

The German attack lasted until 25 September 1941. The defence was hard-fought but the Germans stopped at the Neva River and dug in. Hitler decided to divert his forces to the assault on Moscow. Saved from defeat, the city's population of 3.3 million was in a precarious position. Daily shelling and bombing were maintained. Ration cards were issued but they were insufficient to feed the whole population. By December, workers and soldiers received 8 ounces of bread a day; this was twice the amount given to civilians. People ate cats, dogs and vermin. Thousands died from starvation and cold. Bodies were piled up waiting for those who would dig mass graves to regain strength. Although it was punishable by death, some opted to eat the dead.

Despite serious deprivation, a number of factories remained open producing tanks and munitions until they were mostly closed in December. In the midst of the suffering, Shostakovich wrote what became known as the 'Leningrad' symphony. There was a single means by which to bring in limited supplies: the port of Osinovets on the western shore of Lake Ladoga, which lay to the east of Leningrad. The far shore was still held by the Soviets and a flotilla of small boats brought in 45 000 tonnes of food, ammunition and petrol before the lake began to freeze in November. The city would have been entirely cut off had the authorities not decided to create an ice road running for 18 miles across the lake.

Figure 6.1: Poster (1942) by Alexei Kokorekin, 'Let's defend Leningrad with all our might!'

Voices from the past

Stalin

An extract of Stalin's call-to-war speech given on 3 July 1941, broadcast by radio:[3]

Comrades! Citizens!

Brothers and sisters!

Warriors of our army and navy!

It is I who am speaking to you my friends!

Nazi Germany's treacherous military attack on our Motherland, begun on 22 June, is still going on …

How is it possible that our glorious Red Army has surrendered cities and regions to the fascist troops? Are the German troops really invincible, as the boastful fascist propagandists never tire of declaring?

We must organise a merciless struggle against all disorganisers on the home front, against deserters, scaremongers, rumour-mongers, spies and saboteurs … Anyone at all who gets in the way of our defence with their

scaremongering and cowardice must immediately face a Military Tribunal.

In the event of the Red Army's withdrawal, rolling stock must be removed … not a kilo of bread or a litre of fuel must be left for the enemy … Anything valuable which cannot be moved out must definitely be destroyed.

Partisan unity must be created in the areas occupied by the enemy … We must make conditions intolerable for the enemy and all his accomplices in all the areas that have been seized …

Discussion points:

1. What is the tone of Stalin's speech?
2. What comes across more strongly – admission of disaster or reassurance?
3. There is a marked change in Stalin's language – appearing to avoid the usual references to Marxism-Leninism or class warfare. What has he replaced them with?
4. How useful is this source to a historian studying the first year of the war?

The attack on Moscow: Operation Typhoon

At the end of September 1941, Hitler's attention turned to Moscow. He aimed to destroy the remaining Soviet forces protecting Moscow along the so-called Mozhaisk line, 60 miles from the capital. The tried and tested pincer movement, towards Vyazma in the north and Briansk in the south, would be used to encircle the Soviets and open the route. The southern arm of the offensive, Operation Typhoon, began on 30 September; and the northern arm on 2 October. The day before, Stalin had at last ordered the evacuation of Moscow to Kuibyshev, including the packing up of Lenin's embalmed corpse. Ordering yet another final stand, Stalin again called on Zhukov to address the situation and on 10 October he was given command of all the forces defending Moscow. Amid the increasing panic of the population and preparations for the evacuation of the government, Stalin decided on 17 October that he would not leave Moscow. A state of siege was declared on 19 October. The NKVD was deployed to restore order and supervise the building of defences.

From the end of October and throughout November, German forces advanced towards the Moscow–Volga Canal. Figure 6.2 shows their progress to that point. Despite the lack of forces available, Stalin ordered Zhukov to launch a counter-offensive. His plan was to drive back the northern and southern arms of the now well-established German pincer movement. On 5 December, the Soviet attack began. Zhukov employed concentrated 'shock' armies to break through German lines. By 15 December, the northern pincer had been driven back and, by the end of the year, Tula had been relieved and the German lines had been forced back 80 miles. This campaign involved intense fighting by both sides in the bitter cold. The idea that the German advance was slowed by the Russian winter may be slightly exaggerated. Nevertheless, it is clear that the Soviet forces were better prepared, with the infrastructure, vehicles and kit designed for winter fighting. In mid-December, Stalin announced that the threat to the capital had been averted and Hitler, denying his generals their request for a strategic withdrawal, took personal charge of the army. The fighting to secure Moscow continued well into the new year.

The winter of 1941 marked the beginning of a new stage in the war. The attack by the Japanese on the US Pacific Fleet in Pearl Harbor on 7 December 1941, and the consequent entry of the United States into the war, brought Stalin a new ally, with a vast industrial base. Indeed, Japanese deployments in the Far East against British and American interests had allowed Stalin to transfer troops from Siberia in defence of the capital. What is more, Hitler's failure to take Moscow and Leningrad and to allow a halt to his eastern campaign was arguably one of his costliest decisions.

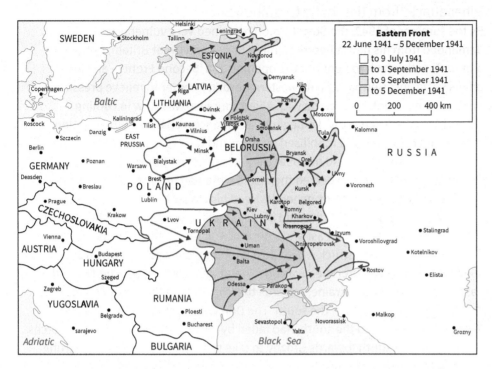

Figure 6.2: German advances by 1941.

Timeline 1941

22 June	German invasion of Soviet Union along entire western frontier: Operation Barbarossa. Martial law declared in western Soviet Union.
23 June	Stavka (Main Headquarters) established.
27 June	Minsk (Belarus) occupied by Germany (300 miles into Soviet territory).
30 June	State Committee for Defence established.
3 July	Stalin gave his first radio address to Soviet people.
10 July	Stalin appointed Supreme Commander.
12 July	Brest-Litovsk (border fortress) fell to Germany.
16 July	Smolensk taken by Germany.
19 July	Stalin replaced Timoshenko as Commissar of Defence.
21 July	First bombing of Moscow by Germany.
17 Sept	Kiev (Ukraine) evacuated by Soviets.
26 Sept	Siege of Leningrad began – encircled on three sides by German forces.
30 Sept	Operation Typhoon launched against last forces protecting Moscow.
1 Oct	Evacuation of Moscow ordered.
10 Oct	Hitler declared victory in the East (prematurely).
19 Oct	Moscow declared to be in a state of siege.

Hitler attacks from the south: Operation Blue

By the summer of 1942, the Soviet Union remained very vulnerable. Stalin demanded from his new allies, the United States and Great Britain, not only materials with which to fight but the opening of a 'Second Front' – an Allied offensive against Germany on its western border, in order to relieve pressure on the eastern front. This, along with Allied supplies, was slow in coming. Nevertheless, the Red Army did begin to experience a changing organisation in the spring of 1942 around mobilised infantry and tank corps along the German model. Such changes would not bear fruit before Soviet forces had faced another existential threat. Stalin expected the next German offensive to be against Moscow. This was in fact where Hitler's generals urged him to strike. Hitler, however, believed that the Soviet Union could be defeated if it was cut off in the south, both from its links to the Middle East and from its Caucasian oilfields. This approach had a certain logic and struck where Soviet forces were weakest. On 28 June 1942, just over a year after the invasion, Operation Blue was launched from the easternmost border of Ukraine, towards the Don River in the north and towards the Caucasus mountains in the south. The Don was reached in just over a week. Rostov, the gateway to the south, had fallen by 23 July. Hitler then split his forces: Group A headed south towards Grozny to take the oilfields and Group B swung north-east towards the Volga River with orders to take Stalingrad.

The battle for Stalingrad, winter 1942–1943

Zhukov was once again sent to devise a solution. Now as Deputy Supreme Commander, he flew to Stalingrad on 29 August 1942 to survey the situation. He then flew back to Moscow and met with Stalin on 12–13 September, where he put forward his plan. He intended to undertake a pincer movement to isolate and encircle the forces that had advanced to Stalingrad under General Paulus. It was based on attacking the weaker flanks of the advancing forces, made up of Romanian, Italian and Hungarian troops. This was entitled 'Operation Uranus', but could not be launched until November. This meant that Stalingrad had to hold out. Chuikov was put in charge of the defence of Stalingrad. The city sat on the eastern bank of the Volga, surrounded by Paulus's forces. It was reduced to rubble. German and Soviet troops were within yards of each other. Chuikov relied on bringing supplies and troops across the river under heavy fire.

Despite his inability to take the city, Paulus continued to make progress, street by street, until mid-November. On 19 November, Operation Uranus (see Figure 6.3) finally began. By 23 November, the two Soviet pincers met at the Don River 60 miles from Stalingrad. Paulus had requested permission to break out and retreat, but Hitler insisted he remain. As a result he was isolated from the remainder of the Reich's forces by a corridor 100 miles wide. Paulus was cut off but was under orders not to surrender. German morale, including that of its commander, was eaten away by cold and hunger although many fought on with fanatical zeal. The assault on Stalingrad began on 10 January 1943. By 17 January, the territory Paulus held had halved. The city was taken one block at a time. On 31 January, Paulus's headquarters within the city were located. Unshaven, listless and lying on his bed, he surrendered.

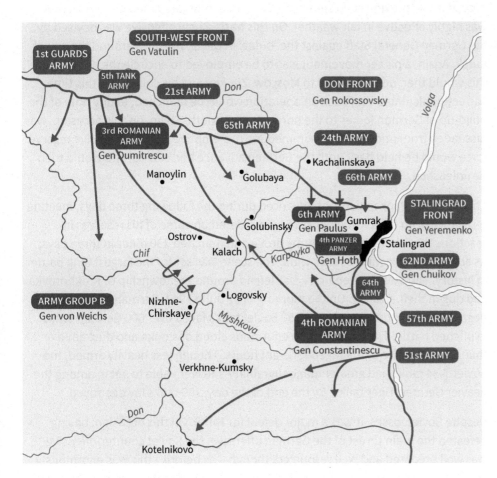

Figure 6.3: The Russian fight-back: Operation Uranus, 1942–1943.

Stalingrad was a turning point in the war for a number of reasons. Perhaps its most important effects were on German morale. It ended the notion of German invincibility in the East; 147 000 German troops were killed at Stalingrad and another 91 000 were taken prisoner. For the Soviet Union, which had lost 500 000 men in its defence, it was the third and final symbolic city to be held and it bore the name of the newly 'promoted' Marshal, Stalin. It was undeniably a heroic defence. Apart from its propaganda value, Stalingrad had proved that the Soviet command were capable of organising a complex military operation run, in the main, by the professional General Staff (political interference in military decisions was waning by late 1942). Towards the end of 1942, the Soviet Staff also recognised the importance of supplies – another lesson they were learning from the failures of German forces. It was at this point that Allied supplies began to make a steady contribution to the Soviet war effort. Alongside, and arguably as a result of increased Allied shipments to Vladivostok in the east and Murmansk and Archangel in the Arctic, Soviet mass production revived in 1943. It was these factors that enabled the first distinct blow against the forces of the Reich and their expulsion from the Soviet Union.

Kursk, summer 1943: the largest tank battle in history

After Stalingrad, the Soviet Union remained vulnerable. A number of German counter-offensives were launched around Kharkov in March 1943. As had been proved in the previous two summers, German coordinated mechanised warfare was highly effective in fair weather. On this basis a new offensive was devised by the German General Staff against the 'bulge' in the Soviet lines around the city of Kursk. Again, a pincer movement was to be employed to encircle the Kursk 'bulge'; this would then open the road to Moscow. Zhukov and his colleagues this time correctly calculated that such an operation would be launched, taking note of the build-up of German forces to the north and the south. Stalin, on this occasion, was dissuaded from undertaking an immediate pre-emptive attack. A massive reserve force would be held back until the German advance had stalled, and would then be unleashed.

Three elite SS Panzer divisions advanced during the following three days, meeting resistance from the 1st Tank Army. Stalin ordered up some of his reserves in reaction. The 5th Guards Tank Army drove and marched 230 miles in three days; its advancing unit was 20 miles wide. The scene was set for the largest tank battle in history. The Soviets prepared a battlefield around the township of Prokhorovka and dug in their artillery. On the morning of 12 June 1943, German bombers began to attack Soviet positions: 850 Soviet tanks faced over 600 German tanks in pitched battle. The result was an enormous cloud of smoke and dust amid a thunderstorm. The battle raged for eight hours. Though less heavily armed, the Soviet T-34 tanks had greater manoeuvrability and were able to get in among the heavier German Tiger tanks. By the end of the day, 700 tanks lay destroyed.

Despite Soviet losses, it was a major defeat for Hitler. On this occasion, having defeated the main thrust of the German offensive, the Soviet counter-offensive was well prepared and well resourced, though – as before – this was enormously costly in life. Overy notes that the Red Army's divisional strength was half what it had been in 1942.[4] For this reason there was no decisive destruction of the enemy, which gathered its strength to resist most strongly in Ukraine. Nevertheless, the remainder of the year saw the reconquest of Orel, Briansk, Kharkov, Smolensk and, by 6 November, Kiev. At this point, Hitler ordered a retreat. Again, this had been won through enormous Soviet sacrifice.

Timeline 1942–1943

1942	
June	Hitler ordered advance in south towards the River Volga and Caspian oilfields.
23 July	Soviet forces under Gordov met German forces under Paulus 80 miles from Stalingrad.
19 Aug	Paulus ready for first assault on Stalingrad.
29 Aug	Zhukov made Deputy Supreme Commander.
12–13 Aug	Zhukov proposed Operation Uranus to cut off Paulus in Stalingrad pocket.
19 Nov	Operation Uranus put into effect.

1943	
10 Jan	Final Soviet assault on Stalingrad began.
31 Jan	Paulus surrendered; Stalingrad regained for Soviet Union.
12 April	Stalin accepted Zhukov's plan to counter expected German offensive around Kursk salient (known as 'Citadel').
5 July	German forces under Manstein attacked at Kursk.
12 July	850 Soviet tanks faced 600 German tanks in largest tank battle in history.
13 July	Soviet counter-offensive unleashed. German forces ordered to retreat.
5 Aug	Orel taken by Soviet forces.
18 Aug	Briansk taken by Soviet forces.
28 Aug	Kharkov taken by Soviet forces.
6 Nov	Kiev taken by Soviet forces.
28 Nov–1 Dec	Tehran Conference between Stalin, Roosevelt and Churchill.

The 'ten blows' and the occupation of Eastern Europe

In 1944 German forces were pushed off Soviet territory, in the way that Stalin had imagined was possible back in 1941, and through Eastern Europe to Berlin itself. The offensives that drove back the invader all along the front were referred to in Soviet propaganda at the end of the year as 'Stalin's ten blows', but it is better to understand them in terms of the major advances made in the summer of that year as part of Operation Bagration, which was launched exactly three years after the German invasion (22 June). Just over two weeks earlier, the Western Allies had at last established a second front by mounting an amphibious attack on the beaches of Normandy (6 June). Soviet progress was rapid. By 4 July, Minsk had been taken. From 13 to 27 July, the German high command experienced what Overy describes as 'a week of disasters'.[5] The drive into Polish territory enabled a convergence on Warsaw, although by this point Soviet forces were worn down and required time to recoup.

In October, the British Prime Minister, Winston Churchill, flew to Moscow to discuss the future of Eastern Europe. Stalin had first made his claim to a sphere of influence from the German border reaching south as early as December 1941, when the British Secretary of State for War, Anthony Eden, had visited Britain's new ally in Moscow. No undertakings had been made at that point. It is, however, helpful to set Stalin's claim in the context of Soviet foreign policy throughout the 1920s and 1930s. While it is possible to see Stalin's domination of post-war Eastern Europe as stemming from a position of strength and confidence, one should keep in mind the web of rather ineffectual pre-war bilateral agreements, which had proved so inadequate for Soviet security.

The banks of the Oder and Neisse rivers had been reached by 24 February. These were to form the disputed newly created western border of a liberated Poland, shifted west as Russia subsumed what it had gained under the Nazi-Soviet Pact. By the end of March the Baltic coast to the east of Stettin was under Soviet occupation. Towards the end of April, Allied and Soviet forces met at the Elbe River and the final assault by the Red Army on Berlin began. Hitler, unwilling to leave the capital, shot himself on 30 April, having transferred authority to Admiral Doenitz. The German High Commander Jodl surrendered to the Western Allies at Reims on 7 May. This caused consternation for Stalin, who demanded that a new version be signed in Berlin in the presence of Zhukov. This took place at midnight at the beginning of 9 May.

Timeline 1944–1945

1944	
6 June	Operation Overlord: Western Allies launched an amphibious invasion of German-occupied France on Normandy beaches.
22 June	Beginning of Operation Bagration: Soviet advance west into Eastern Europe.
4 July	Minsk taken by Soviet forces.
13–27 July	A series of disastrous reverses for German forces from Baltic states to Ukraine, including capture of Vilnius (13 July) and Lvov (27 July) and Soviet forces reaching the Vistula River outside Warsaw.
20–29 Aug	German Army Group South collapsed.
23 Aug	Romania capitulated and joined Allies against Germany.
9 Oct	Churchill met with Stalin in Moscow to discuss post-war Eastern Europe.
1945	
11–17 Jan	Soviet capture of Warsaw and advance on Krakow.
19 Jan	Krakow taken by Soviet forces.
4–11 Feb	Yalta Conference between Stalin, Roosevelt and Churchill.
8 Feb	Banks of River Oder reached.
14 Feb	Budapest taken by Soviet forces.
23 Feb	Poznan pocket (Poland) taken by Soviet forces.
24 Feb	Banks of River Neisse reached.
31 March	Baltic coast to the east of Stettin under Soviet occupation.
18 April	Allied forces reached Leipzig.
25 April	Allied and Soviet forces met at River Elbe.
7 May	Jodl signed act of unconditional surrender at Reims.
9 May (12 a.m.)	Keitel signed a new version of surrender in Berlin in presence of Zhukov. Liberation of Prague.

The USSR under occupation and the fight-back

The Soviet losses of men, machinery and territory were dramatic. By the end of 1941:

- 5.9 million Soviet troops had been killed or captured
- 90% of Soviet tanks were destroyed
- an already thinly spread forward air force had been neutralised
- nearly two-thirds of military supply dumps had been captured by the advancing German forces (this occurred in the first month alone).

Stalin promised a 'wasteland' to the invading forces and ordered the destruction of anything that could not be taken. In the main, however, this suited Hitler who had ordered a *Vernichtungskrieg* or 'war of annihilation'. It is true that in the Baltic States, and in Ukraine especially, German troops were popularly hailed as liberators and men were recruited to collaborate with the Nazi authorities, most infamously in the arrest and murder of Jews and Communist Party members. Nevertheless, invasion and occupation was a brutal process. Villages were burned to the ground and many civilians resorted to living in holes in the ground, like their military compatriots.

Partisan resistance

The German occupation led to the formation of partisan bands. Initially these were formed of Jews and Communist Party members escaping Nazi persecution, by moving to remote and inaccessible areas such as the forest. As such, the partisans were poorly equipped and lacked training as a military force. They were reliant on local populations for supplies and therefore vulnerable to betrayal by civilians, who were offered rewards by the Germans for information. The partisans of the Ukraine were particularly vulnerable, as Ukrainians, many of whom had welcomed German 'liberation' in 1941, had long-standing resentment for the Soviet regime. Some (Ukrainians, Cossacks and other nationalities) even joined the fight against the Soviet Union, while other Ukrainian nationalist groups banded together under warlords to fight both the Germans and the Soviet Union, as had occurred during the Civil War of 1917–1922.

German treatment of anyone suspected of being a partisan was merciless. 'Partisan' became a catch-all term that enabled a total disregard for human life: indeed, atrocities against the Jews in the occupied Soviet Union began as anti-partisan operations. By 1943, Stalin had introduced a centralised military structure to the partisan brigades, including NKVD officers and a General Staff. They were seen as the Soviet Union's crack troops behind enemy lines, and they undertook sabotage operations against German communications. In 1944, as the Red Army advanced west, the partisan units were integrated into the regular army.

The Soviet economy

As has been suggested, the rapid pace of the German invasion in 1941 meant that a great deal of important economic assets were lost and were unavailable for the subsequent Soviet war effort. R.W. Davies notes that, in all, about one-third of industrial capacity was lost by 1942 through occupation, and about 40% of grain,

Speak like a historian

Partisan

Partisan was a term given to groups who found themselves either in enemy territory or in territory not under the control of either side. They were partisan because, even though they were not part of their side's regular army, they were fighting for the same cause (or 'party', whose side they took). Their means of fighting was through raids on the enemy or their perceived civilian sympathisers. This guerrilla warfare relied on ambush, movement and avoiding open and sustained confrontation. They also undertook operations to disrupt the operations of their enemies through sabotage, for example by blowing up railway lines and bridges. This kind of destructive behaviour was typical of anti-Nazi resistance movements across Europe.

sugar and capital.[7] By the same year, Soviet GNP fell to 66% of the pre-war level; industrial output fell to 14% of the pre-war level.

On 24 July, a Committee of Evacuation was created, led by Kaganovich. The task was immense: to move whole factories and their workforces to the Urals, or further east to Kazakhstan and Siberia. This required the hurried dismantling of plant and buildings, their loading onto trains and reconstruction on hastily designated sites. The process often took place under enemy fire from the air. Two-thirds of the newly established industrial sites were on entirely new ground, with very few existing facilities for the workforce.

Around 2600 factories were moved in this fashion in the latter part of 1941 and the process continued as more land was lost. Unsurprisingly, the process was chaotic and arduous and, as had occurred during rushed industrialisation, trainloads of valuable equipment were left to rust for want of sufficient coordination. Nevertheless, only 1 in 27 of those major factories relocated by the end of 1942 were not yet functioning. Following the early catastrophic losses, men and women were removed from the factories to replace their comrades in the forces: in the first 18 months this meant that up to 17 million were recruited. While men and women served in the Red Army, women by and large replaced men in the urban workforce (53% by 1945).

Above all, the economy saw a shift towards armaments and war production. Davies notes that by 1942, 56% of national income was devoted to military purposes, up from 17% in 1940.[8] The conversion of factories from consumer goods, such as bicycles, typewriters, abacuses and teaspoons, to war production, for example flamethrowers, entrenching tools, cartridges and ammunition, meant that Soviet civilian life was disrupted to a greater degree than was life in Britain or the United States. Given the serious blows to Soviet morale in the first two years of the war, it is clear that both the NKVD's terror and an officially sanctioned Russian nationalism played their parts in mobilising a population that faced severe deprivation.

Mobilisation and evacuation of industry

All production came under the control of the State Defence Council. Stalin maintained his eye for detail and intervened in a wide variety of sectors. The centrally planned economy based on heavy industry had essentially been designed to wage war, and early crisis drove the process of centralisation. New quarterly and monthly plans were created, which meant that both the successes and the failures were magnified. However, this drove improvisation and initiative at the local level, as officials attempted to achieve the results demanded by Moscow.

A certain cultural freedom was also granted, including expressions of Russian folk tradition, and from 1942 the re-establishment of a state-sanctioned Russian Orthodox Church hierarchy under the Moscow patriarchate. Vera Dunham describes this as 'a combination of permissiveness with drastic punitive measures … [allowing] some permissive elements into a basically Draconian practice'.[9] Such flexibility was essential to allow the survival of a severely deprived population. Private plots on the edges of cities and semi-legal markets were tolerated. The impact of the war on agriculture was severe. Not only had some of the best agricultural land been occupied by German forces, but the recruitment of agricultural workers to replace those factory workers who had themselves replaced fallen soldiers meant that the collectives were stripped of their most able workers. Between 1940 and 1942 agricultural production dropped by 40%. Many of those left to farm were the old and vulnerable. This stated, the centralised rationing system was far better established and effective than it had been during the Civil War.

 Voices from the past

Western-front soldier

This letter is from a gunner on the western front to a steel worker in Sverdlovsk. The exchange appeared in Soviet newspapers and the men were held up as role models.[6]

Dear Comrade Bazetov,

I read in the paper that in competition with Aleksey Sorokovoy, comrade Bazetov, a steel worker at the Verkh-Isetsk works, achieved an output of more than 10 tons of steel per square metre from the sole of an open-hearth furnace, and that from the beginning of next year you'll be doing only high-speed smelting …

As for me, I can tell you that, like you, I try to do everything using high-speed methods. You smelt steel, I kill fascists …

You're a Tartar and I'm an Uzbek. Your mate in the competition, Aleksey Sorokovoy, is a Ukrainian. You and Sorokovoy at the furnace and me at my machine gun – together let's defeat the enemy who's burst into our beloved Motherland.

If you've got time, write me a couple of lines about yourself and what you're going to do for the Red Army's anniversary.

Bye for now. I shake your hand. Regards to Aleksey Sorokovoy.

Discussion points:
1. Why was this letter printed in a Soviet newspaper?
2. What is the significance of 'You're a Tartar and I'm an Uzbek'?
3. How useful is this source in studying the people of the Soviet Union during the war?

Foreign aid

The shipments of food provided by the United States and Britain were arguably essential in preventing mass starvation – particular among these was the processed meat product, Spam, which played a significant role in feeding the Red Army. Stalin was insistent that more material was required, sending 'shopping lists' to his allies and complaining about the quality of what he received. Despite his complaints, he refused to allow Allied technical support and personnel. Stalin did not wish to publicise the degree of foreign aid to the Soviet people and quite possibly remained concerned about espionage by his capitalist allies. Other than food, the main contribution to the Soviet war effort was not direct provision of foreign munitions (these are reckoned to have been 4% of the Soviet arsenal), but rather communications, transport and raw materials. The complex strategies such as Operation Uranus and subsequent campaigns were only possible because of significantly improved signals intelligence. These were labelled by the 33 000 radio stations, 380 000 field telephones and 956 000 miles of cable provided by the Allies. In addition to these, 77 900 jeeps, 151 000 light trucks and 200 000 army trucks were provided. Furthermore, the Western Allies provided 50–60% of the air fuel, explosives, rails, copper, aluminium and rubber tyres used by the Soviet Union. The great majority of locomotives and railway cars, as well as the track provided, were from abroad.

All this said, the bulk of armaments and fighting vehicles were produced in the Soviet Union, including all of its artillery, seven of every eight tanks and five of every six aircraft. This clearly would not have been possible without the provision of otherwise deficient metals, but some credit must be given to the methods of Soviet production; what Overy refers to as a 'crude mass manufacture process'[10] and to the inventiveness and initiative of Soviet engineers in overcoming obstacles. The T-34 tank, for example, proved the optimal design against heavier German armour. Foreign aid was, therefore, undoubtedly a lifeline that fed a narrowly focused Soviet war economy and enabled the effective deployment of its products in the war effort.

The defeat of Germany

Reasons and results

The reasons for Germany's defeat at the hands of the Soviet Union can be summarised as:

- Hitler's strategic failures
- Soviet military reorganisation
- Soviet materiel, production and manpower
- Soviet propaganda and terror.

Hitler's strategic failures

Although it is obvious that the German summer offensives of 1941 and 1942 were enormously successful in making rapid progress into Soviet territory through mechanised warfare, they were arguably difficult to sustain, as they required supplying over thousands of miles of terrain. Much is also made of the inadequacy of German equipment, particularly soldiers' clothing, in winter conditions. While this can be overemphasised, Soviet equipment was more suited to winter fighting, and the successful defence of Leningrad, Moscow and Stalingrad were all achieved during the winter months.

Although this is most easily stated through hindsight, the failure of German forces to take either of the historic capitals or Stalingrad (highly symbolic in itself) was highly significant. While it is possibly speculative to suggest that the fall of any of these three cities would have proved a fatal blow to Soviet morale and the government's ability to continue waging war, it is fair to suggest that the fact that this line was held played a crucial role in enabling the fight-back from mid-1943. Hitler may well have had good grounds to strike south towards the oilfields in 1942, but it is worth considering what would have occurred if he had followed his generals' advice and renewed the offensive against Moscow during that summer, when Soviet forces were still in a very vulnerable position.

Again, Hitler's obstinacy in denying Paulus the opportunity to break out of Stalingrad provided Stalin with the propaganda coup and demonstrated that the German army was not unconquerable. The military contribution of the other Allied forces to German defeat is obviously also important. Hitler's failures in North Africa, the Atlantic and in France and Italy, his failure to defeat Britain and his audacious declaration of war against the United States are essential context to his failure in the east.

Soviet military reorganisation

Following the disasters of the first 18 months of the war, the Soviet military were substantially reorganised in the spring of 1942. As mentioned, the army was organised around new motorised divisions that were able to replicate German tactics. Even before the onset of dramatically increased production, there were significant changes to the staffing and culture of the military. Vasilevsky was made Chief of Staff in July 1942 and he himself relied on his Chief of Operations, Antonov, who was appointed in December 1942. Novikov was also appointed

---

 Voices from the past

Stalin

This letter from Stalin to Churchill is dated 3 September 1941.[11]

I wish to thank you for promising to sell the Soviet Union another 200 fighter planes in addition to the 200 already promised. I am quite sure that our pilots will soon get the hang of them and go into action. However, I do have to say that these aircraft, which obviously cannot go into action straight away, cannot make a major difference to the situation on the Eastern Front. In the last three weeks our situation has got dramatically worse in such important places as Ukraine and Leningrad …

I think there is only one way out of this situation: open a Second Front somewhere in the Balkans or France this year, able to draw off thirty or forty German divisions from the Eastern Front, while supplying the Soviet Union with 30 000 tonnes of aluminium by the beginning of October, and at least 400 aircraft and 500 tanks per month …

Discussion points:

1. What is Stalin really asking for here?
2. How useful is this source to the historian studying relations between Stalin and the Allies?

that year and reorganised the air force. It had proved ineffective in the first months of the war because squadrons had been dispersed across the front. As Overy describes, Novikov now made sure that 'air armies' were concentrated and available for intervention at 'critical junctures in battle'.[12] Novikov also ensured the construction of dummy airfields near to the front to divert the Luftwaffe.

Stalin slowly began to realise the benefits of listening to the professionals. While he still retained the final word, he insisted on listening to the advice from front commanders and became more open to hearing the harsh truth. In October 1942, political commissars were removed from smaller units, and traditional methods of hierarchy and discipline, including the reintroduction of epaulettes and elite guards units (reminiscent of the tsarist days), contributed further to a professional rather than a political military culture. It is worth noting that this had also proved successful during the Civil War. Much credit, however, is due to those such as Zhukov and Antonov, who knew how to manipulate Stalin. Zhukov's repeated success (having previously been demoted for criticising Stalin) lay in presenting well-designed plans, not necessarily of his own invention, before his political master. Despite promoting Zhukov to Deputy Supreme Commander, Stalin remained jealous of his success and popularity, but this did not prevent him playing a crucial role in victory.

Soviet materiel, production and manpower

As has been made clear, from 1943 onwards foreign aid and dramatically improved production enabled the Soviet war machine to out-produce its German rival. In 1943, the Soviet Union was finally in a position to contend for air supremacy. In addition, Soviet tank production out-did German tank production by a ratio of more than 4:3. Almost two-thirds of those were T-34s, which continued to be modified and improved. The IS-2 'Joseph Stalin' heavy tank was also introduced in 1944. Improved tank use also meant that a previously disastrous loss rate of up to seven Soviet tanks to every one German tank was equalised by 1944.

It would be wrong to argue that, from 1943, the Axis powers were inevitably going to lose as a result of superior Allied production, yet the drive back west would not have been possible without it. Likewise, it would be wrong to suggest that the Soviet population was inexhaustible, but the tireless determination of the Soviet military and civilian population played an enormous part in victory. Put in simple terms, Soviet command was highly accepting of heavy casualties. In one sense, this was extremely wasteful, particularly in the early stages of the war. In another sense, it demonstrated to German forces the high degree of resistance they would face. Stalin was able to enforce a ruthless attitude to the extent that, as German forces advanced with a line of Soviet prisoners in front of them, the order to the Soviet troops was to disregard the lives of their fellow citizens in the higher interests of the Soviet people and open fire. In a similar manner, sacrificial units were formed from gulag inmates, who were told to prove their loyalty through service. This included being sent ahead of their compatriots to clear minefields with their own bodies.

Human losses remained heavy during the bitter fighting to remove German forces from Soviet and East European soil. It is estimated that 26 million Soviet citizens died as a result of the war, either as a result of action (8 million), ill-treatment by German occupying forces, or malnutrition and illness on the home front;[13] this is calculated by comparing the population census at the beginning and end of the war. Adding those who were left incapacitated through injury brings this figure to 50 million.[14] Note also that this figure does not include those who would have otherwise been born were it not for war. It is also essential to note the role of forced labour within the war economy. Davies states that in 1942, around 1.5 million of the 2.5 million prisoners in camps were engaged in forced labour, particularly in construction, mining and timber; this made up one-twelfth of the non-agricultural workforce.[15]

Soviet propaganda and terror

Part of the Soviet population's ability to wage a war had to do with a continued system of terror and a new form of Soviet patriotism. As shown, the NKVD now had full licence to deal with enemies of the state as military threats, which played a considerable part in maintaining order in Leningrad and Moscow during the panic of late 1941. This included apartment managers being made directly responsible for the behaviour of their tenants. Order Number 227 acted to equate 'panic' with desertion, and indeed becoming a prisoner of war was considered an act of treason (the assumption being that every Soviet soldier would fight to the death). This extreme attitude was matched by an increasingly nationalistic tone to propaganda. Stalin was transformed into a national military leader rather than a communist boss. Marxist-Leninism was played down in favour of the imagery of 'Mother Russia'. McDermott notes how Stalin exploited the 'usable past'[16] to engender patriotic fervour with the promotion of Russian language, literature, history and the sacredness of the soil itself. Military heroes of the past, particularly Alexander Nevsky, who had fought against Germanic invaders and Peter the Great, and who was sufficiently distant from his hated Romanov successors, were amalgamated into Soviet identity.

Many responded positively to the opportunity this gave for renewed cultural expression. Above all, following clear evidence of German ill-treatment of the occupied west, a passionate anti-German attitude took hold and added to the motivation of Soviet troops when ordered into full frontal attack. An almost entirely counter-productive deportation programme took place in the autumn of 1941 of Volga Germans, with 450 000 sent to Western Siberia and Central Asia. A further 1 million Chechens and Crimean Tartars were deported in 1943 and 1944. A quarter of a million died in transit.[17] Russian nationalism was therefore not wholly beneficial or accepted, but undoubtedly motivated millions and provided the case to fight for in arduous conditions.

Post-war reconstruction

As much of the evidence here suggests, the Great Patriotic War had a devastating effect on the Soviet population and infrastructure. Evacuation of industry was partially successful, but some factories and most agricultural equipment, housing, bridges and roads in the formerly occupied west lay in ruins. This infrastructure had to be rebuilt from scratch with limited resources. Some 70% of those killed in the war were men – this included a third of all young males. By 1946, women outnumbered men by nearly 22 million at a ratio of roughly 4:3.

As the war ended, suspicion and mistrust quickly grew between the Soviet Union and the Western Allies, and the **Lend-Lease programme** was abruptly stopped in September 1945, once victory over Japan had been secured. Other available means further reconstructing industry in particular were reparations, particularly from Germany. Alongside the looting and rape that took place with the defeat and occupation of Germany, the NKVD organised the wholesale export of industrial and scientific equipment, including German technicians and their families, to the Soviet Union. As with the previous evacuation of industry, waste was inevitable. The occupiers also set up joint-stock companies in their zones, by which they could produce goods and profits for export to the Soviet Union. Despite this, reparations played a minimal role in Soviet recovery – Davies estimates this at about 1.5% of GNP.[18] Reconstruction therefore had to be undertaken in the same manner by which industrialisation had been achieved – through further heavy sacrifice.

As a result of the war, the number of children in post-15 education was reduced, which had implications for a trained workforce. Nevertheless, by 1950, pre-war levels of children in education up to the age of 15 was restored (nearly all urban children and around half of rural children). Furthermore, higher education for an admittedly small elite continued to expand.[19] The war's recruitment of a higher proportion of women into the workforce (from 36% in 1940 to 56% in 1945) was also mainly retained. Although the number of working women matched working men, they remained less well paid and, on the whole, in less senior positions.[20]

Industry and agriculture after the war

A fourth Five-Year Plan was devised for the years 1946–1950. Its emphasis was on heavy industry and capital goods, and it succeeded in slightly exceeding pre-war production levels. Production quickly moved away from armaments, and this was at first a blow, as the Soviet economy had been so focused on this sector. Nevertheless, investment in capital goods increased by as much as 21% over these first five years. By 1950 oil, coal, electricity and steel production exceeded the planned targets.

During these years, factory conditions worsened and discipline was tightened. This set the tone for post-war Stalinism. Industrial recovery was bought with yet more graft, although Graeme Gill fairly claims that, 'the physical demands of the war sapped energy out of the Soviet people'[21] and growth rates remained disappointing. Production of consumer goods fared less well, although the technical advances made by the war and the conversion of armaments factories to certain durable goods production (such as bedsteads, radios and clocks) increased to 250% of the pre-war level by 1950. Other important consumer goods such as textiles and footwear remained below pre-war levels. This deficit began to be addressed after 1950 and began to match capital goods production.

The agricultural sector, however, lagged behind. Despite the production of tractors and combine harvesters (from reconverted tank factories), grain production in 1950 was still below the pre-war level and, per head, was lower than pre-First World War levels. Agriculture was still dependent on a largely ageing and female labour force. Many young women left the villages to find work in the towns. The

Speak like a historian

The Lend-Lease programme

The US president, Franklin D. Roosevelt, originally devised the Lend-Lease Programme to provide Britain with goods and weaponry from 1939 in order to help it resist the threat from Germany. This programme was extended to the Soviet Union in late 1941, by which time all three powers, the United States, Britain and the Soviet Union, were allies at war with Germany.

flexibility of the war years was removed, and collectivised practice was re-imposed and newly imposed in the newly created Baltic Soviet Republics (Latvia, Lithuania and Estonia). In addition, there was a serious famine in the Ukraine in 1946. Rural life remained more challenging than urban life. State payments for compulsory grain procurement remained very low, while the cost of basic commodities had multiplied tenfold between 1928 and 1952. Alongside this, collective farms received very little investment in their social amenities.

Davies states that 'no fundamental shift took place in economic policy' before 1953, but that 'certain tentative signs' had appeared.[22] These included the production of consumer goods nearly matching that of capital goods between 1950 and 1952, a greater emphasis on incentives and profit-and-loss accounting and a relaxation of controls over the movement of labour. Agriculture, claims Davies, remained the 'Achilles heel' of the Soviet economy until investment was rapidly increased by the new leadership following Stalin's death in 1953.[23] Nevertheless, the early 1950s saw a further shift towards an industrialised economy, agriculture falling from 47% of the economy in 1928 to 20% in 1955 and industry increasing from 20% of the economy in 1928 to 37% in 1955.[24]

ACTIVITY 6.1

For some historians, the victory of the Soviet Union over Nazi Germany was accidental; for others it was due to Stalin's leadership and the sheer doggedness of the Russians.

Go through your notes and find evidence to support both assessments. You may want to organise your notes in a table like this:

The Soviet Union emerged from the Great Patriotic War victorious because …		
… of luck, or it was an accident	… of Stalin's leadership	… of the determination and sacrifice of the people of the Soviet Union

Soviet historians tended to emphasise that, although the Great Patriotic War caused great sacrifice, the population was united behind the cause from the moment Operation Barbarossa was launched. While the extent to which this is true has been challenged, the driving force of the home front underlining Red Army victories cannot be ignored. Historians continue to debate the impact of the war on Stalin, particularly as he seemed to emerge from the war stronger than before.

Go over your notes to collect evidence to assess the impact of the war from different perspectives.

Impact of the war on...	Positive	Negative
Stalin as a leader		
support for the Communist Party		
the Soviet economy		
Soviet society		

High Stalinism

The term 'High Stalinism' has been applied to Stalin's form of political and social control that followed the removal of his remaining political rivals and the development of terror into its most indiscriminate form. In reality, it is difficult to date the beginning of such an era, not least because Stalin seemingly never desisted from seeking out enemies and rivals to remove or destroy. Arguably, it was his modus operandi throughout the entirety of his career as a contender for power and then as a despot.

Dictatorship and totalitarianism

As suggested, Stalin continued to maintain control, or keep his colleagues guessing. He remained paranoid about other individuals getting credit. In particular, he ensured that Zhukov and others were demoted following their crucial roles in victory. Beria – head of the NKVD – used evidence from Zhukov's deputy in occupied Berlin, Serov, to compile a case against him. It is true, though, that Zhukov did not help himself and was not modest about his role in the war. In June 1945, he was summoned to Moscow. The compliant Politburo condemned Zhukov as a Bonapartist (as Trotsky had been called), but – thanks to his reputation – he suffered only internal exile to an unimportant military post and almost completely removal from the official history of the war. Beria himself lost his post as head of the NKVD in 1946, to Kruglov, but remained on the Politburo without a power base.

Stalin has been fairly characterised during the post-war years as 'ailing despot'. It is quite true that he suffered from arthritis, rheumatism and high blood pressure, and these were not aided by his tendency to hold late-night informal gatherings at his dacha outside Moscow. To some extent he was becoming more out of touch. In 1946 a Council of Ministers was created, which took on many of Stalin's responsibilities and formalised the Soviet state into a more traditional governmental pattern (in contrast with its heritage of revolutionary 'commissariats'). This created what McDermott refers to as a 'combination of traditional autocracy with modern features of governance' or, as he also calls it, 'neo-patrimonialism'.[25] In this situation, Stalin retained a huge degree of power and an ability to intervene at any point in any matter, but he relied on 'more rational predictable forms of administration at lower levels'[26] run by the young, obedient careerists. He also still had control of the secret police. To maintain control he continued to plot against those closest to him. McDermott emphasises that these were not due to 'blind hatred' but were 'carefully conceived and finely constructed'.[27]

Stalin was still capable of controlling his colleagues through 'divide and rule', as was demonstrated in the Leningrad affair (discussed below). It is suggested that after this, the key contenders for power, including Khrushchev, Molotov and Beria, began to form the embryo of the collective leadership that would emerge after Stalin's death in March 1953. Power remained within Stalin's informal court. He himself was concerned that he would grow increasingly irrelevant, in a sense 'above the system', and therefore played with his colleagues to the end. He also ventured into intellectual pursuits, acting as the judge of what was a legitimate and acceptable part of Soviet scholarship and what was not, and studying the lives of previous despots such as Genghis Khan and Ivan the Terrible. He became increasingly concerned with his own mortality and paranoid about assassination.

Renewed terror

One group most closely associated with 'cosmopolitanism' were Soviet Jews and, as will be shown when we examine the purges and the Doctors' Plot, below, there was a distinctly anti-Semitic nature to the post-war terror. 'Cosmopolitanism' was a label, rather like 'formalist' had been, which suggested an overly broad-minded intellectualism that encouraged deviation from orthodox communist thought. The NKVD, which had played a major part in maintaining control and dealing out repression during the Second World War, was reformed in 1946 as the Ministry of State Security, or MGB, following Beria's dismissal.

It could be argued that the Soviet terror apparatus fed off the war in a similar manner to that of the Nazis, and while it is difficult to claim that there was comparable racially motivated genocide, atrocities were committed. Leningrad again became the focus of Stalin's paranoia and the purge there in 1949 was the foremost example of his continued practice of liquidating threats.

The NKVD under Beria

Lavrentiy Beria had taken charge of the NKVD in 1938 following the removal of Yezhov, who took the blame for the excesses of the Great Terror. As Deputy of the NKVD under Yezhov, Beria was hardly without blame, but he used Yezhov's removal to purge the NKVD and put his own men in place. In fact, as war approached the repressive activities of the NKVD increased. Historians note two

Hidden voices

The Nuremberg trials

One of the most alarming aspects of what has been seen as the 'victors' justice' of the Nuremberg trials held to try those responsible for Nazi war crimes and other felonies under an International Military Tribunal, was that the war crimes of the Soviet authorities were not addressed. Indeed, Andrey Vyshinsky, who had acted as Stalin's prosecutor in the show trials of the late 1930s, was sent to guide the process in Nuremberg in November 1945.

particular massacres by the NKVD under Beria because they were passed off as having been perpetrated by the Germans. The first, at Katyn in Poland which, as it eventually transpired, involved the murder of 21 857 Polish soldiers at three separate sites, is taken to have been committed by the Soviet authorities in April 1940 in order to deal with Polish nationalists. The second of these massacres took place in the Kuropaty Forest outside Minsk in Belorussia. In 1987, a mass grave of up to 200 000 bodies was discovered and, as Overy points out, the method of execution used, a single shot to the back of the skull, was the same as at Katyn.[28] The important point here is that, as a victor in the Second World War, Stalin did not face the same degree of scrutiny as his Nazi enemy. It is well documented that the Soviet authorities occupying Germany made use of Nazi concentration camps for their own purposes, for example imprisoning thousands of political prisoners in camps such as Sachsenhausen outside Berlin until the early 1950s.

Many of those former prisoners of war who returned to the Soviet Union were considered to have been collaborators and under Order Number 270 were subject to the fate of traitors. According to Overy, Stalin regarded them as 'unclean, besmirched [and] potentially traitorous'[29] and as a result they were placed in labour camps. By 1953, almost 5.5 million had been repatriated, yet it is estimated that one-fifth were executed or sent to the Gulag. During these years the population of the labour camps swelled from 1.5 million to 2.5 million. Despite the fact that slave labour had proved economically inefficient, Stalin insisted on using forced labour to rebuild the shattered economy. There were also mass deportations out of Soviet-occupied Eastern Europe into the West. As with previous deportations, Stalin believed it was necessary to deal with potential disloyalty on a massive scale and in a crude manner.

Beria was also put in charge of the Soviet atomic bomb programme, which came to fruition on 29 August 1949 with the first successful detonation. Such progress was a shock to the United States, who, until that point, had enjoyed a nuclear monopoly. It was possible because of two factors overseen by Beria: the use of forced labour to develop uranium mining and the running of an espionage network within the United States atomic programme. Although he resigned as head of the NKVD in January 1946, Beria maintained his influence as Deputy Prime Minister.

Zhdanovism and the cultural purge

An important aspect of the post-war era was the re-imposition of the social conservatism that had abated somewhat in reaction to the pressures of war. Administrative and cultural initiative, which had acted as a lubricant during war, was quickly stifled. Initiative again became dangerous, and this led to bureaucratic stagnation and cultural uniformity. Not least was the continued promotion of the Russian language above others. The official Soviet line was turning strongly against its former Western allies. Capitalism was associated with fascism (the terms became almost interchangeable) against which the Great Patriotic War had been waged. The emergence of the **Cold War** gave rise to a new form of xenophobia (mistrust of foreigners). Stalin was genuinely concerned that those returning from Western Europe, having collaborated with their one-time allies, and having been exposed to their political, social and cultural notions, would look to promote these values within the Soviet Union. All forms of academic and cultural life, therefore, were expected to promote a distinct Soviet cultural paradigm, which reflected the Soviet patriotism developed and instilled during the war.

The member of the Politburo most closely associated with this 'anti-cosmopolitan' programme was Andrei Zhdanov. He was at this time seen as Stalin's favourite and his likely successor. As a result, he was a rival to Beria, who made an alliance with Georgi Malenkov in order to counter the Leningrad boss's influence. Between 1946 and 1948 Zhdanov undertook to censor and promote academics and artists in order to impose socialist realism. The first of his targets were the writers Anna Akhmatova and Mikhail Zoshchenko, whose 'vulgar parodies of Soviet life'[30] were seen as 'ideologically harmful'. They had essentially subtly questioned the stifling nature of Soviet life.

Further victims included theatres that staged Western plays, philosophers who concentrated on Western thought, and composers such as Shostakovich and Prokofiev, who were accused of 'formalism' and 'lack of party spirit' in 1948. For musicians, possibly more than any other artists, whether their work was denounced or praised was really down to the whim of their political masters. One academic who continued to benefit from the promotion of a distinctly 'Soviet' scientific tradition was Trofim Lysenko, who essentially cut off Soviet genetics and biology from the international consensus, which he derided as 'false objectivism'. Zhdanov used party influence to decree that Lysenko was correct. This demonstrates how the party's intention to control and define history, philosophy and economics also sought to define the laws of nature by proclamation. Zhdanov died in August 1948, but his legacy was maintained.

Stalin's cult of personality

It is fair to state that at the end of the war, Stalin's position was completely unchallengeable. His victory over the German invader propelled his personality cult further, and his status became ever more god-like. This said, he did not desist from his characteristic means of control: periodically turning on his closest advisers and thereby instilling constant fear and demanding obedience from them. In Molotov's case, Stalin arrested his wife in order to test the loyalty of this closest of his allies. This also enabled Stalin to rely on a troop of newly appointed, inexperienced and highly obedient young protégés. Stalin's despotism after the war can be understood through three factors: his position in relation to the party and bureaucracy; the enforcement of a cultural and academic orthodoxy; and the methods of terror and persecution perpetrated against groups and those he continued to regard as rivals. (The opening photograph of this section shows Stalin in his later years – in a white jacket and named 'Generalissimo'.)

The Leningrad affair

Leningrad and its Communist Party came out of the war with a good deal of prestige, having been tried and proved by lasting the siege. Several leading communists had their power base in the city, foremost among them Zhdanov, who was local party leader. When he died, in 1948, apparently of heart failure, Stalin acted to remove what he saw as a rival focus of power. Clearly, he wished to prevent another Kirov emerging from the second city. The two men in his

Key term

Cold War is the term used to express the tensions that existed principally between the two superpowers of the United States and the Soviet Union and their allies following the Second World War up to the dissolution of the Soviet Union (1945–1991).

ACTIVITY 6.3

Look back to Chapter 2 at what happened to Trotsky after his successes in the Civil War. Might this explain why Stalin was quick to deal with the war heroes after victory was secured?

sights were Nikolai Voznesensky and Alexander Kuznetsov. The former had been responsible for planning the Soviet war economy and was becoming a prominent theorist; he was second only to Stalin in the Council of Ministers. The latter had been mainly responsible for Leningrad's survival and was second only to Stalin in the party.

Stalin was not the only leading communist aware of their status, and their rival contenders for power began a set of purges to attack the Leningrad party in 1949. In particular, Beria and Malenkov took an active role, seeing an opportunity to consolidate their power through the destruction of Zhdanov's former power base. Evidence was created to charge the majority of local party members, and in the well-established pattern, a show trial was held in September 1950 accusing them of corruption, espionage and debauchery. Neither Voznesensky or Kuznetsov admitted these allegations, but along with their comrades were shot shortly after being convicted.

Beria and the Mingrelian affair

Stalin continued to weaken possible successors. Molotov was dismissed as Foreign Minister in 1949. Even Poskrebyshev, Stalin's secretary and linked to his secret apparatus, was sacked in 1952. In 1951, Beria came close to being purged in the so-called Mingrelian affair. Mingrelians are a distinct Georgian people, whose language is unlike that of their compatriots, and Beria had close links to them. He had, with Stalin's permission, advantaged them against Georgian Abkhazians. Stalin began a purge of them in the winter of 1951–1952, and although it never reached Beria, the former head of the NKVD was made to feel very uncomfortable. These cases indicate how Stalin was able to intimidate his closest advisers until the end.

 Thematic Link: Civil war

Purges and the Doctors' Plot

A particularly notable strain within the post-war terror was anti-Semitism.

There was a broadly anti-Semitic culture, particularly within the army, where Jews found promotion difficult. Despite anti-Semitism being officially banned, the growth of Russian nationalism during the war allowed for the return of traditional insults against the Jews. There was never a clear official recognition of the atrocities perpetrated specifically against Jews from the occupied areas of the Soviet Union. Those Jews who returned to Belorussia and Ukraine were not made particularly welcome, as their compatriots had seized their property. As well as being accused of 'national egotism' when demanding a recognition of Nazi genocide, Jews were also associated with the 'cosmopolitanism' under attack by Zhdanov.

This became most prominent in 1948, when Solomon Mikhoels, a playwright and spokesman for the Jewish Anti-Fascist Committee, which had formed during the war, was murdered in Minsk on 12 January by the local party boss; the official version was that he had been murdered by the US Secret Service. Following the murder, a number of prominent Jews were sacked or arrested. Stalin regarded them as a problematic group: 'I can't swallow them, I can't spit them out.'[31] Zionist sentiment and demands for a specific homeland for Soviet Jews left them open to allegations of having ties with the West involved in espionage. In November 1948 there was a wholesale attack on Jewish culture – schools, newspapers, literature, libraries and religious life. This, of course, can be partially contextualised by Stalin's renewed persecution of the Russian Orthodox Church and other religions after the war. Trials against prominent Jews took place between 1951 and 1953, particularly of members of the Anti-Fascist Committee in July 1951.

The final episode of Stalinist purging involved an alleged Zionist plot that became known in the Soviet press as 'The Doctors' Plot'. Lidya Timashuk, an electro-cardiographer and informer for the newly formed KGB, had submitted a report at the time of Zhdanov's death in 1948 accusing his doctors of misdiagnosis. In 1952, the report was rediscovered and used to accuse Poskrebyshev of lack of vigilance, and to target Meer Vovsi, chief physician of the Red Army during the war.

From this point the supposed conspiracy was widened to a number of senior doctors, who were accused of being responsible for a Zionist conspiracy. The purge gathered pace, leading to the arrest of Stalin's personal doctor, Vinogradov, Stalin's bodyguard, Vlasik, and erstwhile head of the KGB, Abakumov, as well as senior doctors from the Kremlin clinic and around Moscow. The plot was announced to the public on 13 January 1953. Reports claimed that nine senior doctors were responsible for a broader Zionist plot 'to destroy leading statesmen of the USSR'.[32] Other supposed Jewish conspiracies were nursed in the following months, though there was a brief respite when Stalin died in March of that year.

Summary of key events

- The Second World War had been a catastrophe for the people of the Soviet Union, but it proved a victory for Stalin as he emerged from the war a dictator with mass popularity.
- Many of the systems begun under Stalin in 1928 continued after the war, such as the Five-Year Plans and use of repression.
- As Stalin grew older, he retreated from public life and concentrated power even more in his own hands, through fear of enemies.
- Because of the way Stalin had ruled, his succession was problematic and it was unclear how the Communist Party would proceed.

The transformation of the Soviet Union's international position

The emergence of a 'superpower'

Stalin saw the project of rebuilding the Soviet Union as another kind of war – a re-run of 1930s modernisation. Overy states that victory 'plunged the Soviet people into a second Dark Age'.[33] This may be a fair summary of Stalin's domestic policy as explored above, but it could arguably also be applied to the international situation. Victory in the Second World War, through an alliance with the United States and Britain, had properly established the Soviet Union as one of the 20th

Speak like a historian

Zionism

Zionism as a political movement grew to prominence in the early 20th century. It was based on the belief that the Jewish people, having been spread throughout the world through various *diaspora* (moving out in many directions), should be able to return to ancient Judaea in the Middle East and found a state and home for Jewish people. Many of its proponents were on the political left but were mistrusted because of their loyalty to another cause.

century's two 'superpowers'. It is arguable that by 1939, Stalin had established the economic and industrial base necessary to exert influence abroad and, eventually, to support a vast military capable of occupying half of Europe. Cooperation and rivalry with his allies had, however, secured Stalin an international status that he arguably lacked prior to the war. The Soviet Union was a founder member of the United Nations. The post-war settlement agreed at Yalta in February 1945 and at Potsdam in July and August 1945 defined the nature of international politics for the majority of the remainder of the century.

Stalin was determined that the Soviet Union should compete with the capitalist West and eventually prove its superiority. One of the means by which this was achieved was espionage. An early and very important success was gaining intelligence on the US atomic programme. Progress on the Soviet atomic programme was of the highest priority following the USA's deployment of atomic bombs on Hiroshima and Nagasaki on 6 and 9 August 1945. By the following year the Soviet Union had built its first nuclear reactor. On 29 August 1949, the Soviet Union successfully tested its first atomic bomb. This rate of progress alarmed the United States and triggered an arms race, sealing the Soviet Union's reputation as a rival and potential threat.

The formation of the Soviet Bloc

The Soviet Bloc was formed gradually; not properly consolidated until 1949. Stalin may have occupied the countries, but this did not necessarily ensure the creation of sympathetic and obedient regimes. It is important to note that many Europeans saw communism as a potential future model. In some Eastern European countries, the communist parties had genuinely popular support. This was, however, not comprehensively the case. Stalin had actively trained exiles in Moscow during the war with the intention of sending them to their homelands to create sympathetic regimes. This was the task of Walter Ulbricht and his comrades, who were quickly transported to Berlin after victory.

Some of the 'Eastern Bloc' countries established wholly communist regimes from the beginning in 1945 (Romania, Albania, Bulgaria). In others, the communist parties controlled by Moscow had to use more underhand methods; what the Hungarian communist leader Mátyás Rákosi referred to as 'salami tactics', which involved isolating and defeating political opponents one by one, beginning with the centre-right and moving to the moderate left (as if reducing the size of a salami sausage one slice at a time). Yugoslavia and Albania, though under communist leadership, managed to maintain their independence; for the remainder Stalin was able to exercise control by creating direct political links, providing an alternative form of economic assistance to Marshall Aid and, most directly, through continued military occupation. (See Figure 6.4.) It is worth noting that the Western Allies, under NATO, also maintained a military presence in Europe.

Speak like a historian

Superpowers

The 19th century had seen the creation of the European powers, whose status was based on developed industry and the control of their empires across the globe. The United States had grown to be the world's largest industrial power even before the First World War. Following that conflict, the old European powers such as Britain and France struggled to maintain their dominance of the globe. Following the economic depression of the 1930s, the United States recovered mainly as a result of rearmament. Despite the ravages of war, the Soviet Union could rival the United States in terms of global dominance, not least because of its enormous armed forces. Once the Soviet Union had ended the United States' monopoly on nuclear weapons (by the end of 1949), the two great industrial and military powers stood above all others and thus were referred to as 'superpowers'.

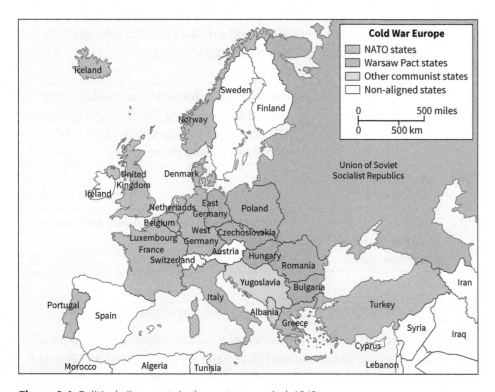

Figure 6.4: Political alignments in the post-war period, 1949.

ACTIVITY 6.4

This timeline shows some of the key events after Stalin's death. However, some domestic developments have been left out. Use your notes to complete the timeline.

Timeline 1945–1953

Year	Domestic events	International events
1945	May: Russians declared victory over Germany.	Feb: Yalta Conference. July: United States tested first atomic bomb – didn't inform Soviets. Aug: Potsdam Conference.
1946		Churchill made 'Iron Curtain' speech – in which he suggested Eastern Europe was being forced under the control of the Soviet Union.
1947	**Cominform** established.	Truman Doctrine announced. Marshall Aid Plan – United States gave Western European countries $47 billion of aid to rebuild after Second World War.
1948		Czechoslovakia became communist. Berlin Air Lift after Stalin blockaded west Berlin from receiving supplies by road or canal.
1949	**Comecon** founded. First Soviet nuclear tests.	NATO formed – military alliance between United States and Western Europe.
1950		Korean war began between communists in the north and those wanting democracy in the south. USSR backs the north along with China. The United States backed the south.
1952	Doctors' Plot unveiled.	
1953	Beria executed. USSR tested the hydrogen bomb.	Khrushchev signed peace deal with Eisenhower to end Korean War.

Key terms

Cominform (Communist Information Bureau): Created in October 1947 to coordinate the actions of communist parties in Europe under the leadership of the CPSU. It was successful in helping Stalin gain control over communist leaders in Eastern Europe and ensuring that they followed Soviet policy in the years after the Second World War when the Cold War was developing.

Comecon: Set up in 1949 in the Eastern Bloc under the leadership of the Soviet Union as a response to the US Marshall Plan. The United States donated $17 billion of aid to Western European countries. Comecon was formed to prevent Eastern European countries moving towards the Americans.

Conflict with the United States and the capitalist West

The three conferences at which the leaders of the United States, Britain and the Soviet Union met (Tehran in November 1943, Yalta in February 1945 and Potsdam in July and August 1945 – see Table 6.1) essentially acted as a measure of how the wartime alliance had cooled. At the end of 1943, US President Roosevelt was keen to ensure good relations with Stalin. The emphasis of Allied cooperation at this point was, of course, on defeating Hitler and the Axis powers. Nevertheless, as victory came closer, the future of particular parts of Europe began to be seen as one reason for the cooling of relations and growing mistrust. Chief among these was Poland – its geographical composition and its future government.

General agreement was reached at Yalta that the Soviet Union would have a broad sphere of influence over Eastern Europe – territory that in any case it was quickly occupying. Poland was a more sensitive area of discussion, because Stalin wished to regain the land once under the Nazi-Soviet pact, and because Churchill was hosting the 'London Poles', who looked to him to facilitate their return to power from exile. Stalin, on the other hand, was looking to put the communist 'Lublin Poles' in power. At Yalta, Stalin assented to 'free' elections in Poland, but in May, once the territory was occupied, he went back on this deal. Churchill, reluctantly, gave in.

The mood among the Allies changed significantly between Yalta and Potsdam, particularly because the more hardline Truman became US President and only the day before the Potsdam Conference the United States has successfully tested the atomic bomb. By mid-May 1945, the Red Army occupied the countries of Eastern Europe, which Churchill designated the following year in his Missouri speech as lying behind 'an iron curtain'.

The US regime became increasingly convinced that a stronger response was required to prevent communist domination of Europe. This was notably expressed in the so-called 'Long Telegram' sent by George Kennan in February 1946. The next steps by the United States in this regard were, first, the formulation of the 'Truman Doctrine' of March 1947. This committed the United States to preventing the spread of communism by promising everything short of military intervention to support those who wished to resist it (thus the United States' intervention in the Greek Civil War). Second was the European Recovery Programme, devised by General George Marshall, which became known as 'Marshall Aid' and was enacted in 1948.

Stalin saw both the Truman Doctrine and Marshall Aid as a direct challenge to the Soviet Union's influence in Eastern Europe. In September 1947, he created the Communist Information Bureau, to which most of the communist parties of the newly liberated and Soviet-occupied countries of Eastern Europe belonged. It was by this means that Stalin persuaded the Czechoslovak government to reject proposed Marshall Aid at the Paris Conference in July 1947. The subsequent seizure of power by a communist government the following year convinced the US Congress of the need to pass the aid bill. Matters came to a head in 1948 and 1949. Stalin, it seems, had hoped that Germany, under the occupation of Britain, the United States and France (each with a Western zone) and of the Soviet Union (with the Eastern zone), could have remained united. His broad wish was for a single, neutral and socialist Germany that would act as part of his Eastern European 'buffer zone' against possible Western attack. Tensions had increased over Germany because the Western powers clearly excluded the Soviet Union from their deliberations over the future of the Western zones. It seemed clear that the Western Allies' vision for Germany was one in which the Western part, at least, would be reconstructed and brought decisively under Western influence.

The introduction of a West German currency into Berlin (which was also split into four zones) was a clear provocation to Stalin, who introduced a blockade on the Western sectors on 24 July 1948. The Western response was to fly in aid to West Berlin at enormous expense. Occupied Berlin was arguably the most dangerous location in Europe at this time: it is where Soviet and Western allied troops were in closest proximity and this 'cold' confrontation was a perfect illustration of how the

Speak like a historian

Who had the right to rule Poland?

In September 1939, when Hitler and Stalin invaded Poland, the Polish government fled to safety in London. Britain had, after all, promised to declare war on Germany if it invaded Poland, and saw itself as a guarantor of Poland's rights. A Polish government-in-exile was therefore established in London and they became known as the 'London Poles'. Churchill wished them to return to run Poland after the defeat of Hitler. It was, however, the Red Army that drove out German forces and occupied the whole of Poland by May 1945. Stalin wished for a group of Polish communists based in Lublin to form a government. They were known as the 'Lublin Poles'.

'Cold War' had the potential to turn hot. The crisis was resolved after 11 months, when Stalin lifted the blockade.

In April 1949 the Western allies had formalised the 'Western Bloc' with the creation of the North Atlantic Treaty Organization (NATO); this was a military alliance formed specifically to react in defence of any one of its members. Germany was formally divided in June 1949, with the creation of the Federal Republic of Germany (FRG; West Germany). In October, the Soviet Occupation Zone became the German Democratic Republic (GDR; East Germany). The communist regime established here was not recognised by West Germany or its allies for many years. The FRG did not become a member of NATO until 1955, when the Soviet Union reacted with the formation of the communist military alliance, including the GDR, known as the Warsaw Pact. By this date there were two armed camps either side of the Iron Curtain.

There is some debate over whether Stalin was 'expansionist' or merely 'defensive' in his intentions and actions in Eastern Europe. Seen from the viewpoint of the increasingly hostile Western Allies under the leadership of Truman, Stalin's aim was clear: to gain influence over as much of Europe as possible and to impose Soviet hegemony (overall control) over the whole continent. The case for this view is not so clear. Between 1945 and 1948, Stalin tolerated the demands from Eastern European communists to maintain coalitions with non-communists on the left. This may have simply represented a patient approach, but the likelihood is that Stalin was cautious about Western reaction. In March 1952, Stalin sent a communication to the Western Allies proposing the possible reunification of West and East Germany as a neutral state. In reality, this had little chance of succeeding: neither side was really prepared to compromise in such a delicate arena of confrontation. It may have been a ploy by Stalin or his last attempt to tip the scales slightly further in his favour, but the episode also demonstrates the intransigence of the Western Allies. Add to this Stalin's record prior to the war of an obsession with the security of the Soviet Union's western frontier, and it is possible to view his actions in the light of a leader ensuring the toughest possible defence.

Conference and context	Main areas of agreement	Areas remaining/ unresolved
Tehran 28 Nov–1 Dec 1943 The war had turned decisively against Germany and Allied victory was far more likely.	Western Allies would launch an invasion of Nazi-occupied France in May 1944. The Soviet Union would launch a major offensive in the east at the same time.	Administration of post-war Europe under Allied occupation.
Yalta 4–11 Feb 1945 Hitler's forces were in retreat and the defeat and occupation of Germany by the Allies was likely within months.	Joint occupation of Germany by Allied powers – each responsible for a sector of Germany and of Berlin. Reparations paid by Germany would be agreed. Soviet-occupied Poland would be allowed free elections. The USSR would join the war against Japan.	The eastern and western borders of Poland. The Soviet Union claimed Polish land up to the Curzon Line in the east. It also supported the eastern border of Poland running along the Oder-Neisse line, taking territory from Germany.
Potsdam 17 July–2 Aug 1945 Germany had been defeated and occupied in May. The Red Army occupied Eastern Europe. War against Japan continued. The United States had just tested an atomic bomb. Roosevelt had died, replaced by the more anti-communist Truman.	The five Ds for Germany: Denazification, Demilitarisation, Democratisation, Decentralisation, Decartelisation. These were designed to prevent Germany being a threat to democracy and peace. Prosecution of Nazi war criminals. Expulsion of Germans from Soviet-controlled territory. Creation of Polish Government of National Unity and the eastern and western borders as proposed at Yalta, but the Oder-Neisse line remained provisional.	The economic future of Germany. The future integrity of Germany as one country. The future allegiance of Germany. A final peace settlement with Germany (this was not concluded until 1990 after reunification). The definition of what would constitute democracy east of the Iron Curtain.

Table 6.1: Planning post-war Europe: the Tehran, Yalta and Potsdam conferences.

Stalin's death and his legacy at home and abroad

On 28 February 1953, Stalin held a late-night party with his closest colleagues, as he was accustomed to do. It finished in the early hours and Stalin showed no

ACTIVITY 6.5

The following concepts have been very important in this section. For each one, write a definition of the concept and give an example of what it means in the context of the Soviet Union between 1945 and 1953:

- intelligentsia
- cult of personality
- conservatism
- Communist Party.

particular signs of illness. The next day, however, he suffered a stroke, paralysing half his body. His minders did not enter his room until several hours later, when they found him on the floor in a pool of urine. For no clear reason he was not seen by doctors until the early hours of the following day. Some speculate that his colleagues saw an opportunity to hasten his demise. It could also be possible that they avoided intervening for fear of the consequences should he recover. Stalin took another three days to die. His funeral was held on 9 March 1953.

The news of Stalin's death was deeply shocking to the Soviet people. Stalin, unlike his fellow dictators of the early to mid-20th century, had not died in disgrace and defeat, but rather only eight years after what must be seen as the culmination of his career, becoming 'Generalissimo' – the focus of Soviet victory and the leader of world communism. Stalin's domestic legacy was clearly one, first and foremost, of inhumanity and disdain for human life. Despite the fact that so many of the sacrifices were made by others, Stalin had modernised the Soviet economy and achieved the solid industrial basis it required to secure the revolutionary regime. In this sense he had achieved Socialism in One Country. Of course, it must be added that this had involved several reverses, mistakes and inefficiencies.

His political legacy was to create a personal dictatorship, a modern form of despotism, which resulted in adulation, conspiracy, fear and stifled initiative, these being part and parcel of political and everyday life. This said, the collective leadership that emerged, while they were still engaged in rivalry and infighting, were capable of maintaining control. Stalin had created a stable, if cruel, administrative system that was to some extent meritocratic and allowed social mobility (especially following the purges). Additionally, having been deified through propaganda, he could provide stability in death and was able to join Lenin in the pantheon of the founders of Soviet socialism.

Stalin remained an inspiration to many of his countrymen, and Khrushchev had to undertake 'de-Stalinisation' cautiously and only once he had stabilised his own position as successor by 1956. Stalin also remained an inspiration for many within the expanding communist world. Indeed, Khrushchev met with resistance from hardline Stalinists, such as Ulbricht in East Germany, who had been schooled in Stalinism, its worldview and its methods of control. The divergence of Communist China from the Soviet Union's pursuit of 'peaceful coexistence' in the 1950s was, to some extent, a result of Mao maintaining Stalin's hardline approach (though in reality this is a far more complex matter). Despite other forms of communism that emerged during the 20th century, it is arguable that 'Stalinism' had defined communism, particularly by making the Soviet Union the 'socialist fatherland' to which all other communists were expected to look. It is arguable that the Soviet Union and its allies were simply incapable of breaking the Stalinist mould.

Further reading

It is very worthwhile reading Richard Overy's *Russia's War* (Penguin, 1999) in its entirety, as it gives a compelling and detailed narrative of the military campaigns and the Soviet Union's experience of the Second World War. Detailed and readable accounts of the experiences of the three main cities are available in Rodric Braithwaite's *Moscow 1941: A City and its People at War* (Profile Books, 2007), Anna Reid's *Leningrad: Tragedy of a City Siege, 1941–44* (Bloomsbury, 2012) and the magisterial work by Anthony Beevor, *Stalingrad* (Penguin, 2007). Robert Service's *Stalin: A Biography* (Pan, 2010) is again very valuable on the dictator's final years and legacy. The post-war international situation is fully dealt with in Tony Judt's *Postwar: A History of Europe Since 1945* (Vintage, 2010).

Practice essay questions

1. 'The victory of the Soviet Union in the Second World War was the result of Stalin's leadership.' Assess the validity of this view.
2. 'By 1953, Stalin had built a system of government wholly dependent on continuous terror.' Assess the validity of this view.
3. 'The Soviet Union was in a stronger position in 1953 than it had been in 1941.' Assess the validity of this view.
4. With reference to the sources below and your understanding of the historical context, assess the value of these three sources to a historian studying the preparedness of the Soviet Union for war.

Source A

Extract from the Nazi-Soviet 'non-aggression' Pact, 23 August 1939 (in Boobbyer, P., *The Stalin Era*, pp. 118–119).

Article 1. The two contracting parties undertake to refrain from any act of force, any aggressive act, or any attack against each other, either individually or in conjunction with other Powers ...

Secret Additional Protocol

1. *In the event of a territorial and political transformation in the territories belonging to the Polish state, the spheres of interest of both Germany and the USSR shall be bounded approximately by the line of the rivers Narev, Vistula and San ...*

Source B

An extract from Nikita Kruschev's account of the war, written in 1956 (in Stacey, F.W., *Stalin and the Making of Modern Russia*, p. 52).

Very grievous consequences, especially in reference to the beginning of the war, followed Stalin's annihilation of many military commanders and political workers during 1937–1941 [...]

During these years repressions were instituted [...] beginning literally at the company and battalion level and extending to the higher military centres; during this time the cadre of leaders who had gained military experience in Spain and the Far East was almost completely liquidated.

Source C

Extract from a top-secret communication written to Stalin by the head of Soviet intelligence on 17 June 1941 (in Boobbyer, P., *The Stalin Era*, p. 121).

We present intelligence received from the USSR NKGB [intelligence services] in Berlin …
Information from Berlin
The source, working in the headquarters of the German air force, states:

1. *All military preparations by Germany for an armed action against the USSR have been fully completed, and the blow can be expected at any moment …*
2. *… The source, working in the Ministry of Economy, states that the appointment has taken place of the heads of military-economic administration for the 'future areas' of the occupied territory of the USSR.*

Taking it further

Having studied Stalin's rise to power and rule up to his death in 1953, do you agree that he should be referred to as the 'Red Tsar'?

Chapter summary

Having studied this chapter you should be able to:

- identify the reasons for, and trace the speed and extent of, Soviet defeat
- assess Stalin's role as a wartime leader
- identify the reasons for, and trace the speed and extent of, German defeat
- define the evolution of the nature of Stalin's dictatorship during and after the war
- identify aspects of Stalin's legacy and the Soviet Union's international status by 1953.

End notes

1   McDermott, K., *Stalin*, p. 123.
2   Overy, R., *Russia's War*, p. 78.
3   Cited in Acton, E. and Stableford, T., *The Soviet Union: A Documentary History, Volume 2 1939–1991*, pp. 64–65.
4   Overy, *Russia's War*, p. 217.
5   Ibid, p. 244.
6   Davies, R.W., *Soviet Economic Development from Lenin to Khrushchev*.
7   Cited in Acton and Stableford, *The Soviet Union, Volume 2*, p. 117.
8   Davies, *Soviet Economic Development*, p. 60.
9   Dunham, V.S., *In Stalin's Time: Middleclass Values in Soviet Fiction*, p. 7.
10 Overy, *Russia's War*, p. 198.
11 Cited in Acton and Stableford, *The Soviet Union*, Volume 2, p. 69.
12 Overy, *Russia's War*, p. 191.
13 Cited in Davies, *Soviet Economic Development*, p. 63.
14 Cited in Gill, G., *Stalinism*, p. 43.
15 Davies, *Soviet Economic Development*, p. 62.
16 McDermott, *Stalin*, p. 133.
17 Ibid, p. 134.
18 Davies, *Soviet Economic Development*, p. 65.
19 Ibid, p. 67.
20 Ibid, p. 69.
21 Gill, *Stalinism*, p. 46.
22 Davies, *Soviet Economic Development*, p. 68.
23 Ibid, p. 69.
24 Ibid, p. 68.
25 McDermott, *Stalin*, p. 142.
26 Ibid, p. 142.
27 Ibid, p. 142.
28 Overy, *Russia's War*, p. 295.
29 Ibid, p. 302.
30 Ward, C., *Stalin's Russia*, p. 241.
31 Overy, *Russia's War*, p. 310.
32 Ibid, p. 319.
33 Ibid, p. 290.

Glossary

Anti-Semitism Racial hatred against Jewish people. This had been prominent in Russia and the Russian state had at times created laws to discriminate against Jews in the Russian Empire and supported attacks (pogroms) against Jewish communities.

Autocracy The system of government that existed in Russia until 1917 under the tsars. All power was concentrated in the hands of the tsar who had no legal restraints on his power.

Bolsheviks Meaning 'majority': these were a group of Social Democrats who split from the rest of the party because they disagreed on the leadership of the party. The Bolsheviks were led by Lenin.

Bourgeoisie The ruling class under capitalism. Often translated as the 'middle class', for Marxists its most important members were the bankers and industrialists who, as they saw it, had power over the proletariat.

Treaty of Brest-Litovsk Treaty of Brest-Litovsk: signed on 3 March 1918 between Germany and the Bolshevik government of Russia and effectively signified a Russian surrender and withdrawal from the First World War.

Central Committee The sovereign body of the Communist Party, elected by the Party Congress. While many of its responsibilities were given to other important bodies such as the Politburo, it was in theory where, ultimately, the policy of the Communist Party was decided.

Central Executive Committee Formed in 1922, this was the highest governing body of the Soviet Union until 1938, when it was replaced by the Supreme Soviet. It was part of the Soviet state apparatus rather than the party apparatus.

Cheka (All-Russian Extraordinary Commission against Counter Revolution and Sabotage), formed on 20 December 1917, was the Bolsheviks' secret police force. It was responsible for carrying out the 'Red Terror' mass oppression during the Russian Civil War of 1918–1922. Its founder and leader was Felix Dzerzhinsky.

Civil War A conflict in which two or more groups within one country fight each other. The Russian Civil War began in 1918 and lasted until 1922. It was fought mainly between the 'Reds' and 'Whites'. Red victory ensured the consolidation of power by the new communist regime. Another relevant example is the Spanish Civil War (1936–1939), fought between socialists and nationalists.

Cold War A term used to express the tensions that existed principally between the two superpowers of the United States and the Soviet Union and their allies following the Second World War up to the dissolution of the Soviet Union (1945–1991)

Collectivisation A policy introduced by Stalin in 1928 which aimed to consolidate individual land holdings into collective farms (*kolkhozy*) in the hope of increasing production. The human costs of this policy were enormous.

Comecon Set up in 1949 in the Eastern Bloc under the leadership of the Soviet Union as a response to the US Marshall Plan. The United States donated $17 billion of aid to Western European countries. Comecon was formed to prevent Eastern European countries moving towards the Americans.

Cominform (Communist Information Bureau) Created in October 1947 to coordinate the actions of communist parties in Europe under the leadership of the CPSU. It was successful in helping Stalin gain control over communist leaders in Eastern Europe and ensuring that they followed Soviet policy in the years after the Second World War when the Cold War was developing.

Comintern (Third Communist International)

An international organisation created in 1919 whose purpose was the promotion of worldwide revolution. The First and Second Internationals had been loose federations of European socialist parties, whereas this was under the direct influence of the Communist Party of the Soviet Union (CPSU). It was dissolved in 1943 and succeeded by Cominform in 1947.

Communist Party of the Soviet Union (CPSU)

The ruling party of the Soviet Union. All other political parties had been banned by 1921. Its power structure was closely integrated with the organs of state in the Soviet Union. Originally, it was the Bolshevik faction of the Russian Social Democratic Labour Party and then the Russian Communist Party (Bolshevik) before the creation of the Soviet Union in 1922.

Constituent Assembly

The first democratically elected legislative body in Russian history, formed just after the October Revolution of 1917. It met for 13 hours before the Central Executive Committee (under Lenin's orders) dissolved it.

Constitutional Democrats (Kadets)

Party formed of liberals in 1905 just after the announcement of the October Manifesto. Led by Pavel Miliukov, they favoured an eight-hour day but were committed to constitutional monarchy, so worked within the Duma.

Council of Labour and Defence

Set up under the authority of Sovnarkom in November 1918 to help administer the wartime economy. It brought together the most important individuals involved in the war effort including the chairman of the Supreme Council of the National Economy.

Dekulakisation

A policy that developed as part of collectivisation. It involved liquidating the richer peasants or those who fought against collectivisation. Under this policy at least 1.8 million peasants were deported and up to 5 million more shot. (Figures from the time are unreliable and historians still debate the numbers involved.)

Duma

Deriving its name from the Russian for 'consider', the State Duma was formed as a result of the 1905 Revolution under Nicholas II. It had legislative and advisory powers, but its power was to be severely curtailed under the Fundamental Laws issued by Nicholas II just before the opening of the Duma in May 1906.

Gosplan

The State Planning Committee which was responsible for economic planning in the Soviet Union, particularly from 1928 onwards. It was set up under the authority of the Council of Labour and Defence in 1921.

Ispolkom

The Executive Committee of the Petrograd Soviet. From February 1917, this body essentially represented the Petrograd Soviet in negotiations with the Provisional Government.

Kolkhoz

The Russian term for collective farms, established after the October revolution of 1917. They were set up spontaneously, and voluntarily in many cases, until 1928 when Stalin decided to force the collectivisation of all individual holdings.

Komsomol

The All-Union Leninist Young Communist League, established in 1918 and a youth division (14–28-year-olds) of the Communist Party. Although membership was voluntary it was almost impossible to pursue higher education without being a member. Younger children could join the Young Pioneers.

Kronstadt

The fortified naval base of Petrograd (later Leningrad), which was situated at the edge of the city's Baltic Sea port. The sailors of Kronstadt were strong supporters of the Bolsheviks in 1917, but turned against them in March 1921, accusing them of betraying the revolution and instead creating a dictatorship.

Kulaks

A group of relatively affluent farmers that grew during Stolypin's reforms. According to Marxist-Leninist philosophy they were class enemies of the poorer peasants. Under Lenin, kulaks meant anyone who refused to hand over grain during requisitioning. Under Stalin they were terrorised during collectivisation.

Left Opposition

This was a general term used to describe those who opposed the Communist leadership in the mid-1920s by calling for more rapid industrialisation and the abandonment of the NEP.

Left SRs

The Socialist Revolutionaries split in 1917, between those who supported the Provisional Government (established during the February Revolution) and those who supported the Bolsheviks (the Left SRs). In 1918 they revolted against the Bolsheviks, who had signed the Treaty of Brest-Litovsk.

Lend-Lease programme

Originally devised by US president, Franklin D. Roosevelt, to provide Britain with goods and weaponry from 1939 to help it resist the threat from Germany. It was extended to the Soviet Union in late 1941 by which time all three powers (USA, Great Britain and USSR) were allied against Nazi Germany.

Machine-tractor stations (MTS)

These provided collective farms with machinery to help mechanise Soviet agriculture from 1928 onwards.

Marxism

The political and economic theory expounded by Karl Marx and Friedrich Engels. Their theory placed class struggle at the centre of historical development.

Mensheviks

Originally part of the Russian Social-Democratic Labour Party, the Mensheviks (which means 'minority') were formed after a split between Julius Martov and Lenin, which occurred at the Second Congress of 1903. The Mensheviks opposed Lenin's idea of a vanguard party and wanted broad-based support within the party.

Military Revolutionary Committee (MRC or *Milrevkom*)

The armed force of the Petrograd Soviet. It was used by Trotsky to organise the Bolshevik seizure of power in October 1917.

Mir

A traditional peasant commune, the basic unit of organisation in the countryside. It decided how land was distributed to each household. Pyotr Stolypin attempted to break the power of the commune by allowing kulaks (richer peasants) to buy their own land before the First World War. It remained popular until destroyed by collectivisation.

NEP (New Economic Policy)

Introduced by Lenin in 1921 after it had become obvious that war communism had failed. NEP was controversial because it allowed the peasants to sell some of their produce for profit and allowed small independent businesses to flourish once more.

NKVD

The People's Commissariat for Internal Affairs – the NKVD – contained the regular police force (including traffic police and firefighting and border guards). It became infamous for running the gulag system after 1934 where it conducted executions, as well as keeping harsh conditions within the camps.

Octobrists

A group of conservative liberals formed during the 1905 revolution who called for Nicholas II to fulfil the reforms of the October Manifesto. However, they were fully committed to constitutional monarchy.

OGPU

The All-Union State Political Administration was the secret police of the Soviet Union from 1922 until 1934. Felix Dzerzhinsky was the first chief of this state security branch. However, by 1934 it became reincorporated into the NKVD.

Orgburo

Organisational Bureau of the Central Committee of the Communist Party of the Soviet Union. Created in 1919, this body was responsible for party administration and membership. It was also in charge of the Party Secretariat which became an important part of Stalin's power base when he became General Secretary of the Secretariat in 1922.

Politburo — An abbreviation of 'Political Bureau of the Central Committee of the Communist Party of the Soviet Union'. Founded in October 1917 by Lenin with seven members who would decide on questions too urgent to await the Central Committee.

Progressive Bloc — Formed when the State Duma was recalled during the First World War – several members including the Progressists and the Kadets formed a political front to push Nicholas II to form a 'Government of Confidence' where they could take control of the domestic war effort.

Proletariat — The industrial working class who, according to Marxists, would overthrow the rule of the bourgeoisie (the ruling class under capitalism) through revolution.

Provisional Government — Formed immediately after Nicholas II abdicated – intended to be a temporary body until the elections for the Constituent Assembly could take place later in 1917. Initially led by Prince Lvov and latterly by Alexander Kerensky.

Radical — Someone who believes in drastic change from traditions or government policy.

Red Guards / Reds — A paramilitary organisation within the Bolshevik Party, made up of factory workers, peasants and ex-soldiers. Reorganised into the Red Army during the Civil War beginning 1918.

Right Opposition — A general term used to describe those who opposed the Communist leadership in the late 1920s and early 1930s by opposing the end of NEP and Stalin's programme of rapid industrialisation and collectivisation, as well as the extent of his personal power.

Right SRs — The Socialist Revolutionaries split in 1917, between those who supported the Provisional Government (established during the February Revolution) and those who supported the Bolsheviks (the Left SRs). When the majority of SRs left the Congress of Soviets in October 1917 when the Bolsheviks took over, they were labelled by the Bolsheviks as 'Right SRs'.

Rightists — Supporters of the tsarist monarchy who were elected to the Duma during its existence between 1906 and 1914.

Romanov — The name of the royal family and household in Russia since 1613. In 1913, Nicholas II (the last of the Romanovs and last Tsar of Russia) celebrated the tercentenary or 300-year anniversary of the dynasty.

The Russian Soviet Federated Socialist Republic (RSFSR) — The name for Russia after the Bolshevik Revolution until 1922, when it became a republic of the Soviet Union.

Social Democrats — The Russian Social Democratic Labour Party was formed in 1898 to unite various Marxist groups within Imperial Russia. Members were Marxists and they opposed revolutionary populism – believing instead that the agents of the revolution would be the working class.

Socialism in One Country — Stalin's theory that the Soviet Union should strengthen itself to resist capitalist encirclement. It followed the defeat of socialist revolutions in Germany and Hungary. The policy was criticised by Trotsky and Zinoviev.

Socialist Realism — A style of realistic art that developed to further Socialism in One Country. It glorified the working class.

Socialist Revolutionaries — Marxists who drew inspiration from the Narodnik/populist movements of the 1870s. The SRs were led by Victor Chernov from 1902 and thought that both peasants and workers could lead a revolution against tsarism. Although they sought to agitate peasants, they relied on political assassinations as a tactic to bring about a revolution.

Soviets — In late imperial Russia 'soviets' were workers' councils – the earliest being the St Petersburg Soviet formed in 1905. They were formed as a movement of workers independent of the government-sponsored Zubatov unions.

Sovkhoz — State-owned collective farms entirely owned and run by the state. Farm workers were employees of the state like factory workers in state-owned factories.

Sovnarkom — Council of People's Commissars formed shortly after the October Revolution in 1917. It was the legislative body, chaired by Lenin, charged with restructuring government systems to build the Soviet Union. There were eleven members called 'commissars' instead of 'ministers'. It became the Council of Ministers under Stalin in 1946.

Stakhanovite movement — A movement formed by workers who followed the example of Alexei Stakhanov, who over-achieved targets set for him (mining 102 tons of coals in under 6 hours). In 1935, under the second Five-Year-Plan, some workers tried to emulate or compete with his achievements.

State Committee for Defence — This body was created in June 1941 following German invasion of the Soviet Union and was put in overall charge of the Soviet war effort with Stalin at its head.

Stavka — General Military Headquarters. This name was used both for the tsarist army during the First World War and for the body created by Stalin in June 1941 following the German invasion of the Soviet Union.

Supreme Council of the National Economy — Set up in December 1917 under the authority of Sovnarkom, this was the first body responsible for attempting to create a planned economy. It set up many subordinate bodies to deal with a wide range of economic issues.

Totalitarian — A political system where the state retains complete control over society and all aspects of citizens' lives.

TOZ — A small-scale farm on which land was worked collectively but peasants retained individual ownership of animals and equipment.

Union of Soviet Socialist Republics (USSR) — Formed officially in 1922 and disbanded in 1991, the USSR was a single-party, communist state consisting originally of the RSFSR, Transcaucasian, Ukrainian and Belorussian Soviet Socialist Republics (SSRs). Other SSRs were subsequently formed and joined the Union. It is often referred to as the Soviet Union.

United Opposition — The term used to describe the faction which opposed the policies of Stalin and Bukharin from 1926 and included Zinoviev, Kamenev and Trotsky. Zinoviev and Kamenev had previously been enemies of Trotsky and allies of Stalin.

War communism — The economic system introduced by Lenin that existed during the Civil War. It was a combination of Marxist ideas and emergency measures and involved nationalising the land and banks.

Whites — The Whites formed as a loose confederation of anti-Bolshevik forces who fought for control of Russia from 1917 to 1922. Some wore the white uniforms of imperialist Russia but some chose white to be distinct from the Bolshevik Reds.

Workers' Opposition — The political faction which formed during 1919 to 1920 to protest against the decrease of influence of working-class democratic institutions under the Communist regime.

Yezhovshchina — The systematic campaign of mass terror organised by Nikolai Yezhov, head of the NKVD in 1937–1938.

Zemstvo — A form of local government created in Russia during the reforms following emancipation of the peasant serfs. Established in 1864, the *zemstva* were small elected councils in rural areas to provide social and economic services.

Bibliography

Part 1 The Russian Revolution and the rise of Stalin, 1917–1929

Chapter 1

Acton, E. and Stableford, T., *The Soviet Union: A Documentary History, Volume 1, 1917–1940*. Liverpool University Press, 2005.

Evans, D. and Jenkins, J., *Years of Russia, the USSR and the Collapse of Soviet Communism*. London, Hodder Education, 2008.

Figes, O., *Revolutionary Russia, 1891–1991*. London, Pelican, 2014.

Fitzpatrick, S., *The Russian Revolution*. Oxford University Press, 2008.

Kowalski, R., *The Russian Revolution, 1917–1921*. London, Routledge, 1997.

Pipes, R., *A Concise History of the Russian Revolution*. New York, Vintage Books, 1997.

Service, R., *Lenin: A Biography*. Basingstoke, Pan, 2010.

Service, R., *The Penguin History of Modern Russia: From Tsarism to the Twenty-First Century*. London, Penguin, 2015.

Service, R., *The Russian Revolution, 1900–1927*. Basingstoke, Macmillan, 2009.

Vernadsky, G., *A Source Book for Russian History, Volume 3*. Yale University Press, 1972.

Chapter 2

Acton, E. and Stableford, T., *The Soviet Union: A Documentary History, Volume 1, 1917–1940*. Liverpool University Press, 2005.

Atkin, N., *Daily Lives of Civilians in Wartime Twentieth-Century Europe*. Westport, CT, Greenwood Press, 2008.

Davies, R.W., Harrison, M. and Wheatcroft, S.G. (eds), *The Economic Transformation of the Soviet Union, 1913–1945*. Cambridge University Press, 1993.

Figes, O., *Peasant Russia Civil War: The Volga Countryside in Revolution 1917–1921*. Oxford, Clarendon Press, 1989.

Marx, K. and Engels, F., *The Communist Manifesto*. London, Penguin, 2004.

Mawdsley, E., *The Russian Civil War*. Edinburgh, Birlinn Ltd, 2008.

Nove, A., *An Economic History of the USSR*. London, Pelican, 1989.

Pipes, R., *A Concise History of the Russian Revolution*. New York, Vintage Books, 1997.

Read, C., *War and Revolution in Russia, 1914–22*. Basingstoke, Macmillan, 2012.

Chapter 3

Acton, E. and Stableford, T., *The Soviet Union: A Documentary History, Volume 1, 1917–1940*. Liverpool University Press, 2005.

Figes, O., *Revolutionary Russia, 1891–1991*. London, Pelican, 2014.

Nove, A., *An Economic History of the USSR*. London, Pelican, 1989.

Pipes, R., *A Concise History of the Russian Revolution*. New York, Vintage Books, 1997.

Sandle, M., *A Short History of Soviet Socialism*. London, UCL Press, 1999.

Service, R., *Stalin: A Biography*. Basingstoke, Pan, 2010.

Service, R., *Trotsky: A Biography*. Basingstoke, Pan, 2010.

Part 2 Stalin's rule, 1929–1953

Chapter 4

Acton, E. and Stableford, T., *The Soviet Union: A Documentary History, Volume 1, 1917–1940*. Liverpool University Press, 2005.

Boobbyer, P., *The Stalin Era*. London, Routledge, 2000.

Conquest, R., *The Great Terror: A Reassessment*. London, Pimlico, 2008.

Davies, R.W., *Soviet Economic Development from Lenin to Khrushchev*. Cambridge University Press, 1998.

Davies, R.W., Harrison, M. and Wheatcroft, S.G. (eds), *The Economic Transformation of the Soviet Union, 1913–1945*. Cambridge University Press, 1993.

Figes, O., *The Whisperers: Private Life in Stalin's Russia*. London, Penguin, 2008.

Fitzpatrick, S., *Everyday Stalinism*. Oxford University Press, 2000.

Gill, G., *Stalinism*. Basingstoke, Macmillan, 1998.

Mawdsley, E., *The Stalin Years: The Soviet Union 1929–1953*. Manchester University Press, 2003.

McDermott, K., *Stalin*. Macmillan, Basingstoke, 2006.

Nove, A., *An Economic History of the USSR.* London, Pelican, 1989.

Service, R., *Stalin: A Biography.* Basingstoke, Pan, 2010.

Ward, C., *Stalin's Russia.* London, Bloomsbury, 1999.

Chapter 5

Acton, E. and Stableford, T., *The Soviet Union: A Documentary History, Volume 1, 1917–1940.* Liverpool University Press, 2005.

Boobbyer, P., *The Stalin Era.* London, Routledge, 2000.

Davies, R.W., Harrison, M. and Wheatcroft, S.G. (eds), *The Economic Transformation of the Soviet Union, 1913–1945.* Cambridge University Press, 1993.

Gill, G., *Stalinism.* Basingstoke, Macmillan, 1998.

McDermott, K., *Stalin.* Basingstoke, Macmillan, 2006.

Montefiore, S.S., *Stalin: The Court of the Red Tsar.* London, Weidenfeld & Nicolson, 2010.

Service, R., *Comrades: Communism: A World History.* Basingstoke, Pan, 2008.

Service, R., *The Penguin History of Modern Russia: From Tsarism to the Twenty-First Century.* London, Penguin, 2015.

Thurston, R.W., *Life and Terror in Stalin's Russia, 1934–1941.* Yale University Press, 1998.

Ward, C., *Stalin's Russia.* London, Bloomsbury, 1999.

Chapter 6

Acton, E. and Stableford, T., *The Soviet Union: A Documentary History, Volume 2, 1939–1991.* Liverpool University Press, 2007.

Beevor, A., *Stalingrad.* London, Penguin, 2007.

Boobbyer, P., *The Stalin Era.* London, Routledge, 2000.

Braithwaite, R., *Moscow 1941: A City and its People at War. London,* Profile Books, 2007.

Davies, R.W., *Soviet Economic Development from Lenin to Khrushchev.* Cambridge University Press, 1998.

Dunham, V.S., *In Stalin's Time: Middleclass Values in Soviet Fiction.* Cambridge University Press, 1979.

Gill, G., *Stalinism.* Basingstoke, Palgrave Macmillan, 1998.

Judt, T., *Postwar: A History of Europe Since 1945.* London, Vintage, 2010.

McDermott, K., *Stalin.* Palgrave Macmillan, Basingstoke, 2006.

Overy, R., *Russia's War.* London, Penguin, 1999.

Reid, A., *Leningrad: Tragedy of a City Siege, 1941–44.* London, Bloomsbury, 2012.

Service, R., *Stalin: A Biography.* Basingstoke, Pan, 2010.

Stacey, F.W., *Stalin and the Making of Modern Russia.* London, Edward Arnold, 1970.

Ward, C., *Stalin's Russia.* London, Bloomsbury, 1999.

Acknowledgements

The authors and publishers acknowledge the following sources of copyright material and are grateful for the permissions granted. While every effort has been made, it has not always been possible to identify the sources of all the material used, or to trace all copyright holders. If any omissions are brought to our notice, we will be happy to include the appropriate acknowledgements on reprinting.

The publisher would like to thank the following for permission to reproduce their photographs (numbers refer to figure numbers, unless otherwise stated):

Cover image: National Geographic Creative / Corbis **Chapter 1 Opener Image TopFoto:** ullsteinbild, **Fig 1.2** The Granger Collection; **Fig 1.3 Alamy Images:** The Print Collector; **Chapter Opener 2 TopFoto:** Fine Art Images / Heritage Images; **Fig 2.1 Corbis: Fig 2.3 TopFoto:** The Granger Collection; **Chapter Opener 3 Alamy Images:** World History Archive; **Fig 3.1** Sandle, M. (1999). *Adapted from A short history of Soviet socialism.* London: UCL Press. Reprinted by permission of Taylor & Francis Ltd; **Fig 3.2 TopFoto:** ITAR-TASS; **Fig 3.3 Getty Images:** Photo by NY Daily News Archive; **Chapter Opener 4 TopFoto:** Fine Art Images / Heritage Images; **Fig 4.1 TopFoto:** Fine Art Images / HIP; **Fig 4.2 Getty Images:** Fine Art Images / Heritage Images; **Fig 4.3 TopFoto:** Fine Art Images / Heritage Images; **Chapter Opener 5 TopFoto:** RIA Novosti, **Fig 5.2** ITAR-TASS, **Fig 5.3a** Fine Art Images / Heritage Images; **Fig 5.3b Getty Images:** Ria Novosti / AFP; **Fig 5.4 TopFoto:** Ria Novosti, **Chapter Opener 6, Fig 6.1** Ria Novosti;

The publisher would like to thank the following for permission to reproduce extracts from their texts:

Chapter 1: p. 25 Source C Vernadsky, G. and Pushkarev, S. (1972). A Source book for Russian history from early times to 1917. New Haven [Conn.]: Yale University Press. **Chapter 3: p. 80 Source B** Copyright © 1937, 1973 by Pathfinder Press Reprinted by permission. **Chapter 4: p. 105 Source A** The Five Year Plan in Crisis (Part 3) Finance and Monetary Circulation by Christian Rakovsky (27 July–7 August 1930). Copyright Critique: Journal of Socialist Theory. Volume 13, Issue 1, 1982, pp 48-49. Translation by Donald Filtzer. Reprinted by permission of Taylor & Francis Ltd, www.tandfonline.com on behalf of Critique. **Chapter 5: p. 133 Source C** Robert McNeal, Resolutions and Decisions of the Communist Party of the Soviet Union, Vol.3, The Stalin Years: 1929-1953, 1974, pp. 188-9. Reprinted with kind permission of Toronto University Press. **Chapter 6: p. 169 Source A** Degras, J. (1953). Soviet documents on foreign policy, selected and edited by Jane Degras. Vol. 3. 1933-1941. London: Oxford University press. Reprinted with permission of Chatham House, The Royal Institute of International Affairs. **Chapter 6: p. 169 Source B** Stacey, F.W., Stalin and the Making of Modern Russia, 1970: Liverpool University Press

Index

Lightning Source UK Ltd.
Milton Keynes UK
UKOW07f0006150716

278456UK00009B/21/P

9 781107 587380